Guide to
Environmental Protection
of Collections

by Barbara
Appelbaum

SOUND VIEW PRESS
MADISON, CONNECTICUT

1991

To my family.

Sound View Press is the publisher of
Who Was Who in American Art
and other reference books on American art.
A catalogue is available upon request.

Sound View Press
170 Boston Post Road
Madison, CT 06443
Telephone: 203-245-2246

All photographs are by the author.

Library of Congress Catalog Card Number (CIP): 91-067042
ISBN 0-932087-16-7

Contents

Part I

The Five Major Issues in Environmental Protection of Collections

1   Temperature and Relative Humidity   25

Part II

Assessing the Needs of Collections

Preface

In the last fifteen to twenty years, the expansion of museums in America has been unprecedented. As a result, collections that had lain untouched in the same storerooms since their acquisition — in some cases for over one hundred years — were brought into the fresh air, cleaned up, examined, and moved into new storage and exhibition spaces. Whatever the virtues or shortcomings of their previous homes, the collections had come into equilibrium with their surroundings. Already covered with dust or dried out, many condition changes had occurred much earlier. Upon examination, the specifics of condition problems came to light, and new clean air-conditioned surroundings with exhibition cases and storage cabinets of modern materials were expected to be a major improvement.

New buildings, particularly those designed by well-known architects for maximum aesthetic impact, sometimes turned out to be unsuitable for the long-term preservation of collections. Subtle changes in the condition of objects were traced to the effects of construction materials, and more obvious problems were traced to climate control systems designed more for the comfort of visitors and staff than for the care of collections. All this was becoming evident at a time when international changes in export laws, the end of many traditional cultures, imperiled wildlife, and incredible price increases in much of the art market cut short the number of new accessions in many different kinds of museums, making existing collections all the more valuable. Simultaneously, the number of professional conservators trained to recognize changes in the condition of collections multiplied (indicated by a six-fold increase in membership of the American Institute for Conservation over the last twenty years), and many museums hired their own in-house conservators for the first time.

In the private sector, awareness of conservation-related issues was somewhat slower to develop, but the increase in market values and increasing publicity for the field of conservation have prompted many private collectors to hire consultant conservators and curators to manage their collections to the highest museum standards.

Meanwhile, Garry Thomson's book, *The Museum Environment,,* first published in 1978, laid out clearly the hazards to which museum collections are subject, and became a bible for museum personnel who were trying to upgrade the care they were providing. Detailed information specific to the North American climate, both political and physical, has been scattered throughout technical and non-technical literature. Conservators, and experts in other fields who work with them, are feeling their way in dealing with many technical questions that remain unresolved. Although the publication of a book on this subject may seem premature, the author hopes that a systematic compilation of information from numerous sources, written and verbal, will help to clarify what we know and what we think we know but cannot yet prove. Meanwhile, those who care for collections need to have as much information as is available to move ahead with confidence in making decisions that will affect the well-being of collections for many generations to come.

The author wishes to thank all those colleagues whose writings, research, and observations over many years have contributed to the body of information in this book. I wish to extend particular thanks to all those colleagues whom I have the privilege of having also as friends; without their encouragement this book would never have been written.

Special thanks are due to Paul Himmelstein, my business partner, who started us in the serious study of environmental control by perfecting the art of extracting information from anyone in possession of it, and who is always as willing to share knowledge as to collect it. William Lull of Garrison/Lull, Princeton Junction, N.J., has been unceasingly generous with his wide knowledge and experience in museum environmental work. Thanks are also due to Steven Weintraub, Louis Sorkin, and Michelle Gewirtz for agreeing to review chapters in their areas of expertise.

Many clients, both private and institutional, have provided me with insight into the difficulties incurred by diligent but technically untrained people who want to provide optimal care for a wide variety of objects with limited funds and staff time. I hope this book will help them. Many manufacturers and suppliers have also been generous with their knowledge.

To me belongs the responsibility for all errors; I hope none are serious.

BARBARA APPELBAUM
New York City

Introduction

The Role of the Non-Conservator in the Preservation of Collections

This book is intended for use by anyone who cares for or about collections of art, historical artifacts, or any other kind of cultural material, or for natural history collections. It is written for those with no technical background who find themselves in the difficult position of having to make decisions concerning the physical care of those collections. This includes owners of private collections, museum curators, registrars, and administrators.

The term conservation embodies three activities: analysis, treatment, and preservation. The field of technical analysis has become increasingly complex, and rests largely in the hands of scientific specialists. Conservators rightly reserve the treatment of objects for their own ranks. The subject of this book is the activity of preservation. One act of carelessness or purposeful destruction can end an object's existence; hundreds of individual acts of caring repeated over decades and even centuries are required to assure its survival. All the conservators in the world could not preserve our cultural heritage without help in this vital area of preservation. The custodians of cultural and historic items, rather than professional conservators, hold the power to assure the future of what we have come to call the world's cultural patrimony: curators, museum administrators, private owners, historical societies, municipalities, universities, archives, and libraries. Conservators can only provide technical assistance in these matters but cannot do the job themselves.

It is vital that you learn more than you probably were taught in school about the physical needs of the objects in your care. You may have suffered through some kind of disaster - an insect infestation, water damage, or breakage. Someone may have pointed out damage that you had never noticed. But you may still have difficulty in getting a full explanation of what happened, why it happened, and what you should do about it. It is hard to know whom to believe, as there is so much conflicting information in newspapers and magazines. Many people who have helped you to learn all the things you know about your collection may have no more training than you

9

in these matters; some may even have a financial interest in your not learning more about the physical state of your purchases or about complications involved in their care. On the other hand, some conservators have been known to lapse into jargon and tell you what the objects need without providing any information that would help you to take appropriate action.

If you have tried to get information from books or articles, you may have found it both sparse and contradictory. Some of the information is out of date, some of it is ill-advised; some is too specific, and some, not specific enough. You may read something with recommendations about the care of leather, for example. Does the advice apply equally to undecorated harness leather, to gilded book bindings, beaded buckskin shirts, 1920s shoes, 1880s trunks, bearskin rugs and the heads of African drums? Obviously not. Because of the difficulties of generalization when the subject under discussion is the total output of mankind (and, if we add natural history specimens, everything *not* produced by mankind), this book will not make any recommendations about what to do to specific objects. That is up to a conservator to decide, based on an examination of a particular object.

This book is designed to provide explanations that everyone can understand about the various phenomena that affect objects, how the objects respond, and how you can decide what to do. There are few blanket recommendations here; every object, every building, every circumstance is different, and the decisions on what to do are yours. The book should help you understand which kinds of objects are the most susceptible to damage and deterioration, and under what circumstances professional help is most crucial. But even when outside conservators, designers, engineers, framers, and other experts in their own fields work with your collection, the decisions on whom to hire, what to have them do, how much money to spend — are yours. Therefore, it is important that you have in hand a guide to the basic facts, a way of separating major from minor issues, and a roadmap to the most common pitfalls others have encountered in implementing protective measures.

I have written this book because I firmly believe that the information that conservators have can benefit the objects in your collection and can add to the enjoyment you get from them. Not everything in this book is fascinating or easy to read. Feel free to skip over sections that do not apply to you, but give some of it a try.

The book consists of two basic sections: the first, on issues in preservation, and the second on ways of assessing the needs of objects. There is some unavoidable repetition between topics in the two sections. For example, some of the information on the light-sensitivity of wood appears in both the chapter on light and in the section on wood. Most of the information is not original, and is the most specific I could get without getting too technical for the general reader. Topics for the book were derived from two sources: information that I as a conservator would like custodians of collections that I work with to have, and questions that I get from museum staff and private clients. I have tried to draw examples from everyday life to de-mystify as much as possible the processes that happen to all objects in this world. Much in learning about conservation is learning to see things that were in front of you all along, but that you never noticed.

Much of what is in this book is also propaganda for conservation, both for the field and its practitioners, and for the idea of conservation as a function of society. As you see and recognize more, you will, I hope, become more convinced of the measures needed to preserve our collections. And the more you observe objects, the more you want to preserve them.

Much is riding on your stewardship of the objects in your care. The past, the present and the future all have an interest in their preservation. The people of the past who made these things, used

them, and loved them, have a stake in this. Their immortality rests in them, and our best understanding of the people of the past rests in their objects. Their things show us how they felt about themselves and the world around them, and provide physical clues for how they lived, what they wore and ate, and what they knew. Original objects are important because they transcend time — whether George Washington's love letters or a seat from Ebetts Field, Tutankhamun's throne or a prehistoric bone with astronomical markings — they were there when history was not yet history. They provide a link to the reality of the past. We owe it to their makers and users to keep these things looking as close as possible to their original as-used condition, and physically intact.

For us and for people in the future, whether or not we are related to the makers of the objects by ethnic or national history, works of art and other cultural material give us a measure of the race of which we are all members — the human race. They provide for our lives what we have come to call "roots." Non-cultural objects, the group of things commonly called natural history specimens, hold within them all our clues to the history of our planet and to the evolution that created us. In the case of meteors and moon rocks, this could be broadened to include the history of the universe.

There are of course reasons other than the moral, social, or scholarly for preserving collections. Aesthetic concerns are also important. For a museum there are legal responsibilities, part of the charter of the institution. For private collectors, there are financial incentives. Objects in deteriorating condition lose monetary value as well as their aesthetic and research value.

For whatever reason we choose to preserve the things we do, it is important to think of the objects we may own or be in charge of as part of a continuum of time. Our ownership or care of these things is a brief stop for them between the past and the future. We are figuratively, and sometimes literally, holding them in trust for our children and their children and a thousand generations to come. The attrition rate is not encouraging. How many Rembrandts, for example, did the artist paint? How many were there in existence one hundred, or two hundred, or three hundred years after his death? And how many will there be in another three hundred years? How many full-size Classic Greek sculptures are now in existence two thousand years after their creation? It is important to save the things we can — even though much is beyond saving, much will be destroyed by accidents, wars and natural disasters, and much will be altered beyond recognition by time itself.

As in the environmental movement, those who care for things must learn that the things we value in this world, although they may seem eternal and unchanging - the oceans, the sky, as well as the Acropolis, Lascaux Caves, and the *Mona Lisa* - are not immune from decay or disfigurement. Benign neglect will not assure their healthy futures.

The preservation of whatever group of things we as individuals or our institutions have singled out for permanent protection is a major undertaking. In addition to the forces of nature, our most powerful enemies are human stupidity, indifference and destructiveness. Where is the ancient library of Alexander the Great; where is Pennsylvania Station? The melting down of Pre-Columbian gold in 16th century Spain, periodic Chinese book burnings, and the persistent rumors of the destruction of erotica of several major artists by their families after their deaths should all remind us of how much has been irretrievably lost. Religious intolerance, political repression, and pathological vandalism have cost us countless treasures. Much of mankind's legacy to the future has been destroyed on purpose; extraordinary effort is necessary to protect what is left in as good condition as possible.

How can we best protect collections? As we are coming to learn — not too late, we hope — people and animals cannot remain healthy in an unhealthy environment, and the same is true of objects. There is no treatment that will keep a textile from fading in the light, or keep silver from tarnishing in acidic air, or keep a wooden statue from cracking in dryness. Once such damage is done, no treatment actually reverses the damage, and it would take more conservators than exist in the world to perform whatever treatments become necessary. As with people, prevention is always preferable to disease — even a curable one.

Conservation treatments, even the best ones, entail a certain degree of risk. They can alter the physical properties of object, like the acoustic qualities of a musical instrument. The degree of intervention required by pieces in poor condition may reduce our access to parts of the object, or adulterate the usefulness of the object for scientific analysis. It may destroy the religious value of sacred objects. Much environment-induced damage cannot be "restored" by any means now known. Faded colors and embrittled fibers cannot be made "like new". Rusted iron cannot be reformed. Cracks in wood and paint cannot be joined together. Broken objects can be repaired, but not brought back to an unbroken condition. When treatment is necessary, more serious intervention may be required if the piece is going back into a hostile environment.

It is important to realize that in trying to preserve objects for a long time, if not forever, we are fighting one of the most persistent forces of nature - entropy, the tendency of all matter to return to chaos. The organized forms created by living things are a short layover between ashes and ashes, dust and dust. Non-conservators tend to think of objects as having a strong tendency to stay put: placed on a shelf, they will simply wait there unchanged until picked up again. But close study of objects tells us this is not true. This is one of the hardest notions for conservators to instill in the minds of those who care for collections. Most objects are in a continuous state of flux; they are expanding and contracting, fading, gathering dust; they are conglomerations of chemical reactions.

Consider, for example, a woolen textile. Wool as produced by the sheep has a limited lifetime. Lanolin secreted by the sheep's skin keeps it supple and helps it to shed water; the wool is part of a living system, and is shed when the time comes. When we take the wool, wash the lanolin out, comb it, spin it, dye it, knit it, and wear it, we are trying to prolong its existence past the life evolution created it for. The wool has enough strength so that during the normal lifetime of a sweater, problems of aging are not apparent, although a certain amount of careful washing in cold water and protection from moths is necessary to preserve the properties that make it useful to us. When these properties are gone, we discard the sweater. However, when we take a wool textile from a tomb in the desert caves of Peru where it has lain for hundreds of years in a completely stable dry environment, bring it to a museum in the northern hemisphere, mount it and exhibit it with the desire to preserve it just as it is forevermore, we run into trouble. Handling turns the fibers into powder, light fades the colors, heat from lights embrittles it even more, changes in relative humidity send the fibers into a tizzy of twisting and untwisting. If we put it aside in the dark without periodic inspection, we run the risk of finding it later - eaten. Attempting to keep it whole and in as good condition as posssible is fighting nature.

For non-organic materials, the story is similar in outline if not in detail. Minerals exist in nature in their most stable state. They have reached equilibrium with their environment. When taken from the ground, changed from ores into metals or exposed to different environments, they are no longer at equilibrium and can be expected to change. If the role of the museum is to preserve objects unchanged, then this is unacceptable.

It is important to keep permanently in mind both the differences and similarities between the things we are talking about, whatever they are, and normal everyday things. If the paint on your bathroom ceiling starts to peel off the plaster, you know what should and can be done to remedy the problem. If the ceiling in question had a famous fresco on it, the solution would not be the same, even though the problem might be. The materials of art and history are not physically any different from items around our houses, and they suffer from the same physical problems — but the problems cannot be dealt with in the same ways, because their historic authenticity is just as important as their appearance. A photocopy of a Beethoven manuscript would serve the same purpose as the original if we wanted to play the music, but would no longer be an object of veneration. A reproduction of a Rembrandt, no matter how attractive, does not fascinate us the way the real painting does. Our desire to preserve things, the real original things, intact, looking as much as possible like they did originally, can create some very difficult problems.

These problems are philosophical, scholarly, and aesthetic — as well as technical. That is why conservators need you, and the objects need all of us. "An endless struggle against the forces of nature" — this might be a legitimate, if pessimistic, definition of conservation. The monumentality of this task may be what makes conservators so often cranky and unyielding.

I am often asked to advise owners and curators on how they can perform conservation treatments on objects in their care. Other than describing the obvious dangers in having non-conservators do conservation work, I often respond that if non-conservators were doing all they could to preserve their collections, they would have no time left to worry about gluing pots together or cleaning paintings. This book will provide information, perhaps more than you ever thought you wanted to know, on some of the technical and practical issues in providing a safe environment for collections.

"But still," you ask, "What else can I do?"

For private collections, for small museums, and not-so-small museums, there is much aside from treatments that non-conservators can, and should, be doing. Collections management is a term usually used for institutions rather than for private collections, but it is a valid notion in both settings. The basic idea is the creation of a step-by-step plan for both physical and administrative methods of improving the condition of a collection and arranging for its appropriate use. Most of the items on the following list, and most of the ideas in this book, could be included in the term collections management. It might include consultation with experts in fields like conservation, pest control, and insurance to review the collections, prioritize problems, and arrange for step-by-step improvement. Much can be done in most areas without major expenditure of funds; more expensive projects can be undertaken a little at a time. The emphasis here should be on the active participation of the owner or custodian of collections. If nothing is done, if none of these matters are attended to, some of the potential of the collection for enjoyment and for providing knowledge will be wasted, and the physical condition of the pieces will undoubtedly suffer.

The following is a summary of various ways to keep yourself busy in the service of preservation.

1   Take a Close Look

The first, and probably the most important thing, is to spend some time looking at your objects. You may do this all the time: you may admire the richness of color in a sunset, stare into a little girl's eyes, or note the abstract silhouette of an African sculpture against your wall. But look again. Look for all the things that you would not see in a photograph in an art book. Look, first of all, for signs of the maker. Look for fingerprints, brushstrokes, toolmarks. Look at the backs of things, and the insides. A small well-focussed flashlight will help you here. With a magnifying glass look at the raised lines of ink on a print or the weave patterns in a textile. If the piece is small enough to carry safely, bring it to a window and turn it around in the bright light. Look at it in raking light, with the light almost parallel to the surface, to see the surface texture.

Look at the condition of the piece. See what you can detect of breaks, scratches, and previous restorations. Do you see the remains of insects (this may be almost inevitable in wooden objects brought from a tropical climate)? Are fingers or toes broken off? Are there thin vulnerable areas that have been broken and repaired? See how the piece may be different from its original state. Is a painting on canvas flat and tight on its stretcher or is it rippled or "dished"? Can you see brighter colors between the threads of a textile or in the seams than in exposed areas? Are there surface layers that are cracked or lifted up from the surface? If necessary, a gentle touch with the tip of a long fingernail or a small tool will tell you if the layer is flaking and loose. Think of how the piece may have been used and see if you can see any signs of use. Are there sweat marks on the inside of a mask, scuff marks around the bottom of chair legs, or normal wear on drawer runners?

Where will this get you? With patience and perhaps some reading about the way the pieces were made, you should learn to appreciate the objects in ways quite different from the distant view of the average museum-goer, ways that may give you an increased feeling of rapport with the people who made them. You will undoubtedly spot anomalies that necessitate further inquiry. The more you know about the objects in your care, the better you will be at choosing the best consultants, scholars and curators as well as conservators, and the more you will be able to profit from their expertise. The more you know about how your collection looks, the better you will be able to detect condition problems as they arise.

2
Maintain Your Building

Another activity that will provide a major boost to your ability to protect your collection is building maintenance. In my experience, more damage to collections has occurred from building problems than almost any other source. Make sure that all necessary servicing is carried out on your heating plant. Do periodic checks on the roof drains and gutters. Replace defective wiring and corroded pipes before disaster strikes. Bring in professionals for annual (or more frequent) cleaning of air conditioners. Fix leaky faucets and radiators. Make sure windows close well, and locks are sound. Eliminate bird and insect nests from the perimeter. Provide fire extinguishers and smoke alarms and make sure they remain in working order. If at all possible, keep collections away from water pipes, just in case. In basements where flooding is always a possibility, keep all objects at least four or five inches off the floor. In buildings with flat roofs, no amount of inspection or maintenance is too much, as periodic leaks are next to inevitable. Keep an eye open for the beginning of problems — water stains around skylights, for example. When work is being done, be extra watchful of workmen when in the proximity of collection material, and supervise them carefully. Many disasters have started from accidents with welding torches, or with workers who smoke while using flammable materials. Construction workers and repair personnel of various kinds do not understand the need for extra care when working near collections.

3   Document with Photographs

Another important activity is photography. Photographs will allow you to record and monitor the changing condition of objects. They will help to document collections for insurance purposes. Having photographs will allow easier consultation with various experts including conservators who may not be close at hand, and will give you something to carry with you to compare your material to similar things you may see elsewhere. They will provide immeasurable help in case of damage or theft, and will reduce the need for handling of stored collections. For basic black-and-white photography of collections, you will need an undisturbed space, a decent camera (a simple 35mm will do nicely), a tripod, and standard photographic lights. Some study and a few trials will allow you to produce perfectly adequate record photographs. Whoever is doing the photography must understand precautions for handling objects. Lights must never heat the objects. Care must be taken that the light stands do not fall onto the objects. If professional photographers are hired to do this, you must make sure that they understand the differences between record photographs and "art" photography. You do not necessarily want photographs that make the pieces look as good as possible. You do want detailed photos of inscriptions or signatures. You may want color slides or prints to better represent the appearance of the pieces, but remember that color pictures are not very permanent. Some color prints may change color noticeably within ten years, even in the dark, so for long-term use black and white is preferable.

If you decide to take on this tedious job, you should remember the amount of bookkeeping that is involved. Undated or inadequately labelled photographs lose a great deal of their usefulness. You will make the job easier if an identifying label with the date included is in the photograph. To be up to museum standard, all photographic prints or slides should also be labelled with the medium and measurements of the object, artist and title.

If you prefer a different method of documentation, video tape should be considered. This medium does not provide all of the benefits of archivally processed photographic prints, but it is much quicker, easier, and cheaper, entails much less handling of objects, and requires less storage space. Because information about the pieces can be read into the audio, there is no need for labelling. Basic information about the identity of collection items can be stored easily, and the information is available for purposes of comparison of condition, or for documentation of loss. Collections can be previewed by potential borrowers or researchers from the videotape to minimize handling of actual objects. Video tape is not considered permanent and will never replace methods that produce a high-quality print, but can be a second choice if traditional photography of every object is impractical.

4 Keep Records

Record-keeping is a well-known function of a museum, although all institutions do not necessarily fulfill their obligations in this area. It is important to keep and to organize all records relating to the objects in your care. These include official ones like receipts, informal material like correspondence with artists or previous owners, copies of catalogue entries, conservation records, ar any other information that might be interesting. Some owners like to record, together with the price they paid, prices of similar pieces as they come on the market. Museums generally give each object a unique number to aid in both identification and the organization of information, although this is seldom done in private collections. However, if your collection reaches a size where it is getting hard to remember which piece is which, it may be time to do the same. When you acquire something, you should routinely inquire about its history. How long has it been it the previous owner's hands? Do they know anything about other owners, or exhibitions the piece has been in? Did they ever have a conservator examine or treat it? If so, try to contact the conservator to get additional information. Records of condition and treatment will become even more valuable as time goes on.

If the artist is alive, you might consider contacting him or her directly and asking for information. Some museums have forms they routinely send to living artists to elicit various kinds of information. An example of such a form is reproduced in the Appendix. For collectors of contemporary works, personal contact with an artist or craftsperson can add a rewarding dimension to appreciation of the piece.

An important part of record-keeping for an institution or large private collection is attaching accession numbers to the pieces. Damaging materials like acidic inks on paper, nail polish, labels sewn to fragile textiles, painted numbers on the fronts of paintings, and numbers too large or in an awkward place must be avoided. Numbering should be done directly on the pieces if at all possible. Tie-on labels often do not last long enough. Although paintings, for example, are easily recognizable with or without numbers, some kinds of objects may be difficult or impossible to identify without clear numbers. For most objects, either carbon-based India Ink or a permanent red oil paint is appropriate. If the surface of the object is very porous, a coat of non-yellowing varnish should be used under the paint or ink. For paper, a very soft pencil should be used to avoid pressing into the paper. For most textiles, twill tape with the number printed on can be sewn onto the piece. For very fragile

objects, a conservator or registrar should be consulted.

5 Monitor Condition

Monitoring the condition of a collection is a job best done by the person who sees the objects most often. Photographs aid greatly in this process, as does knowing what to look for. Even experienced conservators sometimes succumb to the "Was that there before?" syndrome, so do not assume that you will remember every detail of an object without notes or photographs. It may be difficult to differentiate new scratches from old use-marks on furniture or to recognize minor damage on a large abstract painting with apparently random surface patterns.

Metal objects and framed works on paper should be inspected most carefully at times of high humidity. Painted wooden objects should be watched most carefully around the time that the weather starts to turn colder in the fall. Insect-susceptible objects should be looked at most carefully in the spring when the weather starts to warm up. Inspections for condition should include looking behind and under objects, particularly when looking for insects. Wood-eating insects will most commonly get into furniture, for example, through the rough uncoated wood underneath rather than through highly polished areas, and many kinds of insects prefer the dark, so examination of the undersides with a good light is important.

Special inspections should follow mechanical breakdowns, accidents, or other possibly harmful events. For example, if the heating system fails, relative humidity will increase suddenly, possibly causing condensation. Any objects in sealed containers, like textiles or works on paper framed behind glass or acrylic, should be checked for drops of water or spots of mold. After workmen are on the premises, or after large parties, everything should be checked for minor contact damage. When an accidental splash of liquid occurs near collection material, the drops often travel further than you would expect; look systematically for damage you didn't anticipate.

Most sources recommend monthly inspections for objects at risk. For collections on public display, daily rounds are recommended to check for vandalism or theft. All personnel involved with a collection should be trained to recognize damage and deterioration. Cleaning or security staff in museums or historic houses often spend more time with the collections than curatorial or administrative staff, and are therefore more likely to identify problems at their earliest stages.

Inspection of collections in storage is particularly important, because various kinds of deterioration, including insect damage and water damage from leaks, must be caught early in order to prevent severe and possible widespread damage to collections. Although storage is usually thought of as a problem only in institutions, many households have valuable family heirlooms in storage in closets, attics, and basements. Because basements and attics have such extreme environmental conditions (in the first case, cold and damp; in the second, hot and dry) objects stored there may be subject to serious problems. Many families have old clothing, photographs, and family documents in storage; these things are particularly sensitive to poor environments. Photographs and clothing are also particularly difficult to restore after damage has occurred.

Although museum-quality storage may seem like an overwhelming job for a private individual, if you wish to preserve the things you have put aside, then the same criteria that govern museum storage should govern yours. Rewrapping things for the greatest possible protection may spell the difference between having these things in the future and not having them.

Look both at the objects and under them for any small pieces. A small fragment that may have been part of an object should be put into a small envelope or jar, labelled and dated, and saved for a conservator to look at. With a magnifying glass, you should be able to decide whether it is part of the object, insect debris, or something else. A telephone call to a conservator who knows your collection should help you figure out what is happening, what should be done, and how quickly it should be done. In general, water damage requires immediate professional attention; mold and insect infestation require fast, but not emergency, response.

6 Hire a Conservator

Conservation treatments can be expensive; you may have stayed away from conservators for this reason. However, conservators with experience in environmental control and collections care can be an important source of information that will prevent damage and therefore save money. Most conservators are willing to look at collections with no commitment on your part for having treatments done. For an hourly fee, you can have conservators in different specialties examine the objects in your collection for condition and comment on possible treatments. They should be clear in specifying which pieces should be treated to prevent damage or to slow ongoing deterioration, and which ones would benefit aesthetically from treatment. They should be able to comment on the quality of the environment and give concrete suggestions for steps that could be taken to make improvements, and should be able to prioritize these steps. If you are looking for written information, perhaps including addresses of suppliers or bibliographies, expect to pay for the additional time.

If you could use some help in learning how better to examine your collection, this is a good time for instruction. Let the conservator know this in advance, since it may alter his or her estimate of how much time the visit will take. A conservator may be willing to look through your collection with an ultraviolet ("black") light and explain what this examination method reveals. Proper interpretation of the appearance of objects under ultraviolet light is particularly difficult to learn without guidance. In paintings, for example, paint added by a restorer usually appears a dark purplish-black; the same color on ceramics usually indicates original material. Many non-conservators who try to use an ultraviolet light make errors in interpretation that convince them that they see restoration when they are actually looking at original artist's work; this leads to unfortunate suspicions about the object when there should be none. The accurate interpretation of ultraviolet examination requires some training.

Do not clean up specially for visiting conservators or hide your worst problems. You may think you have the worst conditions they have ever seen, but they have undoubtedly seen worse. It is difficult to shock an experienced conservator. You deserve credit for trying to remedy problems, so don't be embarrassed.

The formalized version of the conservator visit, what I sometimes refer to as a "walk-through," is called either a conservation survey or, increasingly, a conservation assessment. Grants are available from a number of federal and state agencies to pay a conservator for this kind of visit to museums, historical societies, or other not-for-profit institutions. With or without a grant, it may be one of the most efficient ways to gather information. A formal assessment must be followed up with a written report. Although this will add to the total cost of the consultation, the report will become a valuable source in drawing up a long range conservation plan. Having information in writing will assure that you have correctly understood what the conservator has said. It will give you something to show to other people who deal with your collection. If you have any doubts about the conservator's judgment or knowledge, the report can be shown to others for their opinion. In addition, the writing of a report will give the conservator a chance to organize his or her thoughts and to present the material in the most effective way.

Once a conservator has seen your collection, he or she can often supply further information over the telephone. Although most conservators will answer simple questions over the telephone without charge, expect to pay some fee when doing a more complicated consultation.

Most conservators are also willing to inspect pieces before purchase to determine their general condition, the extent of previous restoration, their physical need for treatment, and how their appearance might be improved. Any reputable dealer or other seller should be willing to allow this. Information from the conservator may help you to decide if the asking price is reasonable, based on the condition, and if expensive treatment will be necessary. Conservators can also help to protect your pieces if requested for loan, consult on proper framing and mounting, and give advice or refer you elsewhere on any other issue that touches on the physical welfare of your collection.

Don't expect conservators to offer appraisals of your collection, as this is generally regarded as a conflict of interest and usually not within their expertise. Avoid putting them on the spot by asking them what they think of the quality of your things. Many clients ask conservators if a particular piece is worth treatment. It is hard to know exactly what this question implies, but I generally assume that it calls for some kind of judgment on the dollar value of the piece compared to the cost of treatment. Market values are very nebulous things; certain kinds of pieces may be fashionable one year and not the next. Most nineteenth-century portraits, for example, no matter how beautifully painted, seldom fetch prices anywhere near what comparable landscapes cost, because few people want portraits of people other than their own ancestors. This sort of valuation by market price is something few conservators have sympathy with. For collections like textiles which fetch relatively low prices, it is not unusual for a treatment to cost more than the market value of the object. Does that make the treatment not worth doing? In some other cases where an object was purchased in poor condition, the obvious necessity for treatment may have lowered the price, so that the market value of the piece after treatment may exceed the purchase price plus the treatment cost.

Many treatments will not add to the market price of a piece, but it is also not true that a proper treatment will detract from the value of a piece. Treatment of a painting that has been restored repeatedly may reveal damage that was not visible before; it is, however, the damage and not the treatment that is responsible for any devaluation. Conservators can and should be able to tell you how much a treatment or a consultation would cost, what the expected results would be, and

what might be expected to happen without treatment, but the ultimate decision is yours. They should offer to put in writing a condition report, proposal for treatment, and estimate, and should insist on having it signed by you before any work is begun.

How do you find a conservator? The best place to start is usually a local museum, or a major one somewhat further away. If the museum has a conservation department, try to get a referral directly from a conservator. Conservators tend to cluster in major urban areas, so if you are far away from a large city, you may not be able to find one close by. If the institution gives you a name (or more than one), find out what kind of work the person has done for the institution or how well their work is known. When you contact a conservator directly, feel free to ask about their training or request a resume. Most professional conservators are members of the American Institute for Conservation of Historic and Artistic Works (AIC). This is no guarantee of competence, but it indicates that someone is interested in continuing to learn. A brochure from AIC (See *Sources of Information*) entitled *Guidelines for Selecting a Conservator* should help you know what to look for, and a copy of the AIC *Code of Ethics and Standards of Practice* should help you further in knowing what to expect. AIC also has a referral service.

Ultimately, your best way of choosing a conservator should be the same as the way you choose a doctor: after getting a good referral, trust your instincts. Does he or she seem like someone you can trust? Do you feel comfortable asking questions - even questions that *seem* stupid? Do you get respectful thoughtful answers free of jargon? If you visit a conservator's laboratory, does it look clean and well-organized? Are objects handled with care and respect? Does the conservator have experience with the kind of collections you have? Don't forget to describe your collections and what you see as their primary problems. If your primary concern is with the environment, make sure you look for someone with this specialty; as with medicine, the field of conservation is getting much more specialized.

doubt be an excellent source of information.

❦

Greater involvement in the physical care of your collections will benefit them greatly. It will also benefit you by deepening your appreciation of aspects of objects that many collectors and curators do not see. Historical and art objects have obvious aesthetic, intellectual, and spiritual components. They are also concrete things that somebody made. It has always seemed to me that dealing with their physical aspects brings us closer to their makers.

7 Plan for Disasters

Planning for disasters such as fire and flood has become an important part of a proper collections care policy. Libraries and archives have led the way in this area, largely from unfortunate experience. A few conservators have become expert in disaster planning, although much of the recent literature in this field has come from non-conservators. Any institution in your area that has had a fire or flood will no

Temperature and Relative Humidity

The subjects of temperature and relative humidity are surrounded by more misconceptions than any other area in the field of conservation. The first one is simple: most people assume that temperature is more important than relative humidity in its effect on objects. This is completely untrue. In fact, the most important thing about temperature and its effect on collections is its effect on relative humidity levels.

Inappropriate levels of relative humidity or widely fluctuating relative humidities are implicated in the deterioration of almost every kind of object, organic and inorganic, wood and textiles as well as metals and glass. Poor conservation treatments are often damaging simply because of their effects on the response of the object to changes in relative humidity. Under most conditions, people are much less sensitive to RH levels than to temperature, and it is therefore difficult to get them to take seriously enough the effects of relative humidity on collections.

What is the Relation between Temperature and Relative Humidity? ... What is Relative Humidity?

Proper understanding of these questions is crucial to understanding much about the condition of objects, so please excuse a certain amount of repetition in these beginning sections. Relative humidity is a measure of the amount of moisture in the air relative to the amount the air is capable of holding, expressed as a percentage. If the air at a particular temperature contains half the water vapor it can hold at that temperature, the relative humidity is 50%. This figure is much more important that absolute humidity, a simple measure of the amount of moisture in the air. Put in human terms, if the air in a room is holding only a small percentage of the moisture it is capable of holding, it will "want" to pick up moisture from its surroundings; if the relative humidity is very high, it will not do so, and will, in fact, be close to ready to give some up. The tendency of air to take up or give off water is expressed by the relative humidity; absolute humidity has nothing to do with this.

What happens when the temperature in a closed space changes? Think of air molecules doing a juggling act: their rapid movement picks up water from their surroundings and holds the molecules in suspension. As the temperature rises, the air molecules move faster and can juggle more water. As the temperature drops, the air molecules slow down and find it more and more difficult to keep the water molecules suspended. As an enclosed body of air cools down, the relative humidity gets higher; the temperature at which it hits 100%, or saturation, is referred to as the dewpoint temperature. This is the point at which condensation occurs.

The lowering of relative humidity as air temperature increases can create extremely low wintertime relative humidities in cold climates. As outside air at 30° F., 50% RH, is heated to a room temperature of 75° F., the relative humidity falls to about 10%. Drastic reductions in indoor humidity levels during the winter are therefore due directly to the difference between outdoor and indoor temperatures.

Objects that are sensitive to changes in relative humidity, that is, "hygroscopic" objects, are better preserved in unheated buildings. Outdoor relative humidities in temperate climates tend to stay within a narrower range than indoor ones. Objects, unlike

people, do not suffer from cold. This is another important fundamental point that causes endless misunderstandings in the design of environmental controls for collections: people are very sensitive to temperature and much less sensitive to relative humidity; objects are much more sensitive to relative humidity levels and much less sensitive to temperature.

It is important to differentiate between water vapor, a gas, and tiny droplets of liquid water. Relative humidity relates to gaseous water. Changes in energy that occur when water droplets actually evaporate into the gaseous state are crucial to understanding the processes of humidity control. What we call steam that we see coming out of a pot of boiling water is not a gas, but gaseous water condensing as it cools in the air.

The relationship among temperature, relative humidity, absolute humidity, and dewpoint temperature, as well as a few other things that are irrelevant at the moment, is illustrated in a complex-looking thing called a psychrometric, or hygrometric, chart (See Fig. 1). The lines we are most concerned with are in the scale across the bottom, labelled "dry bulb temperature", and the lines curving upward to the right, which are the lines of relative humidity. The curved line at the left is equivalent to 100% RH, that is, the dewpoint temperature. Lines representing changing temperatures where no moisture is added or taken out of the air are horizontal.

This chart can give us answers to some important questions. For example: moisture-sensitive works of art are being shipped in a truck in cold weather. Should the truck be heated? As we shall see later, cold in itself does not affect most objects, but we wish to avoid condensation. Suppose the crates will be sealed at 75°, 30% RH. If we find this point on the graph, and follow it to our left, we find that, as we expect, the relative humidity increases until we hit the dewpoint temperature of about 40°. If, therefore, our truck is out in the cold long enough for the temperature inside the crates to drop to 40°, we will find wet objects in the crates when they reach their destination.

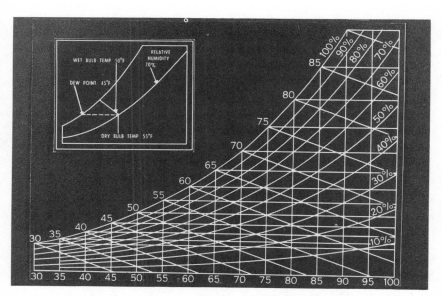

Fig. 1   Hygrometric chart. Also called a psychrometric chart, this is a simplified version. A hygrometric chart shows, among other things, the relationship among temperature, relative humidity, absolute humidity, and dewpoint temperature. Chart courtesy of Belfort Instrument Co.

How is Relative Humidity Measured?

This is not an easy question to answer. Difficulties with accurate measurement of RH outside a laboratory are not easily resolved. They are so pervasive that many projects involving adjustment of environmental controls have the production of accurate readings as their first task. I have attended and heard of many meetings on environmental control where participants - conservators, engineers, museum representatives, consultants of various kinds - each pull out their favorite instruments and try to agree on what the RH level actually is before the discussion can begin.

The "real" relative humidity is measured by laboratory equipment not at all suitable for museum use. The most basic piece of equipment portable enough to use outside a laboratory is the sling psychrometer. This consists of two standard glass thermometers mounted side by side in a device that allows the operator to swing them through the air. One thermometer has a fabric sock over the sensing end. The sock is wet with distilled water, the device is swung, and water evaporates from the wet bulb. The less moisture in the air, the more water evaporates, and the lower the temperature reading will be on the "wet bulb" thermometer. After an appropriate amount of time, both thermometers are read, and a chart is consulted to produce the magic number.

One of the first hazards of this instrument is that the swinging is tiring, and after a few readings, the operator's aim tends to deteriorate, leading to broken thermometers when the instrument hits a wall or doorway by accident. In order for readings to be accurate, swinging must be continued for two to three minutes at two to three revolutions per second. Body heat and moisture can change the readings considerably, so the instrument must be swung at arms' length rather than close to the body. The solution to this problem is a battery-operated version, where batteries run a small fan that blows air past the wet sock. This is a major improvement in ease of operation and is highly recommended, even though the price (about $120-$160) is more than that of a sling psychrometer (about $40-$60).

Even with a battery-operated psychrometer, measurements must be taken very carefully. Batteries must be strong enough to produce an acceptable fan speed. The two thermometers must have exactly the same readings before use, and must be read immediately after use. Only distilled water should be used, and fingers should never touch the sock, as any dirt or grease on the fabric will slow evaporation. Frequent changes of the sock for a new clean one should avoid problems from this cause. The sock must be in close contact with the thermometer. Most experts recommend that three readings be taken one after the other as a check. When operated perfectly, readings on a wet-and-dry-bulb instrument are excellent at high RH levels, but much less accurate at lower levels. Below 25%, they are very inaccurate, with no readings of below 10%. A great deal of variation in RH readings can come from a very small change in temperature readings, so the accuracy of the thermometers is vital. For example, a dry bulb reading of 69° and a wet bulb reading of 65° indicate 81% RH; 70° dry with 64° wet indicates 72%, almost 10% difference with only one degree difference in temperature! It is important to remember, as we shall see later, that most errors will result in a higher than actual RH reading. Although the psychrometer is still one of the most reliable instruments for the money, its defects are magnified when an institution uses psychrometer readings to calibrate other instruments.

A common instrument for direct measurement of relative humidity is the dial hygrometer. These are inexpensive; even the best cost around $100, and cheap ones are available for under $10. Many dial hygrometers simply do not indicate either very high or very low RH levels. Their needles do not go much above 70% or below 30% or 40%. Some of the more advanced models are somewhat better, although subject to damage from careless handling, but dials should not be used unless

they can be intitially calibrated and monitored repeatedly with other instruments. The danger with these or any other inaccurate measurement is that custodians of collections will assume that their collections are safe when they are not. This is not an imaginary scenario, but a very real and constant problem.

One small dial meter, the Arten Meter (See *Sources of Supply*: Art Preservation Services), may solve some of these problems by including humidity-indicating paper strips in the unit. Calibration kits are also available for this instrument.

The standard for continuous readings of temperature and relative humidity is the recording hygrothermograph. The sensing device for relative humidity is a harp of human hair or a synthetic membrane either of which expands and contracts in response to RH changes. The movement is recorded by a pen on a moving chart. Many instruments run for one week at a time on a manually wound mechanical system; some operate on batteries or electricity with charts that record a month of information at a time. A range of features creates a range of prices from about $500-$1000 (See *Sources of Supply*). Hygrothermographs are vital for surveying environmental conditions in a building prior to designing environmental controls, since they show the changes caused by daily lighting and heating cycles and weather changes. Placement of the instruments is crucial, since some parts of a room will have naturally stagnant air and will not show changes occurring elsewhere. Hygrothermographs situated near a ceiling may show the effects of hot lights; those situated lower may risk being bumped. In certain situations it is valuable to use several instruments in one room to investigate the differences between environments in different parts of a room. Hygrothermographs in several adjoining rooms will show the movement of exterior air through the building when sudden weather changes occur.

Before planning environmental controls, it is obviously vital to have readings from many parts of a building in all seasons of the year. Too many institutions plan climate control based on assumptions rather than fact; this does a disservice to collections and budgets alike.

When doing environmental surveys, any occurrences which affect either temperature or relative humidity should be marked on the charts. These include rainstorms, direct sunlight, floor-mopping, and large influxes of people. Dates and exact locations for the instruments must also be marked clearly on the charts, and notes should be made when the machines are calibrated.

Once environmental controls are installed, hygrothermographs are vital during the period of testing and balancing of mechanical systems, and as permanent monitors for the system. Sensors that control the system should not be the same ones that monitor its performance.

Hygrothermographs have become a common sight in museums, but they do nothing for collections unless the information is in a usable form and someone is available to read and act on it. Keeping several hygrothermographs in operation is time-consuming, with calibration, winding, changing charts, cleaning and re-inking pens. Dealing with an ever-growing pile of charts is daunting. Handling the mass of data that hygrothermographs produce is an unsolved problem. Several systems have been proposed for summarizing data, but different uses of monitoring equipment require different kinds of information, so it is impossible to set a single standard. There is no point in operating many instruments if nothing is to be done with the data that is gathered. Before spending a lot of money and time on hygrothermographs, it is necessary to decide exactly what it is that you are trying to find out.

As useful as hygrothermographs are, they are not perfect instruments, and need repeated calibration, every one to two months, against another instrument. In areas with very polluted air, the sensing elements will need to be cleaned, as pollutant gases may affect their sensitivity. Very low relative humidities will affect the hair; some manufacturers recommend re-hydrating the hair by laying a damp cloth over the instrument before re-calibration. Hygrothermographs do not show an immediate response; although RH levels may change within minutes in response to outdoor weather changes, hygrothermographs may take many times that long to register the changes. Hygrothermographs also show hysteresis effects. This means, in short, that readings in the same environment will be different if the RH is approaching the target level from a lower level or a higher one. For temperatures very different from normal room temperature, some corrections to the readings should be made; specific information should come from the manufacturer.

There are several electronic hand-held direct-reading instruments that have become available in the last few years. They are generally modest-sized instruments, in the $500-1000 range, that provide excellent results in all ranges except the very low. Guarantees on accuracy from the manufacturers often do not extend to levels below 25%, and accuracy is much worse below about 15%. Many have their own calibration devices. They are simple to use, and can provide relatively idiot-proof calibration for hygrothermographs.

Recent advances in electronics have produced a system where electronic sensors in a building connect to a computer that records readings from many sensors at once. Data can be transferred via phone lines to another location periodically. These solid-state data loggers will make it easier to monitor environment in small institutions where no staff is available to service hygrothermographs. Since the information is already on a computer database, work can be done directly to translate the raw data into a more easily usable form. These systems have not yet (1989) been used in many different settings, and future development of standardized software will undoubtedly make this kind of system easier to use. In any building that would need half a dozen or more hygrothermographs, a solid state data logger may be less expensive.

We have so far a variety of instruments, all of which perform poorly at low relative humidities. What is the point of calibrating one instrument against another that may be just as inaccurate? Remember that normally-heated buildings without wintertime humidification may have RH levels well below 20% during almost the whole heating season, just the levels at which most instruments are unreliable.

A partial solution to this problem is humidity-indicating paper strips. These are familiar pink-and-blue indicating papers, which can be purchased as small cards with squares that give readings in steps of 10% from 10% to 100% (See *Sources of supply*: Conservation Materials and Humidial Corp.). Reading the RH is not an exact science. It is impossible to tell 37% from 39%, but the cards are capable of producing reproducible readings in dry conditions; unlike hygrometers, they will not read 35% when the RH is actually 15%. It may be useful to tape a card onto the outside of each hygrothermograph. This will warn when the hygrothermograph needs calibrating, or when it is simply not working properly.

The paper indicators are useful for several reasons. They are extremely inexpensive, so they can be used liberally. They are small and quite inobtrusive, so they can be placed inside exhibition cases without disturbance. They can be cut into smaller pieces, or the writing can be cut off to make them even less aesthetically disturbing inside cases. They are quite permanent, but need to be replaced if they get dirty or wet. To repeat: they may be the only devices that give close-to-accurate readings at very low RH levels. In my normally heated laboratory, cards that have been tested recently in an environmental chamber are all blue, that is, below 10%, virtually all winter unless humidifiers are working. No instrument I have confirms this reading; even the Arten Meterdoes not read below about 28%. It is vital to be aware of RH levels as low as 10%, because they are so damaging to collection material. The consistent failure of sensors to react at very low RH levels is in itself evidence of the anomalous behavior of materials in those conditions.

The difficulty of getting good RH readings makes accuracy an absolute first priority in any project that will involve spending money on mechanical systems. People who spend their careers involved in climate control projects often have a number of instruments they calibrate against each other; this matter does not get easier the more you know about it. However, it is vital to know where errors might creep in, so that corrections can be made.

A large number of institutions consistently overestimate their wintertime relative humidities by as much as 30 or 40%. This can lead to a whole series of faulty decisions which impact badly on collections. After all, objects will respond to what the relative humidity really is, not to what you think it is.

Setting Standards for Relative Humidity

What level of relative humidity is ideal for collections? This is an even more difficult question than "How is relative humidity measured?". In fact, there is no answer to this question. As we shall see, attempting to answer it draws us into major complications. The museum literature has put us all off on this subject, because most of the work on museum environmental control has been carried out in a climate very different from that of most of the United States. Garry Thomson, who is largely responsible for making the museum community worldwide aware of the importance of environmental control in the preservation of collections, carried out much of his research in a country where the outdoor RH ranges from 70 to 90% all year round. British winters are quite mild compared to those in much of the United States, and unlike Americans, the British are not addicted to the massive use of central heating. Many English house museums are not heated at all.

English concerns with relative humidity center around counteracting "rising damp" and holding RH *down* to safe levels to avoid mold. Much of the museum literature therefore recommends year-round RH levels of 50 or 55%, levels which in U. S. winters would require incredible amounts of water being added to the air at a tremendous outlay of energy. 50 or 55% should not be considered an ideal wintertime level for most American collections. There is little or no evidence that gives these numbers any magic quality of preservation.

As is shown in the chapters on materials, various materials have their own chemistries that may make certain levels theoretically best for their long-term preservation, or may produce the most desirable characteristics. However, an ivory that was acclimated to a tropical climate, carved, and then brought to the United States to spend twenty years in a hot attic is not the same as one that came almost directly from a living elephant; each object has its own history. In addition, although we tend to refer to objects by their principle material, few works are without additions of other media, whether original or from later restoration. A wooden chair may have been originally joined with animal glue and coated with linseed oil. Iron nails may have been added as repair, and a synthetic adhesive may have been used more recently. Many chairs have upholstery which incorporates horsehair stuffing, fabric, steel tacks on the inside, brass tacks as decoration, and jute webbing. Very few objects consist of only one material. In those that do, the original material may have been altered enough by the process of aging so that its chemistry is significantly different from that of the new materials usually tested in laboratories.

It is important to differentiate between two different modes of response to relative humidity. One is seen in a material like iron, where corrosion occurs at high RH levels. Published data for humidity levels below which iron will not corrode are not reliable, because the presence of pollutant gases and the presence of dirt or existing rust on the iron surface may promote corrosion. However, within these complications, any low RH is equally protective, and changes in RH within these limits will not cause any problems. Rapid fluctuations are of no concern.

This kind of object fits a common industrial model of RH standard. If, for example, a candy factory needs to have a RH between 40 and 60%, fluctuations between these limits do not matter. HVAC (heating, ventilation, and air conditioning) engineers, and the equipment they recommend and install, can fulfill these requirements.

Hygroscopic materials adapt to changes in ambient RH by changes in their moisture content. Each material has its own behavior pattern, and each has an equilibrium moisture content (EMC) corresponding to any RH level. Ordinarily expansion of the material accompanies an increase in the moisture content. Particular problems from fast changes in EMC involve internal stresses created by differentials between the exterior and interior of materials as moisture slowly diffuses into or out of the surrounding air. The cracking and warping of wood are direct results of this. One sheet of paper will equilibrate quickly to a changing RH level. A tightly closed book, on the other hand, may take months to reach its EMC. The sheet of paper may ripple at a higher RH, while the covers and leaves of a book may be permanently distorted by the stresses created when exterior and interior are at very different levels. The damage to hygroscopic

materials resulting from fluctuations in RH is damage from the physical stress of dimensional change.

Differences in response between materials can create havoc in compound objects like paintings. Linen canvas is extremely responsive to changes in RH; aged oil paint films are almost completely unresponsive. The combination causes paint to crack and eventually to flake off its support. Veneered furniture is particularly susceptible to RH changes. Because of the thinness of the veneers, they expand and contract readily, while the underlying wood responds more slowly; the animal glue holding them together loses its grip as it dries out and fails to re-hydrate.

The expansion and contraction of textile fibers in response to changes in RH can accelerate aging of the textile because of the internal abrasion they cause. Materials like chipboard are weakened by RH fluctuations for the same reason.

The overriding importance of RH stability rather than any particular RH level is definitely not a typical industrial standard for RH control. Architects and engineers do not readily accept it, nor will they have had experience in fulfilling it. If you are asked what level of relative humidity you require for your collection, the answer should be "Whatever level can be maintained without fail, 24 hours per day, twelve months per year."

Some familiar examples will illustrate this point. Most of the collections of old things we enjoy have been preserved by environments that have remained steady for centuries or millenia, even though they may have been at levels considered highly undesirable. Egyptian tombs, for example, have preserved thousands of artifacts both organic and inorganic in excellent condition, until they were removed from their "final resting place". Panel paintings have come to us in excellent condition after centuries in exceedingly damp castles and churches, and have only come to grief when exposed to the dryness produced by central heating. If environments could be tailor-made for objects, we might conclude that objects recovered from such stable environments be kept in their historic conditions.

As we shall see later, there are many reasons why keeping the RH level steady year-round is exceedingly difficult, but it is still important for those responsible for environmental control in museums and private collections to understand the difference between requiring a steady RH at whatever level can be best maintained and requiring 50 or 55%. 55% RH, maintained most of the time, with perhaps a few incidents every week with sudden drops to 40% will be worse for collections than 40% consistently maintained.

A steady RH every day and night of the year at any feasible level between about 40 and 60% would be virtually ideal for most collections. For reasons we shall see later, this may be prohibitively expensive and difficult to manage. A reasonable alternative that would provide significant protection would be to provide a steady RH of about 35-40% in the winter, a steady 60% in the summer, and to raise and lower the levels between the two in the fall and spring, with daily fluctuations of no more than a few percent, and monthly levels that change no more than 5% per month.

This may be an excellent compromise between object safety and energy use, although it may still not be easy to maintain. It would produce the rather daunting prospect of a system that would be asked to provide a different level almost every month of the year. For example:

Month	Average RH
Jan.-Feb.	35%
March	40%
April	45%
May	50%
June	55%
July-Aug.	60%
September	55%
October	50%
November	45%
December	40%

These changing levels would probably require an extraordinary amount of constant tinkering to produce the desired result. I am not familiar with any system designed to produce a range of readings like this. The in-between seasons would still be quite difficult, since 55% for September would require massive dehumidification. As soon as heat goes on (in New York City, landlords must provide heat after 15 October if necessary), massive humidification would be required to provide 50% in October. In terms of the relationship between temperature and relative humidity, the idea of a variation of RH in winter with its lowest point in the coldest weather makes sense in helping to avoid condensation. A variation in RH levels from month to month during the summer does not have the same kind of justification, since the hottest weather does not necessarily correspond to the dampest weather.

The above example clarifies the difference between annual, daily, and monthly variation. Given a figure of 50% ± 5% as a specification for a particular climate control system, does that mean that the RH might be 45% in winter and 55% in summer; does it mean that there would be a gradual change from day to night of 45% to 55%; or that readings would bounce back and forth between 45% and 55% every few hours? The first choice would be virtually ideal; the last, possibly ruinous.

Changes in relative humidity need to be gradual for hygroscopic materials. To repeat: this is not industrial standard, since the operation of typical air conditioning equipment involves cycling. A simple feedback system governs the machinery. When the temperature hits one set level, the machinery turns on, and when it changes to another set level, the machinery turns off again. Temperature variations produce even wider RH variations, and each cycle can be under an hour (See Fig. 2). Unless every object in such an environment is containerized to buffer the short-term changes, this environment would be very hard on objects.

How gradual is gradual enough? This is another question that does not have a simple answer. Suppose an environmental system had a malfunction, and the winter RH plummeted from 50 to 15% within a few hours. Should the RH be brought back to 50% as soon as possible, or should it be phased in gradually? In other words, have objects responded to the change fully in whatever time had elapsed since the change? Some objects may respond fully within minutes, others not for weeks. Some may readjust without evident damage; others may require substantial conservation treatment to avoid loss. This is the kind of question that may come up in real life, and that puts conservators on the spot.

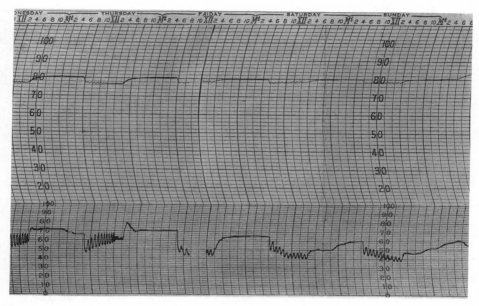

Fig. 2   A hygrothermographchart from a gallery with a standard window air conditioner turned on only during the day. The upper line (temperature) stays at around 80° at night, and drops to around 77-78° during the day. Fluctuations of less than a degree produce swings of up to 15% in relative humidity (lower line). Local weather records and records of museum activity would have to be examined to determine the causes of other shifts in RH.

Reaching an answer for a particular collection would be no more than an educated guess, based on an immediate examination of the pieces and a knowledge of their condition and treatment histories. Most conservators would probably advise that a conservator be present periodically for the readjustment period, would prepare for the worst and hope for the best.
Conservation is not an exact science.

In addition to rapid cycling of temperature and relative humidity, mechanical systems can create serious damage to collections by any sort of malfunction. Complete shut-off of a system, malfunction in a controlling sensoror switch, or any other malfunction, can cause rapid and extreme shifts in RH, or rapid shifts in temperature that cause rapid shifts in RH. If a humidification system that provides 45% RH in a space that, without humidification, would be below 10%, a change of 35 percentage points could occur within hours. Any hygroscopic material not containerized, particularly painted wood, could sustain immediate damage, and a piece in an exhibition case might show damage within twenty-four hours. Wood has been heard to split in conditions like these, with a sound like a rifle shot. On the other hand, malfunctions in switches or sensors have allowed RH levels close to 100%, producing overnight metal corrosion and condensation.

In buildings where equipment malfunctions or disruptions in electrical service are common, collections may well be safer without centralized HVAC systems. If a building housing sensitive materials can be protected from external fluctuations by well-sealed doors and well-insulated walls, with some easily-maintained and cheaply operated localized humidification and de-humidification, the objects may be better off than with a centralized system expensive in energy and manpower. If particularly sensitive material can be protected by well-sealed cases, the actual outlook may be far superior. We will return to this point repeatedly: more expensive and more complex is not necessarily better.

To return to the original question, the concept of the ideal RH for a particular object may have been a faulty one from the start. For a whole collection of objects, the question simply pales beneath the ponderous question of what levels can possibly be maintained.

If we are determined at least to avoid extremes of RH, how can we decide how high and how low are too much? In addition to physical stresses caused by low levels, unacceptable build-up of static electricity and irreversible desiccation of some objects occurs at low RH (below about 40 or 45%). What time period is required for these irreversible changes to take place is not easy to ascertain. Wood and textiles from Egyptian tombs are the extreme cases, being quite brittle and powdery after thousands of years at an RH close to zero. Shorter-term desiccation, say under 20% seasonally for fifty to one hundred years, definitely leaves baskets in a desiccated condition. Data are lacking to answer this question, but it is complicated by the fact that most organic materials undergo permanent desiccation after long periods at low RH but have the capability for significant moisture regain, and a reversal of most of their physical properties, with short-term shifts in RH. It should be noted that animal glue, the traditional adhesive for furniture, loses much of its strength at low RH levels, resulting in the separation of parts and the loss of inlay.

Low RH levels are, of course, desirable for metals, and precise figures exist for the levels necessary for the growth of various corrosion products. As has been stated above, the figures assume unpolluted air and a clean metallic surface, neither of which are apt to exist in collections. Stagnant air can produce a higher humidity around certain objects, and the warmth of lights can lower it. Some conservators have observed that any level below 50% will prevent corrosion in clean collections; in other cases much lower levels may be necessary. Often in museums metals are the one material for which a separate environment is maintained in storage, if not in exhibitions.

Specific numbers for how high is too high are somewhat easier to defend, and have been agreed upon based largely on the experience of archivists and librarians. Mold becomes a potential problem for susceptible material at about 70% and a pretty real possibility at about 75%. Again, stagnant pockets of air can create locally higher RH levels, and hygroscopic dirt can promote mold growth at somewhat lower levels, so 60% is often considered a reasonable upper limit.

Let us return again to the original question: what RH level is ideal? We have several competing interests, for the moment leaving out the question of how we are going to achieve the levels we desire. Most hygroscopic materials will settle at any given level within reasonable limits (say 40-60%). The corrosive effects of air pollution increase with higher RH, as do the harmful effects of light. Deterioration promoted by acids in the object, like those in poor-quality paper and red-rotted leather, accelerates with higher RH.

The action of many harmful insects increases with higher RH, powderpost beetles not reproducing below about 55%. Objects with chemically incompatible elements like wood and metal, or oil paint on raw canvas, deteriorate more quickly with higher RH. There is substantial evidence that an ideal relative humidity for a mixed collection would be on the lower rather than the higher end, possibly 40-45% rather than 50-55%. This would allow most metals to be kept in the same environment as other objects.

Holding year-round relative humidity levels at 40% rather than 55% would, of course, be more difficult in the summer and easier in the winter. It is unlikely that either level, kept year-round, would be worth the expense and trouble it would cause in most museums or private collections. When plans for environmental control are being made for a specific collection in a specific building in a specific climate, with specific operating and capital budgets and a specific level of staffing, many different factors will contribute to the final decision. It is vital to realize that there is no intrinsic virtue to the higher figure, and that arguments could be made for the lower one, even though it goes against museum orthodoxy. Steadiness of relative humidity and reliability of equipment are still overriding concerns.

Setting Standards for Temperature

Temperature levels have an effect on objects, but less than most people think. The major effect of temperature on objects is its effect on relative humidity.

Desirable temperature levels for collections are usually given in the literature as 68-70° F. This is low for American buildings, and may in the winter provoke complaints, particularly from staff and elderly visitors. However, using these figures in the winter instead of a more common 75-80° will help keep RH levels from plummeting, without any of the hazards or expense of humidification. Temperatures below this, or as low as anyone can stand, would help even more. There is no advantage to cooling to this level in summer, and temperature levels should be set to drift between seasons gradually.

In exhibition spaces or offices, human comfort gives little leeway for temperatures, but temperature is an important factor in deterioration and, where possible, lowering it should be considered. A commonly quoted rule of thumb states that every 10° C. (18° F.) increase of temperature doubles the average rate of organic reactions, so setting wintertime temperatures in storage areas in the low 60's will be a significant advantage, and will save energy. This is an arbitrary figure; reactions would be even slower at lower temperatures, but

greater distances between temperatures in different parts of a building make the possibility of condensation on cold objects brought into warmer air more likely, and the suddenness of changes between one space and the other may cause problems. Sensitive objects moved between areas with widely varying RH levels should be moved in well-sealed containers and allowed to acclimate slowly.

For certain materials, notably color photographic materials, unstable film stock, and furs, cold storage is highly recommended. At temperatures in the forties or below, condensation on the objects when they are moved into warmer spaces may be heavy, and photographic materials are easily damaged by water, so water-proof containers are vital.

For long-term storage of paper, cold storage might also be considered, since research shows that the lifetime of paper is increased by many times in low temperatures. Similar reactions could probably be expected with textiles. Only a few institutions nationwide have tackled the technology involved with massive cold storage. If the technology is refined and developed further, cold storage with moderate or low RH would be an excellent strategy for preservation.

If artificially induced cold storage is beneficial, then it should be clear that installing heating systems in unheated buildings is not beneficial. For mixed collections, it may be said that keeping the temperature above freezing could avoid problems, but the worst problem with unheated buildings is not the cold but the lack of protection from the elements that many such buildings provide. In order to improve conditions in buildings that are unused in the winter, a system that controls heating by means of a humidistats has been proposed. This would probably be ideal, but unheated buildings in most climates would actually leave RH levels year-round steadier than in a heated building. Objects do not get a chill.

General Strategies: Using the Natural Properties of the Space

By using the natural properties of different spaces in a building, it is often possible to improve the environment of collections without *doing* any environmental control. This strategy should always be used first, even when buildings are centrally controlled, because no system is perfect, and because certain parts of buildings retain unique properties. For example, basement spaces are often more stable year-round, and cooler and damper than other parts of buildings. Exterior walls generally work against stability of either temperature or relative humidity, particularly if there are windows; interior spaces will therefore be more stable. Large rooms with high ceilings will have better air movement, even without forced air circulation, than smaller spaces. Small rooms or closets near furnaces will undoubtedly be hot and dry all year round. Some rooms will be naturally less dusty than others. Some spaces will always be subject to possible leaks in pipes or roofing.

The use of hygrothermographs together with a little common sense will indicate the conditions in different spaces. Combined with the susceptibilities of collections, this information can provide signficant benefit. For example, metal objects can be kept in a constantly warm closet. Attic spaces with wide fluctuations can be used for porcelain. Dusty spaces can be reserved for, say, boxed collections of arrowheads, or cartons of out-of-date catalogues. Just as galleries for light-sensitive objects are generally interior spaces without windows, humidity-sensitive pieces can be placed in the most appropriate setting. Spaces with the worst relative humidity can be reserved for storage of office furniture or packing crates which would, however, have to be equilibrated in the galleries before being reused.

The extension of this principle can be used to upgrade environmental conditions one area at a time. For example, storage or exhibition of very sensitive material could be restricted to a few rooms which are relatively well insulated from outside air conditions and would therefore be easy to condition further using room humidifiers or de-humidifiers. Offices could be kept at a comfortable temperature but without humidity control. Separating a building into individual climatic zones is an important strategy no matter how much or how little environmental control is actually contemplated. As important as it is to provide optimal conditions for each object, it is pointless, not to mention expensive, to provide environmental conditions *better* than any object requires.

This principle, that is, defining the conditions in each space and then assigning the most appropriate materials to each, requires collections to be segregated by material rather than by provenance or style. In many institutions, this may be difficult for political reasons, since curators are accustomed to having all of their collection material stored together. For storage to be efficient, however, collections requiring similar conditions need to be kept together.

Another simple way of improving the environment for collections care is to reduce the winter temperature. Although almost all conservation sources recommend 68-70° F., and we customarily nod and assume that our indoor winter temperatures are indeed in that range, some checking is in order. One British conservator refers to "the hot rooms that our American friends demand"[1]. In fact, indoor temperatures are often well over 75°. A reduction of this to 68° could raise RH levels considerably, as well as saving energy. Lowering the temperature can also raise the RH level without increasing the risk of condensation. For storerooms, a further reduction to 62 or 65° would provide additional advantages without the risk of condensation that results from cold storage.

Another simple procedure which will improve environmental conditions for all buildings and, incidentally, will reduce energy usage, is sealing openings better. This includes weather-stripping around windows, providing revolving doors or double doors with a vestibule between instead of one door that opens directly into the museum, and filling cracks in walls and roofing.

---

[1] Baynes-Cope, A.D. "Climatic Considerations in Conservation." The Conservator Vol.1: 22-23 (1977).

Buffering Relative Humidity

Because sudden changes in relative humidity are much more damaging to many kinds of objects than a steady level, at any level, buffering relative humidity changes is an important process. The process generally involves putting objects into containers where air exchange with the outside is slow enough so that the inside air is protected from the peaks and valleys of RH changes on the outside. The simplest example is putting collections into a building. A second line of defense is the ubiquitous exhibition case. This does a commendable job in keeping out dust, gaseous pollutants, insects, heat from lights, curious fingers, and air currents, and in levelling relative humidity changes even further. Other common containers in museums are picture frames for matted and mounted works on paper, storage cabinets, and cardboard boxes.

If, however, we take great care to seal the exhibition case or other container to do an even better job, we run into trouble. The moving air that we are cutting off carried away the pollutants created by case materials and by the objects themselves, and helped avoid condensation in climatic extremes (like sudden failures of a heating system). The more we seal up the objects, the more careful we must be in choosing high-quality construction materials.

Tightly sealed exhibition cases can be expected to allow about one air exchange per day. This will buffer daily changes in gallery RH, but will not buffer seasonal RH levels. To reduce annual fluctuations, more buffering is required.

Silica gel is an often-recommended way of increasing the buffering capacity of a container. Silica gel is an inert material with an unusually large moisture reservoir. Dry silica gel is familiar as a desiccant, used to prevent condensation in packing containers for moisture-sensitive equipment like cameras, but if it is conditioned to an ambient RH level, it will act as a buffer. As the RH goes down, it gives up water vapor to keep the RH steady, and if the RH goes up, it will take up some of the water vapor to maintain equilibrium. If used as a buffer, it does not require periodic removal and reconditioning, but will help flatten the changes in relative humidity.

Unfortunately, silica gel has become somewhat of a buzz-word and is routinely misused. The first thing to understand is that silica gel can be used in two ways, as a buffer of whatever the ambient conditions are, or as a provider of a particular RH level that is not the average of ambient conditions. These two functions have somewhat different requirements in the areas of conditioning and monitoring. Buffering has somewhat less capacity for creating harm if done incorrectly.

In order for silica gel to do much good, the container must be sealed as well as possible. For most cases, gap-free seams in plastic sheeting are good enough for this purpose, although inevitable gaps in seams allow some air exchange. The other sides of a case can be of normal joinery, provided, of course, that the materials are as safe as practically possible if the objects are sensitive to acids or other pollutants.

The volume of the case should be as small as possible. Setting up a silica gel-buffered case is enough trouble that we want to keep the work at a minimum. The silica gel should be about 2% of the volume of the case. This is a number arrived at both by calculation and by experience. A more accurate number for a specific case would depend on the rate of air exchange, the needs of the objects, the buffering capacity of other case materials, climatic extremes outside, etc. Since too much silica gel cannot cause problems, and 2% seems to have worked in the past, we will continue to recommend it.

The layer of silica gel should not be more than about one and one half inches thick to allow enough access of case air. Several different approaches to holding the gel have been used. In museums where cases are designed for silica gel, the design generally incorporates a drawer under where the objects rest. The objects rest on a pedestal-like construction and a small gap around the outside of the pedestal allows for air exchange with the tray of silica gel beneath. In cases where objects are suspended or hung on the back wall of the case, the bottom of the case can be a hollow panel with fabric stretched over a framework that incorporates honeycomb or egg-crate material filled with silica gel. Fairly light objects can rest on such a panel. It is also possible to construct vertical panels that can be used as the back of cases or can be hidden behind a false wall in the case.

Small tiles covered with Gore-tex® and filled with pre-weighed silica gel are available ready-made (See *Sources of Supply*: W. L. Gore & Associates). These are quite a bit more expensive than silica gel itself, but are of course much easier to use. They take up somewhat more space than silica gel in a tray. Silica gel is also available in bulk, in porous tubes, and in brick-shaped cassettes (See *Sources of Supply*: Art Preservation Services, Conservation Materials, and W. R. Grace & Co.).

Another sometimes convenient form of silica gel is a synthetic paper impregnated with a powdered form of a kind of silica gel (Art-sorb® made by Fuji-Davison Chemical Ltd., a Japanese firm, and available from Conservation Materials, Ltd.). In addition to ease in handling, the paper provides an additional margin of error in that the powdered form in the paper responds faster than regular silica gel.

Before using silica gel to buffer RH, it should be conditioned to the RH of the room. Silica gel generally arrives from the manufacturer completely dry, close to 0% relative humidity. This will need to be brought to ambient conditions before using it near works of art.

It is obviously important that there be enough air circulation in the case to provide continuing contact with the silica gel. This is difficult to predict, but cases should be tested carefully before objects are exhibited in them to assure that there are no pockets of dead air. If necessary, small fans can be used to circulate the air.

Silica gel comes in many different forms; the standard form, called "Regular density - A type" is less effective than some others at RH levels above about 50%, but few objects will require RH levels above this, so it is most commonly used. Particle sizes of 3-8 mesh are commonly chosen. The choice of specific material is one of those questions that should be referred to a knowledgeable conservator. One special form of silica gel should be mentioned; it is a variety impregnated with the same kind of cobalt salts that are used in humidity indicator papers. Since it is significantly more expensive than other kinds, a little can be purchased and mixed into

uncolored kinds if the indicator would be useful.

Buffering will produce case fluctuations smaller than those of the room. For the most sensitive pieces, a buffered case in an uncontrolled environment of, say, 20-80% will still result in wide annual variations. A buffered case in a room conditioned to 35-65% will produce a much safer environment.

The benefits of containerization, in storage or on exhibition, are too great to give it up because of air quality problems. Individual containerization of objects can minimize virtually every ill that objects are heir to: damage from handling, light, dust and gaseous pollutants, insects, water, and changes in RH. In addition, containers require no energy outlay and are faithful through black-outs and brown-outs and lack of maintenance. With considerable care in the choice of materials, collections can be protected at minimal long-term cost.

Several museums have created storage containers for textiles out of acid-free corrugated cardboard, or ragboard. These are similar in principle to the mats and mounts used for works on paper, but are constructed to accommodate the greater thickness of textiles. Even though such containers are somewhat permeable to air movement, the amount of hygroscopic material surrounding the object has been shown to provide a very steady relative humidity while eliminating pollution and risk from handling, and keeping the items accessible. Although storage containerization is not a major topic of this book, such projects are strongly recommended for many kinds of sensitive objects.

One possible problem that can be encountered with containerization, with or without silica gel, is in the case of heating system failure. Because of the interdependence of temperature and relative humidity, when temperatures plunge, RH levels will increase abruptly, and condensation can result. Regular-density silica gel responds slowly to temperature change, probably too slowly to prevent this problem. Large amounts of hygroscopic material, particularly types with large surface area, will help to mitigate drastic changes under these conditions. In most buildings, however, heating failures are much rarer than humidity-control failures or leaks of water, so the probability of this occurring is small, and should not be a deterrent. In buildings where heating system failures are more common, paper impregnated with the Japanese gel should be considered.

Localized Controls

The use of silica gel to provide an RH level higher or lower than the ambient average requires about the same set-up as using it as a buffer, but the silica gel must be conditioned to the desired RH, and a monitoring system must be established to be sure that the silica gel is re-conditioned as necessary. The container should be sealed as well as possible, and a replacement container of silica gel should be available, properly conditioned and ready for use when the other is removed. With Gore-tex® tiles, cylinders, or other smaller containers, one or two out of a larger set can be rotated out and re-conditioned, leaving the others in place. Small cut-outs from humidity-indicator cards can be used inside the case for monitoring.

The silica gel must be pre-conditioned to the appropriate relative humidity. Several methods have been used for this. Some provide the appropriate level in another container and allow the gel to equilibrate in the desired environment; others provide moisture content directly. One method of conditioning gel is to use saturated salt solutions. Solutions of various salts will condition the air above them to specific RH levels. Containers of such salts can be made up and stored until required. Some museums have used such salt solutions directly in controlling RH in exhibition cases, and they work very well once set up. Handling large volumes of liquids can be awkward, however.

An automatic environmental chamber would make conditioning silica gel easy. One chamber most of us have access to is the refrigerator. I have used a non-frost-free refrigerator as a chamber for conditioning silica gel, since the refrigerator maintains a steady 50%. The gel goes into the refrigerator for a few days in shallow pans (foil cake pans work fine). In order to test the gel, some can be sealed in a plastic bag with a paper humidity indicator. Tests of frost-free refrigerators indicate that the RH is much lower, but crisper compartments appear to be closer to 50%. Regular-density silica gel does not accommodate temperature change perfectly, so as the gel warms to room temperature the RH drops to a few points below 50%. For many objects this level is just fine.

The direct way of conditioning silica gel is to use equations or charts that give the percentage moisture content for silica gel at different RH levels. The appropriate amount of dry silica gel is weighed out, and the appropriate weight of water is added. The mixture is allowed to steep for several days in a sealed container. This is a simple method for those comfortable with a certain amount of arithmetic.

In order to assure that the silica gel starts out dry, any moisture can be removed by putting it in an oven at about 150° F. for a few hours.

One relatively new method of controlling RH in an exhibition case is with a piece of machinery called a relative humidity control module. This is a sort of movable black box about the size of a refrigerator with a hose that can be fitted into a case or series of cases. The module puts out constant-RH air. Constant temperature must be provided by other means. These modules are quite expensive (in the over-$5,000 range) but are low-maintenance and so far extremely reliable (See *Sources of Supply:* Kennedy-Trimnell Co., Inc. and Micro Climate Technology Inc.).

Microclimates for Metals

Provision of low-RH microclimates, that is, contained environments maintained at a level different from ambient levels, for metals is relatively easy, since levels do not have to be steady. In exhibition cases, lights can be arranged to heat the air. Small metal objects can be segregated in storage as well, in cases fitted with incandescent lamps as a heat source. A heated case must be tested first in an easily observed area to see how hot it gets when a light is left on continually. Do not risk fire. Use of the hygrometric chart should provide some guidance as to how much heat is needed. For larger objects, a well-sealed room can be provided with a dehumidifier. Dry silica gel is another possibility, and can be replaced when the RH drifts too far upward.

Low RH levels for metals are an obvious choice for rusty iron and for bronze. Do not forget that the tarnishing of silver is another form of corrosion, which will likewise be lessened at lower humidities. Like bronze disease (a specific undesirable corrosion product on copper and copper alloys), silver corrosion requires both impurities and moisture, so the use of low RH can be an alternative to coatings or to air filtration.

Dishes of Water

The idea of putting little dishes of water into closed cases is an old one, and still commonly recommended. Don't do it. Open containers of water can either do nothing or, if they do something, do it in an uncontrollable way. In a small case situated in an area of constant temperature, there is very little movement of air, and even a small amount of water in a dish is unlikely to evaporate into the air very quickly; if it does, the amount of water will be unlikely to raise the RH very much, and the act of opening the case to refill the container will, of course, allow an air exchange with the air in the room and let out any added water vapor. If larger containers of water are used so that more moisture is available, the RH will rise unpredictably, and under certain conditions can quickly get high enough to cause mold growth. For example, if a beam of sunlight falls on a case for a couple of hours, or if a bright light is turned on, the interior temperature will increase, encouraging more evaporation of the water, although perhaps with little or no effect on the RH. When the heat source is withdrawn, the added moisture in the air will cause an increase in the RH. The possibility of spilling water in a case with objects is another reason not to do this.

Room-by-Room Controls

Portable humidifiers and dehumidifiers are good ways of improving conditions room by room without a major investment. The kind of humidifier that is appropriate for collections spaces has a reservoir of water in the bottom, a drum covered with a belt of absorbent material that dips into the reservoir as it rotates, and a fan that blows air through the belt. Because this type of machinery relies on actual evaporation rather than on spraying a mist of liquid water into the air, impurities in the water are left behind in the reservoir rather than sprayed into the air. Vaporiser types can spray impurities into the air along with water; this has been known to drop white powder onto objects. The newer ultrasonic type also distributes impurities along with water droplets.

Belt-type humidifiers generally have simple humidistats for control. They are quite safe pieces of equipment because no heat is used, and they are unlikely to overheat and cause fires. If they malfunction and continue to operate when the reservoir is empty, no harm is done. If they fail to turn off, and keep operating in humid air, they cannot cause dangerously high RH levels, because the water will simply not evaporate from the belt.

Portable dehumidifiers operate like air conditioners, condensing water on cooling coils, and then collecting it.

Both humidifiers and de-humidifiers must be operated twenty-four hours a day to avoid producing rapid fluctuations. A great deal of water can be involved in both. It is highly desirable, unless twenty-four hour monitoring is feasible, to have both connected directly to building plumbing. There is no purpose in having dehumidifiers pull water from the air and then spill it onto the floor. Humidifiers may need refilling more than once a day in cold weather; plumbing connections make this unnecessary.

Manufacturers' literature should be consulted to make sure that the number of instruments is appropriate to the cubic footage of space. It is also important to be sure that the space being controlled is sealed. If there is a great deal of air leakage in the room, the machines can be in operation twenty-four hours per day while attempting to control the whole building. A dehumidifier placed in a basement that has water infiltration from the outside will be pulling water through the walls forever, and a humidifier that pumps moisture into a room and out the door will be working overtime to little effect.

Both humidifiers and dehumidifiers need periodic maintenance to make sure that mold, algae, or inorganic scale does not build up. Filters need to be kept clean. Sensors and electrical contacts may need periodic cleaning or replacement. Models purchased should be as heavy-duty as possible. Regular inexpensive household models are not built to be run continuously, and make more noise than more expensive models.

Hygrothermographs should be used for several weeks before either machine is put into use, and then while they are being used, to assure that they are operating properly. Too many people install humidifiers or dehumidifiers simply because it seems like a good idea, or because everyone else seems to be doing it. This can produce more harm than good. It should be unnecessary by now to state that environmental control does not always work the way we expect; any attempt at control must be monitored carefully to assure that the effort is not wasted or that, conversely, there are no unforeseen consequences.

Major Issues with Centralized Environmental Control Systems

Although some reference has been made in previous sections to "real-life" situations, much has been devoted to the laws of nature. When major building projects are contemplated, the laws of nature are quickly overtaken as a cause for concern by factors such as massive fund-raising campaigns, public relations on an international scale, artistic temperament, and Board politics. It is almost impossible before a project begins to envision the number of people and competing interests that will become involved.

Let us take first the architect. "Museums are the prestige buildings and prestige architectural commissions of our time."[2] This is not only true of "world-class" institutions. Architects may want to make a major comment on contemporary architecture using the building that they will then turn over to you to house your collections. Under the best of circumstances, museums are difficult projects. They contain almost every kind of space that

architects design, and some that few architects have any experience with. Museums need a full range of public facilities: an auditorium with backstage space, gift and book shops, food service, restrooms, public telephones, and check-rooms. Education departments need classrooms, lecture halls, and art studios. All staff need regular office space, sometimes with a separate lunchroom. Modern registrars need computer rooms and packing and shipping facilities to accommodate the largest things in the collection. Each curatorial department may need a workroom, and the Director may need a separate suite with Boardroom. The Conservation Department needs a technical laboratory with fume extraction equipment; photographers need a studio with developing and printing facilities. Building workers need shops for carpentry and painting. Staging spaces may be needed for large parties. Storage spaces will be needed for office supplies, packing crates, and shop inventories. This formidable list does not include exhibition galleries and collection storage!

---

[2] Reichardt, Jasia. "Museum Tomorrow" *The Architectural Review* Vol. 168, p.35 (1985)

Providing all of this with spaces interconnecting so that each gallery section can be closed off without impeding traffic flow through the building, with separate entrances for different functions, handicapped access, elevators and corridors big enough for the largest collection object, and all the other logistical complications that come with a complex institution is quite a project. Making a major architectural statement besides, perhaps fitting the exterior with the style of an older museum building, is quite enough without worrying about designing spaces for easier environmental control, pest control, security, and other practical matters discussed in this book and elsewhere. And, of course, museums have very limited budgets with which to accomplish their goals.

The architect is fighting a battle from the start, because he or she is not a mind-reader. Each museum department must know precisely what it needs. Museum executives must agree on every detail, and on long-term collections policy as it relates to future acquisitions and the storage or exhibition galleries that must be set aside for them. Only if the museum Board, its administrators, staff, and consultants agree in advance and can describe exactly what they need in terms the architect can understand will the architect have the least chance of giving them what they want.

One ticklish problem in the constant give-and-take of the preliminary discussion is the wide disparity in status between the parties. Architects are hired by the museum's Board. In well-run institutions, staff are considered an important part of the professional team, but even there, when a conflict arises over conservation matters among curators, conservators, architects and engineers, a comparison between their respective hourly fees will often predict the outcome. The architect's *per diem* is apt to be well more than a curator makes in a week. In this case, as in many others, if conservators and others whose primary attention is focussed on the well-being of collections do not have support from the Director and Board, the whole process will deteriorate into name-calling, whining complaints, snide remarks, and nasty power plays, and conservators will once more reinforce their reputation as being people who, no matter what is proposed, always say "No".

One necessary strategy that will help to protect collections in major construction projects is for a consultant conservator knowledgeable in environmental controls together with a technical consultant, *both of whom are paid by the institution*, to be included in the planning process from the beginning. Collections too often have no advocate. This is no time to ignore their welfare; it is for the sake of the collections that the institution exists in the first place, and they can too easily become the victim of the process long after everyone else has gone on to other projects.

Environmental matters are simply not a major concern for most parties in this complex undertaking, whether constructing a new building or renovating an old one. Many architects hired for museums are not experienced in museum design, and the HVAC engineers they use may know little or nothing about how museum requirements differ from those of office buildings or dwellings. To make it worse, few conservators have been trained in environmental control. And to make the process impossible, museums that have gone through the process of centralized environmental control in new or existing buildings have not published any of their experiences, good or bad, so no one has had a chance to learn what works and what doesn't. In the worst cases, the situation has become so embarrassing that institutions have forbidden their staffs to discuss the details with anyone outside the building.

From the host of rather self-congratulatory articles that appear in the popular or architectural press about new museum buildings, it would seem that perfect conditions simply require the outlay of huge sums of money. This has not turned out to be true. In some of the best cases, proper controls require from one to two years of constant tinkering by a local firm after the building is complete before the system

functions properly. In some worst cases, whole systems have had to be removed and replaced within a few years after construction or the system is simply shut down and never used.

There are ways to bridge the wall of silence. Probably the best is to make telephone calls to every institution in your area that has gone through a major climate control project. Do not speak to the Director's office or get put off onto the Public Relations staff. You do not want the grand tour. Try to speak to either the Conservation Department or the building facilities manager, someone who deals with the system and its disasters. If you are not a persistent sort, find someone else who is, and make sure they follow up on whatever they hear. As plans proceed, it is a good idea for staff and Board to make more official visits to other facilities, but do not let the red-carpet treatment cloud your vision. Other people's successes may not prove useful to you because of differences in your circumstances, but other people's mistakes are worth *not* repeating.

One major problem in the process of museum design has been that the responsibility of the architect and engineer traditionally ends when the building is turned over to the client. Generally, this is before any HVAC system is turned on, and almost always before it is monitored. If no staff member is assigned to monitor the new system, it may be a long time before anyone finds out that it doesn't work as promised. Not only are clients left with a building they do not understand, but the engineers and architects never get a chance to learn the consequences of their designs.

Building staff is commonly not prepared for the large amount of necessary routine maintenance, much less the long initial period of shake-down, balancing and adjusting of air volumes, humidistats, and thermostats. It is generally considered that at least one full-time staff member will be needed for routine maintenance, in addition to a contract with an outside firm for repairs. The building contractor has an obligation to furnish a notebook with the manufacturer's recommendations for maintenance of all installed systems. Seldom, however, is the administration apprised of the enormity of this while attempting to calculate in advance the expense of a building project. The almost inevitable result is that even if a system can be made to work properly, few museums maintain it, and breakdowns follow. As Garry Thomson has said, "Evidence for extremely poor maintenance is worldwide in museums."[3]

The high energy costs involved in running an environmental control system have been responsible for several institutions turning them off. This

is another factor that few institutions are prepared for. At this point in the history of the world, it may very well be folly to take on such an energy-inefficient burden.

Maintenance and energy costs, the need for a long period of "fine-tuning", and the possibility that the whole thing may not work as promised are all issues that should be dealt with long before an architect is involved, and even longer before the first spadeful of dirt is turned. Major projects have a momentum of their own, and often no staff is involved until plans have been drawn up. As unwieldy a process as it may be, large numbers of people must be involved in planning as early as possible. The need for the project should not be a foregone conclusion. Particularly in the case of retrofitting an existing facility with centralized environmental control, listen to people who say that there may be responsible alternatives.

Another side of the coin that many institutions would rather not discuss is what happens in the case of malfunction or complete breakdown. All supply-air grills should have the capability of being closed to stabilize room environments if the system is off or is putting out unsuitable air. Fans should be shut off if the output of the equipment is inappropriate. Staff should have sources readily available for rental of emergency fans, portable humidifiers and dehumidifiers,

---

[3] Thomson, Garry. "Climate Control Policy" *ICOM Committee for Conservation Fifth Triennial Meeting, Zagreb, 1978* 78/18/1, p.3 (1978)

pumps, etc. Procedures must be established both for monitoring the system and for notifying responsible parties when something goes wrong. I know of an institution where a curator noticed that several paintings on cardboard were warped, and only then learned that the humidity controls had been out of order for two weeks!

Even a properly working system will not solve all problems; it cannot prevent local microclimates from forming between objects and outside walls or in stagnant pockets that might be created when partitions are moved. Large numbers of people can overload a system, so access to popular exhibitions may have to be limited based either on calculations[4] or on experience in monitoring a specific gallery. Floor-washing, plant-watering, and caterers' steam tables will still induce local variations. The temptation to take all objects out from behind protective glass or Plexiglas® because of improved ambient conditions can leave collections at increased risk from vandalism or theft.

Proper diffusion of air from supply ducts may be difficult. Air speed and volume must be high enough to keep air in all parts of a room circulating, but quickly moving air must be directed away from objects.

---

[4] Nardi, Roberto. "On Temporary Exhibitions" *ICOM Committee for*

To take a more positive point of view, the matter of providing proper relative humidity controls is not a complete mystery. There are certain standards that are agreed upon as a starting point for HVAC systems. The kind of system we are talking about is a constant-volume system that delivers clean air at a set temperature and relative humidity via ducts to all parts of a building. In a building of any size, several different systems are usually installed, providing different climatic zones with different specifications. Separate equipment provides humidification in the winter and dehumidification in the summer, with the two systems sometimes working almost side-by-side in the fall and spring when outdoor temperature and humidity levels are so variable.

The most common type of humidification is steam injection, which introduces steam into a moving stream of air. Dehumidification is generally done with equipment that removes moisture from the air as an air conditioner does. Filters for both particulates and gaseous pollutants are placed in the ducts, and large fans provide enough air speed so that circulation is maintained. "Used" air returns to the equipment through return ducts. Most of the air is recirculated, with a commonly recommended figure of 15% outside air added in to avoid the building up of harmful

---

Conservation Sixth Triennial Meeting, Ottawa, 1981 81/18/3: 7 pp. (1981)

gases (the "sick building syndrome"), although a lower figure, 10-12%, is often recommended to conserve energy.

Assuming that decisions are finally made in a reasonable manner, and that all goes well in the construction phase, the big moment is when the collections move in. It cannot be said too often: do not plan to move collections into a newly climate-controlled building. Even after an initial phase when ventilation is maximized to let out construction fumes, environmental control systems need a lot of adjustment before they can be trusted to care for objects. People who do this repeatedly say that at least a year, one full change of seasons, is needed with all mechanical systems in full use before it is safe to move objects in. Museum professionals have heard too many stories of newly-installed bronzes turning into fuzzy green balls overnight and have seen too many schedules that show systems being turned on the day before installation begins. Do not do this.

In addition to testing of HVAC systems, at least two to three months with maximum outside ventilation are required to purge the building of paint fumes and other volatile components of construction materials including moisture from concrete and plaster. After this purging cycle, all filters should be changed and sensors should be cleaned. Any "new building" smell should be eliminated before collections are moved in. Comparable precautions should be taken after every gallery repainting or laying of new floors.

Although the pitfalls of centralized environmental control are many, knowing what they are will help to avoid them. There *are* institutions that have made environmental control work. There is no question that the better relative humidity control an institution can maintain, the healthier its collections will be. One of the primary difficulties seems to be in learning enough *before the project is undertaken* so that the magnitude of the committment of money, time, and effort is not underestimated.

Humidification

In cold climates, humidification in the winter is probably one of the most commonly recommended feats of environmental control. There is no doubt that the very low relative humidities caused by winter heating are damaging to many different kinds of objects. However, the dangers of the condensation that often accompanies humidification are equally devastating to the building that houses these objects. We see condensation often on windows, where the water drips down and rots wooden window frames and sills. The same process goes on inside walls. Imagine a cross-section of the exterior walls of a building, with a gradient of temperatures between the inside and outside. If the outside is 30° F., for example, and the inside is 75°, the structural temperature, that is, the temperature of the building materials, will range from 30 to 75° at different positions within the wall, depending on the insulating properties of the materials. If the building is artificially humidified, the humidified air diffuses outward through the materials of the wall (or leaks out through cracks in the materials) and cools to its dewpoint, where water will condense. Depending on wind speed and permeability of the exterior surfaces, the water may evaporate through the wall to the outside or spread in the wall and drip downwards.

This water rots plaster and wood and causes corrosion of hardware inside the wall, including the reinforcing rods in concrete, plumbing, wiring, and structural hardware. It increases the emission of acid vapors by wood, and reduces thermal insulating properties. Evaporation of the water through exterior masonry causes the formation of crystals (efflorescence) and the loosening of surface material (spalling), particularly

when ice forms. Because a mechanical system of some kind is pushing moisture and heat into the air at one end of the cycle, and both are escaping through the walls, air leakage and the accompanying condensation put an unnecessary double burden on energy use. These are not remote possibilities; they have, and do, occur with astonishing regularity in major buildings, old and new.

When plans are made for any kind of humidification, serious discussions on where the water will end up must be a basic part of the plan. It is important to realize how damaging water inside structural materials can be: with no air movement and no ventilation to the exterior, water that condenses inside walls will stay there, possibly undetected, for a very long time.

The solution to condensation problems seems simple: provide barriers to water vapor so that the humidified air does not go far enough into the wall to reach its dewpoint. A material commonly used for this so-called vapor barrier is likewise simple: polyethylene film (6 mil is usually recommended). The installation of the material so that it functions properly is not simple. The first requirement is the installation of adequate insulation toward the outside of the wall to keep the structural temperature as high as possible. The vapor barrier then needs to be installed near the interior of the wall, and it needs to be air-tight. Installing the plastic sheeting so that there are no gaps to allow leakage is extremely difficult. There can be no nails or staples piercing the plastic; taped joins are not considered adequate to prevent air leaks. Where pipes, ducts, or electrical conduits pierce the barrier, they must be insulated so that the portion inside the barrier is not cold enough to cause condensation. The polyethylene must be sealed permanently and without air spaces to the ceiling and floor.

Even slight flaws in construction that either bring cold air toward the building interior or allow warm moist air to escape toward the building exterior can cause condensation. Certain details of construction, like slab floors that project to the outside and therefore bridge insulation, or projecting upper floors, provide what architects call "cold bridges" and can nullify the protective effect of vapor barriers. Outside corners of buildings can be colder than straight walls, and provide another condensation hazard. Flat roofs can be a problem because the vapor barriers are commonly installed on the cold side to prevent seepage of liquid water into the materials of the roofing.

Part of the insidious nature of this problem is that an adequate solution lies in craftsmanship as much as design, and proper supervision of construction workers on the spot is difficult at best. Many major museum buildings in the last ten years that have experienced condensation problems were designed with vapor barriers; they were installed improperly. So difficult is it to do this properly that a recent article in a British architectural journal, referring to buildings *without humidification systems,* said "Early advice on vapour barriers underestimated the difficulty of making them work and so the term vapour check appeared. . .

Vapour retarder is probably a better term."[5]

In some cases, calculations have been faulty. The figures for permeability of construction materials are based on laboratory tests of flawless materials, without cracks, bubbles, or other openings. Water vapor moves much more quickly in the flow of air through cracks than it diffuses through solid materials. In many cases, it has been the small details of construction that have caused problems. In one major museum project, nails that pierced the barriers conducted cold toward the interior and the nailheads became the focus for condensation. So much condensation occurred that water dripped down inside the walls and formed puddles under the parquet floor, causing buckling of the wood. Various problems with condensation have in some cases caused lawsuits and the complete dismantling and rebuilding of interior walls.

---

[5] Anon. "Construction Risks and Remedies: Condensation Part 2." *The Architects' Journal* 185: 72 (1986)

The installation of vapor barriers in historic or other houses is clearly out of the question; retrofitting for building-wide humidification entails a major construction project. Some major institutions with imperfect barriers have settled on a balancing act in which the humidification levels are changed based on daily readings of the outdoor temperature. In other buildings, humidification has been done only in interior rooms, so that moisture leaks slowly into galleries with exterior walls. In cases like this, vapor barriers in walls and well-sealed doors are needed to keep the humidity from spreading quickly into other rooms, but the barriers do not have to be perfect.

Calculations by engineers are usually required to establish safe limits for humidification in a particular building. An interior condition of 70° F., 50% will create condensation on single-glazed windows at an exterior temperature of 37° F. and on double glazing at 15°. On the other hand, interior conditions of 70°, 35% will allow single glazing to be condensation-free as low as 20°, and double glazing, above -10°.

Condensation can occur even in buildings without mechanical humidification. Ornamental pools, cooking on the premises, or mixing water used in new construction can all add enough moisture to the air to cause problems. Single-glazed windows and skylights can get cold enough to reach the dewpoint of un-humidified air. Poorly insulated exterior walls can get cold enough so that in the microclimates created, for example, behind paintings hung on the wall, condensation can occur. And in buildings that are heated intermittently, condensation can occur when the air gets warm before the walls do.

On a smaller scale, objects that are sealed in plastic bags or other air-tight containers without sufficient hygroscopic material can experience condensation during a drop in temperature if they were sealed during a period of high RH. This sometimes occurs with textiles or paper framed behind glass. If the object is touching the glass where condensation occurs, mold growth is often the result.

The dangers of condensation in buildings cannot be overstressed. Without appropriate vapor barriers, building-wide humidification cannot and should not be carried out. The damage may be difficult or impossible to detect at first; the absence of windows in most museum galleries leaves us without a reminder of the problem. The damage is however real, and serious. When humidification is contemplated for a new building, many details of the design of the building must be adjusted to allow for safe and efficient humidification. When any kind of humidification system is turned on, all staff must be aware of the potential problems so that careful monitoring can be carried out. If necessary, instruments that detect moisture levels inside walls should be used.

Steam injection is the humidification method generally recommended for museums. Steam is generated at a central point and is injected into a moving air stream in the ducts. Any mineral fallout takes place within the steam generator, and must be cleaned out to avoid clogging the equipment, but at least it is kept away from ducts and objects. Many steam generators have a blow-down cycle that allows dumping of accumulated minerals. Still, monitoring of the cleanliness of water reservoirs must be a routine maintenance chore.

The theory of steam injection is that the steam will be mixed with the air while staying in the gaseous state; in practice, the mixing is not that efficient and some condensation occurs. In typical systems, about nine feet of straight run of duct are required for all water to be picked up into the air stream; failing this, liquid water tends to build up and drip out of the ducts. Some systems have separators that take the liquid water droplets out of the steam; "dry steam" is the term used for steam that has no liquid water in it.

Ductwork that stays clear of liquid water is an important requirement of museum systems, much more important than in other settings. Besides the possibility of drips, stagnant water inside ducts provides a welcoming environment for many kinds of insects and for algae and bacteria.

Steam itself will not corrode metal parts, but liquid water will. Corrosion of any metal parts that come in contact with liquid water, primarily steam lines in boilers, can seriously diminish the efficiency of the system. As a result, engineers typically introduce some type of corrosion inhibitor into the water supply. Corrosion inhibitors are commonly used in steam generators for closed heating systems, that is, those where the steam stays inside pipe radiators. In a well-known case at Cornell University, centrally generated steam intended for closed heating systems was used for museum humidification. It was noted only later that the anti-corrosive, commonly known as DEAE (diethylaminoethanol), was a human health hazard and caused skin and eye irritations, as well as the possibility of long-term health risks.

DEAE was finally detected in a white crystalline haze that was found on the surface of paintings in a large museum in the Midwest several weeks after a new humidification system was turned on and after cleaning personnel reported a slimy residue on gallery surfaces. In this case, engineers first claimed that no anti-corrosive had been used, then admitted that DEAE had been used, but continued to insist that it could not possibly have gotten into the air of the galleries.

The sliminess that probably is the result of salts deposited on surfaces when DEAE reacts with acids in the air is one problem reported in the museum literature from anti-corrosives. Problems specifically traceable to other chemicals used for this purpose have not been reported, but at present, conservators strongly recommend that no anti-corrosives be added to water used for humidification. Alternatives include accepting a certain amount of corrosion in the steam generating equipment or working to keep chemical use to a minimum.

Another possibility is disposable vapor generators. These are small, relatively inexpensive boiler units which can be placed very near the galleries they serve. Duct runs can therefore be short, and the units can be replaced when necessary. The output of these units is at a low vapor pressure, so some augmentation of air circulation in the galleries may be necessary.

DEAE is still a very common additive. Manufacturers recommend that it not be used for direct humidification, so any legal liability related to it rests with the user. No federal regulations prevent its use, probably because levels in the air tend to be low. Since DEAE films build up on walls and other surfaces, long-term skin contact is the main exposure route.

There are firms whose expertise is the health implications of steam purity (See *Sources of Supply:* Mogul Corp.); they should

be consulted early in the design phase if possible. For systems where chemical additives are already in use, alternative chemicals may be possible. Improved monitoring for DEAE concentration should be put into effect; common methods are not accurate and often result in an excess of chemicals being added to the system.

The above is a simplified sketch of the issues involved in mechanical humidification systems. The choice of equipment and design of humidification systems are obviously complicated tasks that must be done by HVAC engineers well educated in their own field and also sensitive to the special requirements of museums. The problems of condensation inside building structures, condensation inside ducts, and corrosion control must be dealt with in all systems. Do not expect that these matters will be satisfactorily addressed at first. Do not hesitate to ask questions and do not hesitate to consult others at the design stage. You should know enough to make sure that these problems have been given their due before any construction is begun.

Dehumidification

Most dehumidification is done with equipment similar to room-size dehumidifiers, but on a larger scale. Large chillers bring the air to its dewpoint, draining off the condensed water. In smaller spaces where RH must be kept very low, a desiccant-type dehumidifier is sometimes recommended. Because of the possibility of salt contamination, silica gel rather than calcium chloride should be used in desiccant dehumidifiers.

Cooling air to a desirable temperature with a regular air conditioner will not produce a desired RH; cooling may raise RH rather than lower it, even though water is being removed from the air. If a humidistat turns on the cooling whenever the RH is too high, and the cooling actually raises the RH, the building will get very cold indeed. A reheat system is necessary so that the cooled air can be warmed up to desirable levels, thereby lowering the RH again. Adjustments at the reheat stage must assure that the end-point has both the desired temperature and the desired relative humidity. The lack of a reheat system has been a common error, even in major museums. It has taken complaints from half-frozen visitors in some cases to have this mistake corrected.

The energy costs involved in simultaneous cooling and heating are enormous. It would be nice to be able to recommend a better method of dehumidification, but apparently there is none.

Dealing with Changes of Seasons

In much of the United States and Canada, dehumidification is necessary for most of the summer months, and humidification is required for all the months that heating is used. The transition seasons are even more difficult. At these times, when temperatures are in the 50's or 60's, the air can be either dry or extremely humid; heating may be required sporadically for short periods, alternating with cooling.

If an institution is trying to allow RH to drift from 40% at the end of the heating season to 60% in June or July, more complications arise. This is a time when constant supervision is needed. Even with a complete centralized environmental control system, at these times of the year it is highly recommended that the objects in a collection most sensitive to RH changes be containerized.

Specific Design Problems

Several architectural features in museum buildings can provide particular problems for environmental control. Buildings with a central atrium or large lobby with galleries opening off it are almost impossible to control. If the galleries have doors that can be left closed, the large space can be a valuable buffer between outside and inside, but an open plan can leave collections defenseless. Any museum design where galleries cannot be closed off from other spaces will make RH control much more difficult and even more expensive than it would be otherwise.

Buildings that do not provide reliable protection against the elements are simply a menace. Any buildings where the surface of exterior walls is cold to the touch or where the roof leaks or where basement water infiltration is a recurrent problem is going to foil any attempts at RH control. Flat roofs and fancy roof forms like multiple set-backs seem to make leaks virtually inevitable. Do not attempt RH control until everything possible has been done to deal with these more obvious, if unglamorous, problems.

Auditoriums or other spaces which may be empty one minute and full of people a few minutes later may be controlled by what is called a variable air volume system (VAV). Engineers often recommend these systems for some museum galleries where, similarly, the load may be very light at night, and very heavy during opening hours. Engineers who work mainly with museums recommend strongly *against* the use of VAV systems, as they are complex and require constant attention, more than most museums can muster.

Environmental Control in Historic Structures

Environmental control in an historic building adds another level of complication to an already complicated business, since the building itself may be the most important item in the collection. Small amounts of condensation which may be permissible in another type of structure should not be risked in an historic building. Taking down walls in order to install vapor barriers, or breaking holes through ceilings for ducts should be out of the question. Ducted air conditioning should probably not even be considered for historic structures.

Improvement of conditions in an historic building should begin with a building survey by an architectural conservator, perhaps in consultation with a restoration architect. Other conservators should survey the movable collections to investigate the sensitivity of the objects housed in the building. Decisions to be made involve many competing interests including historic accuracy and interpretation. Should historic textiles or wall coverings be replaced by modern reproductions? How much can light-sensitive objects be moved to where they will be protected from sunlight? Are there any measures that can be taken to buffer the humidity around hygroscopic objects that do not violate the period qualities of the interior?

Any efforts possible to stabilize RH may be minimal, although turning down wintertime heat as much as is tolerable, and reducing sunlight by use of period shutters or shades, may help significantly.

Summary

Centralized environmental control is expensive to install and expensive to run. There are many pitfalls in its design and installation, and constant maintenance is necessary. When such systems work, they can provide optimal temperature, RH, and air quality. When they do not work, conditions for collections can be worse than if the system had not been installed at all.

A great deal of informed discussion must take place before deciding whether such a project is advisable. Do not allow those who design, sell, or install such systems to make the decision for you.

A facility that does not provide centralized environmental control can still do a great deal to improve conditions for individual objects and groups of objects. It is no disgrace to reject a central system in favor of simpler, less expensive measures. Conscientious application of other measures for control of light, and room-by-room or case-by-case RH control for sensitive objects is an admirable goal, and in itself not necessarily simple. If you think you could do more for your collections, hire a conservator experienced in these matters and find out. Proceed slowly and get as much outside advice as you can before acting. Don't be discouraged in advance; you may already be doing a better job than you think.

Light and Lighting

Deterioration from light is cumulative and irreversible. No conservation treatment can restore the damage done by light. Probably more than any other source of deterioration, light can be said to "use up" objects, to take them to a point where they lose any aesthetic value. It is vital therefore that we understand light and its power to destroy, so that we can show objects at their best while slowing their deterioration as much as possible.

The lighting of collections is an activity that often creates conflict between conservators and non-conservators. All things must be lit to be seen. It may be difficult enough to light things in an attractive and flattering way without having a conservator come along and tell you that the lights are too bright. Making a collection look inviting while following conservation standards requires knowledge, skill, and experience. Turning down the output of existing fixtures will not be satisfactory.

Few conservators are trained in lighting design, and few lighting designers are aware of the special problems of lighting collections. Taste is also a factor here; museum people have very different ideas about what kind of lighting makes a collection look good. In this crucial area of lighting, then, you may be forced to take an active role in the choice of fixtures, their placement, and the overall lighting design.

Light is a potent factor in the deterioration of artifacts in both the fading of colors and the deterioration of materials. The heat from certain light sources affects many objects adversely and produces sudden shifts in the relative humidity of the air around them. The energy from the light enhances many other modes of deterioration. At the same time, light has a positive impact: many insects don't like it, good housekeeping practice requires it, and the constant inspection that prevents problems from getting out of control demands it.

Fading

Damage from light shows itself in two direct ways, and other indirect ones. The type of deterioration most familiar in our daily lives is fading. Almost all colorants are subject to this (ceramic glazes, vitreous enamels, and other mineral colors are an exception), although their sensitivities vary. In general, dyes are more sensitive than pigments. Thin or transparent paint layers are more sensitive than thicker or more opaque layers because the light reaches a higher percentage of the pigment particles. Natural vegetable dyes tend to be more sensitive than synthetic dyes (although many people seem determined to believe the opposite). Pigments encased in medium, like those in oil paintings, generally fade more slowly than those exposed to the air, like those in watercolors. Bright or dark colors show fading faster than subtle ones. The chemistry of specific pigments or dyes also determines their sensitivity; each may respond to a particular wavelength of light.

A great deal of research has gone into determining the exact sensitivities of various pigments and dyes. This is important for artists who have their choice of materials, for colorant manufacturers who work to produce more permanent pigments and dyes, and for art historians who seek to ascertain the original appearance of objects. Since we seldom know the identity of every pigment or dye on an object, it cannot help us to set standards for exposure.

The fading of colorants from light is a terrible process. Some people may say that the mellowing effect of light on colors enhances the attractiveness of certain kinds of objects, like Oriental carpets or Old Master paintings. As a conservator, with the stated goal of preserving as much as possible of the intent of the original artist or maker, I cannot agree. Whether we like the actual object or not, we must allow the artist his or her prerogative; there is no evidence to date that an artist ever made a piece brighter than desired, knowing that it would fade. In the history of technology of colorants, people all over the world have consistently chosen the brightest colors they could get. Mosaics, which are virtually immune from fading, and manuscript illuminations, which have been protected from light as long as they were left in a book, are two art forms which have retained their color over long periods, and provide evidence of a persistent preference for bright colors. Our romantic notions of ages past may condition us to prefer the muted colors that often characterize old things, but we should not make the mistake of assuming that they were made looking old.

Although the fading rate slows down as it proceeds, it does not stop. Faded watercolors may stay at their present tonality longer than they stayed looking bright and new, but their fading continues.

The classic example of works of art destroyed by fading is the pictorial tapestries that museum-goers so often pass by in museum corridors without a second glance. It is almost impossible to imagine that these bluish and brown wall coverings were once brightly and subtlely-colored decorations. Yellows are among the most fugitive of natural dyes; the fading of the yellows out of the greens, leaving them blue, is an indication of this.

Some textiles are exhibited in ways that makes their fading worse because of uneven exposure. Many military collections bear witness to what can happen when dark blue uniform jackets are exhibited pinned to a wall so that the front is exposed to bright light while the back is protected. The fronts and backs of these pieces can be two entirely different colors.

Watercolors that have been matted for a long time with some of the painted area hidden under the mat tell a similar tale; although the matted piece may look perfectly respectable, when unframed, the difference between the original and faded colors becomes apparent. Colored baskets also often show a radical difference in hue between the inside and outside surfaces.

Other Forms of Light Deterioration

The second major type of deterioration from light involves accelerated aging of the material itself: embrittlement and weakening of the structure, often accompanied by discoloration. A common example is the aging of newsprint. Old newspapers cannot be even slightly bent without breaking; they eventually crumble into dust. Anyone who has left a stack of newspapers near a window can testify that the process of deterioration happens in the absence of light, inside the stack, but that in the presence of bright light, at exposed edges, the process is hugely accelerated. Deterioration of paper, which on a chemical level involves the breaking of the long cellulose molecules, is greatly accelerated by light. With other cellulosic materials, like cotton and linen, a similar process occurs, and with proteinaceous materials like silk and wool there is a corresponding process of embrittlement, weakening, and discoloration.

All organic materials suffer from light exposure. Wood can either fade or darken, depending on the wavelength of the light. Light can make the colorants in wood water-soluble. The linseed oil used as a medium in oil paintings hardens faster with ultraviolet irradiation, and becomes brittle more quickly. Natural resins traditionally used as varnishes for paintings and furniture are sensitive to deterioration from light, becoming darker and more difficult to remove. In addition to the fading of colors in Oriental lacquer from light exposure, the lacquer breaks down and becomes more soluble, risking damage from even normal cleaning solutions. Oily materials that cause stains on paper and textiles may be light-colored when new but darken considerably upon exposure to light.

The tapestries that have been so badly faded have also been physically affected. Their fibers are often so brittle as to feel like sandpaper, mainly on the front of the piece, not as much on the reverse. The fibers have weakened so much that the tapestries almost inevitably have undergone massive and repeated restorations just to make them strong enough to hang on a wall without shredding. Many have a spotty appearance due to the differences in fadingbetween original yarns and yarns used in later restorations. Modern re-restorations can take several years and tens of thousands of dollars of work, and after all that effort, the object remains just as faded and brittle as before. It is important for those responsible for the care of light-sensitive collections to keep in mind an example of deterioration as sad as this one, pieces which can only be described as shadows of their former selves. The difference between brittle and faded remains and textiles still vibrant with color is only a matter of time and light.

Although the rate of fading slows with time, the rate of deterioration does not; it increases in most materials. When one wavelength of light initiates a particular chemical reaction, the reaction proceeds like a tree. Each reaction creates more than one chemical product; each product may be subject to a different kind of reaction. As a wider variety of chemical types are produced, more different types of reactions occur. The total rate of reaction therefore increases, and the object also becomes sensitive to deterioration under a wider variety of conditions.

The energy from light accelerates some other forms of deterioration. Acid-related damage like that of wood-pulp paper (our newspaper example is one of the worst) is speeded up by light, by humidity, and by various pollutants. The red rot of leather, a common form of leather deterioration, is likewise accelerated by light. The shredding of old silk curtains is a common example of light deterioration assisted by mechanical damage and air pollution. Although most light damage occurs in organic materials, some inorganic materials like clear glass and argillite, a soft black stone used by Northwest Coast Indians for small carvings, can be affected by light, as can some minerals. It is possible that some metal corrosion mechanisms are enhanced by light.

In any one case, it may be impossible to assign a precise contribution of any one of several different deterioration sources. For example, wooden furniture kept near windows often shows uneven areas of aging, characterized by cracking and flaking of the varnish and bleaching of the surface. Is this primarily from high levels of exposure to sunlight, from the periodic heating caused by exposure to direct sun, or from the RH shifts that accompany the temperature changes? Is it due to exaggerated expansion-contraction cycles of the wood or to embrittlement and loss of adhesion of the resins in the varnish? Although furniture conservators might each have their theories it would be difficult indeed to apportion blame in any precise way. This cannot keep us from designing a solution to the problem: window shades and heavy drapes.

This might be an opportune time to explain something of the state of the art in preventive conservation, a term often used for the field that includes environmental control. There are many specifics that are at present unknown. Choosing the optimal environment for a particular work of art cannot be accomplished by calculation. The intertwined roles of different factors in deterioration often cannot be unravelled. The effect on objects of very small amounts of pollutants is a particularly complex question, just as it is with people or animals or trees. You may have noticed that a disproportionate number of sentences in this book have a "usually" or "often" or some other qualifier in them. I would be happier to be able to leave them out, but generally (there I go again!) cannot. However, just as with human health or with the health of our outdoor environment, the broad outlines are quite clear. We know that the cleaner the air is, the better. We know which objects live longer in lower light, and which do better at stable levels of relative humidity. Although we cannot predict which out of ten objects, dropped on the floor, will break, we are smart enough to know that we should not drop even one. We know enough to guarantee perhaps 95% of the methods we should employ to preserve the things we care about. Many of these methods require no more than knowledge, common sense, low-tech (or no-tech) methods and small amounts of money. The 5% uncertainty need not deter us from doing what we should.

Reducing Light Damage: The Amount of Exposure

The degree of deterioration from light is dependent both on the amount of light and on the duration of exposure. The interrelationship between these two factors follows what is called the reciprocity rule; that is, a particular amount of light for two months will produce essentially the same amount of deterioration as twice the amount of light for one month. It is important to remember that the time and brightness (non-scientists tend to refer to this property as "intensity", but this word should be reserved for something else) carry equal blame. It is meaningless to specify desired light levels for the exposure of objects if we do not at the same time specify the length of exposure.

How do we measure the amount of light? The traditional measure of light in this country is the footcandle, originally defined as the amount of light falling on a surface one foot away from a candle. In Europe, the lux is the preferred measure, a footcandle being equal to 10.76 lux. This is generally rounded off to an even ten for purposes of simplifying the mathematics. Because of the adaptability of the human eye, it is difficult for us to "read" light levels around us, but for some perspective, the human eye loses its capacity for color distinction at about three footcandles. The illumination in museum print galleries, usually the darkest in the building, normally measures from five to ten footcandles. Industry recommendations for offices are in the one- to two-hundred fc range, and the amount of light coming in a window can easily reach five hundred fc.

Footcandle meters are similar to photographic light meters. Reliable models can be purchased for around one hundred dollars. It is important to purchase a model that gives readings down to very low light levels. A typical meter has three scales for a wide range of readings. A footcandle meter should be a commonly used item whenever exhibitions are being re-lit. For museums or private collectors who do not wish to get involved with this, find a conservator or designer who will.

Because total exposure over an extended period of time is a better indicator of damage than a single light reading, it is important to measure actual exposure levels. There are two ways to accomplish this. One is the integrating light meter, an electronic device that provides total readings over specified periods. (Some expensive footcandle meters have this capability.) The other is the International Standards Organization's Blue-Wool Fading Standards, more commonly referred to as the British Blue Cloths (See *Sources of Supply:*

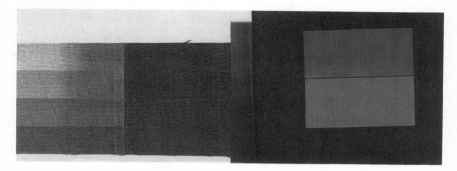

Fig. 3 British Blue Cloths. The eight cloths are shown at the left, with the gray scale on the right at scale number 1. This set had been hung in an east-facing window in New York City for three months in the spring, with one half of each cloth covered.

Talas). These consist of a series of eight textiles of about the same color. Each of the numbered cloths is about half as sensitive to light as the previous one. (Numbers seven and eight are so slow to fade that they are usually used only in aging tests.) Exposure cards with samples of the first six cloths are mounted together in a gallery, with either one half covered or with a matching set left elsewhere in the dark (See Fig. 3). The amount of observed fading of the cloths is in some settings enough to convince staff or administration of the existence of a problem.

For more precise measurement, the exposed cloths are compared with a gray scale. Gray scale number four is "just perceptible fading", and gray scale three is "very definite fading". Although the cloths were originally designed to provide standards for characterizing the light sensitivities of various dyes and pigments, their use has been extended. Research has provided some approximate figures for exposure levels. For example, the no. 1 cloth fades to a gray scale #3 in an exposure of about 104,000 footcandle hours.[6] The fading of blue-wool no. 3 to a gray scale contrast of 3 represents about 500,000 footcandle hours.[7] The fading figures are standardized for 50% RH.

---

[6] Krill, John. "Monitoring of Light at Winterthur" *Textiles and Museum Lighting* p.59-60 (1980)

[7] Feller, Robert L., and Johnston-Feller, Ruth. "Continued Investigation Involving the ISO Blue-Wool Standards of Exposure" *ICOM Committee on Conservation Sixth Triennial Meeting, Ottawa, 1981* Vol.18/1, p. 3 (1981)

There is some disagreement about the sensitivity of the blue cloths to ultraviolet light. Based on existing research, they should be used primarily for measurement of visible light rather than UV.

The museum literature has an oft-repeated recommendation for limits of light exposure: five fc for the most sensitive material, fifteen for intermediate material, and thirty to fifty for slightly sensitive or non-sensitive material. Because of the interrelationship between the amount of light and the time of exposure, these numbers are misleading when presented without further clarification. A unit like footcandle-hours per year, which includes light levels, exposure time, and exposure frequency, would be more accurate. The Japanese, for example, recommend no more than 5000 fc-hours per year for their most sensitive objects.[8] This could result in exhibition conditions of five foot-candles for eight hours per day, seven days per week, for about eighteen weeks out of the year. In contrast, the new Wilson-Turner collection at the Tate Gallery in London was designed for a limit of 500,000 lux hours per year (46,000 fc hours).[9] If this were divided out during a year of permanent exhibition, comparable figures would be about 17 footcandles for eight hours per day, seven days a week, fifty weeks per year.

To give some additional perspective to these numbers, research has shown that at about 6.5 million fc-hours, many natural dyes would have almost no color left. Serious damage to cellulose in paper and cotton occurs by 4.5 million fc-hours.

Generally accepted definitions list the most sensitive materials as all works on paper (See Fig. 4), textiles, and dyed leather. The middle category includes oil and tempera paintings and wood (See Fig. 5). The third category consists of glass, stone, ceramics, and metals.

---

[8] Ibid., p. 1

[9] Wilson, Peter. "The Clore Gallery for the Turner Collection at the Tate Gallery. II. Lighting Strategy and Practice" *The International Journal of Museum Management and Curatorship* Vol.6, p.37-42 (1987)

Fig. 4 An old paper backing for a sampler. This is a piece of good-quality paper, probably late eighteenth-century, which was glued to a wooden stretcher used as an original support for a sampler. The fabric of the sampler was transparent enough to allow significant discoloration of the paper beneath by light. Embroidered areas were more opaque, and protected the paper from light damage. The paper has also broken through from the stresses resulting from dimensional changes induced by RH fluctuations.

Fig. 5 Fading of wood. This was a mount for a set of filigree ivory plaques. Areas of wood protected from light by the ivory kept its original dark color, while the exposed wood faded significantly. Dark tropical woods, including mahogany, are particularly susceptible to fading.

Lighting the Most Light-Sensitive Material

Common practice in departments of prints and drawings in art museums actually follows these figures quite closely, keeping light levels around five to ten fc, with lights turned on only during visiting hours, and with changing exhibitions that last for three to four months each. Given a certain percentage of loan exhibitions both in and out, and the large numbers of prints or drawings in many collections, many works on paper will be on exhibition only once in perhaps twenty years, some, never. For this one situation the museum field has done well. Scholars of prints and drawings have become used to low light levels and expect only temporary exhibitions; galleries are designed for this purpose without windows and with low ceilings that make good lighting at low levels relatively easy. The duplicate nature of prints means that pressure for repeated exhibition and loan of one piece is lessened, although the danger remains for drawings.

Outside this connoisseur's world, however, conditions can be quite different. The pressure for travelling exhibitions that include popular drawings or watercolors can subject them to harmful light levels. This is particularly true for watercolors, which stand to lose a major portion of their artistic appeal as their thin washes of color fade, and their stark white paper turns brown. Works on paper which are exhibited for their subject matter in other kinds of exhibitions, particularly in non-fine arts settings, are seldom accorded the same care as valuable artistic works, and are often seen on permanent exhibition under lighting designed for much less sensitive objects.

Textiles and costumes are commonly part of permanent exhibitions, even though they are among the most light-sensitive material. The best that can be accomplished for their protection may be to design displays so that textiles can be rotated. This requires a collection of some depth and a designer who can create an installation with enough flexibility to accommodate pieces of different sizes in the same spot. The idea of rotating textiles on exhibition has some desirable side-effects. For either museum or private collections, it entails periodic inspection of material in storage and often conservation treatment of a collection one object at a time. Pieces on permanent display are often ignored; changes of exhibition command our attention and make us more vigilant in noting condition changes and possible hazards. We also tend to enjoy the objects more.

Costumes are especially at risk because their structure requires that they support their own weight.

Many important costumes are made of silk, the most light-sensitive textile fiber. Very brittle and weak paper can be backed with Japanese tissue for strength and can then be mounted on a solid support and matted so that it need never flex or even be handled. Similar treatments can be carried out with flat textiles, but costumes depend for their proper appearance on the textile qualities the textile industry calls drape and handle. A skirt that cannot flex without splitting the fabric is not much of a skirt. In institutions with well-established costume collections, conditions of display have improved in the past several years to a point where their policies are similar to those of prints and drawings departments. However, many small museums and historical societies still have costumes on mannequins on permanent display. When their deterioration is noticed, little can be done to "restore" these pieces.

Protection of the most sensitive materials requires careful planning of every aspect of an exhibition and sometimes special display techniques as well. The first requirement is total elimination of glare. Viewers' eyes must be given time to adapt gradually to the lower levels, and views of brighter galleries through doorways must be eliminated. A traditional method of limiting exposure for watercolors or small objects in table-top cases is the use of heavy curtains that can be moved aside by the museum

visitor. Other possibilities are light switches on timers that can be turned on by visitors, or automatic switches that are triggered by a sensing device under a floormat near the object. Some museums have tried using photocells to close curtains or louvers on skylights, but the results have not been a complete success. The sudden noise is unnerving to visitors, and the reliability of the equipment has sometimes not been high enough to make the trouble worthwhile. It is particularly important in situations where lights are turned off and on repeatedly to assure that lights do not heat up the objects or the air of a case. Frequent cycling of temperature and consequent rapid changes of relative humidity are deadly.

One possibility for reducing light levels is the use of dimmers on circuits for incandescent fixtures. Another is the use of neutral-density filters. Neutral-density filters are transparent gray materials designed to filter out a certain percentage of light. They can be purchased as either flexible plastic film or acrylic sheet in different densities. The color gray is designed not to change the color of light passing through it. Because neutral gray sometimes looks too cool at low light levels, a warmer copper tone is also manufactured. Filtering material that cuts out a specified percentage of light can be used in laylights between exhibition cases and fixtures, as covers for fluorescent fixtures, as window coverings, or in interior skylights. It is important before such materials are purchased to review the technical specifications to assure that ultraviolet as well as visible light is being controlled.

Dimmers and neutral-density filters are excellent measures to provide the final level of control in a lighting installation. Since neither save energy, it is highly preferable not to use them as the only way to produce conservation standards from an unplanned collection of fixtures. Neutral-density filters will also not reduce heat levels.

Many conservators would say that the best protection for light-sensitive objects lies in better education for curators and designers. In this as in other conservation matters, there is no fooling mother nature. Light deterioration will occur upon exposure; the more exposure, the worse damage. To lessen permanent damage, reduce light levels or reduce exposure time, or both.

Before we discuss exhibition conditions for moderately sensitive objects, it is important to mention that there are objects that recent research indicates should perhaps not be exhibited at all: certain kinds of photographs. The first step in identifying the relative sensitivities of different kinds of historic photographs is to identify the different media involved. There is a substantial body of recent literature on this subject which should be consulted before any work is done on photographic collections. However, many old, and some new, photographic processes can be categorized as more sensitive to fading even than watercolors; some have been shown to have measurable fading in low light levels after a week of exhibition! Exhibit these with the utmost caution, if at all.

Lighting for Moderately and Non-Sensitive Collections

The five-footcandle recommendation has a basis in actual measurement, three footcandles being the limit of human color discrimination, but the 15- and 30-fc limits have much less basis in fact. Perhaps consequently, they are much less followed. Oil paintings are generally listed as moderately sensitive to light damage, but traditional skylit paintings galleries have readings easily in the several hundreds of footcandles, light cannot be blocked off when the museum is closed to the public, and oil paintings are likely to be on virtually permanent exhibition, making their annual exposure around one million fc-hours. Although oil paintings do not fade to the same degree as watercolors, they are not immune from fading or accelerated aging. A small number of widely used pigments either fade or discolor in light, and the oil medium itself ages more quickly with strong light exposure. It is not unusual to see paint in better condition and with a slightly different tonality at the very edges of a painting where it has been protected from light by the rabbet of the frame. Contemporary paintings with exposed canvas are extremely sensitive to light damage.

Subtle changes in only some paintings may not seem to be enough evidence on which to base the lowering of light levels for pieces in the 15-fc category, and the lowering of light levels for metals, glass, and ceramics may seem nonsensical. However, lowering light levels will lower energy costs and lessen the load on summertime air conditioning. Less light also involves slower deterioration of non-collection materials like wall paint, wooden panelling, floor coverings and window coverings, upholstery and wallpaper. In addition, as museum-goers' eyes become slowly adapted to light levels lower than those outside, the five-fc levels where required will be much more easily tolerated.

Lighting manuals recommend no more than a threefold change of light levels between rooms to accommodate the easy adaptation of viewers' eyes. This would allow 5-fc galleries as a core to be surrounded by 15-fc galleries,

leading to 45-fc rooms. These three levels would provide for high, moderate, and low-sensitivity objects. With the addition of perhaps a daylit lobby area, offices, shops, or other non-collection spaces at about 150 fc, a theoretical floor plan would thereby include lighting zones for all uses.

What do limitations on light exposure mean for the long-term survival of collections? If we wish to be pessimistic (and that sometimes seems to be the crux of a conservator's job), we can only say that they delay their deaths. There is no safe amount of exposure. There is no threshhold under which objects do not fade or deteriorate. Studies of certain sensitive dyes and pigments have filled in some numbers, so that researchers can say that a particular watercolor or dyed textile will show noticeable color change in five years, or will have little color left in fifty or one hundred years of normal gallery illumination. The numbers are not easily transferable into real life; with any one object, we do not know what the colors looked like originally or how much light exposure it has already had. The quantification of the death of a work of art can be chilling, however. We must not forget: damage by light is cumulative and irreversible and involves the most fundamental aspects of the object.

Reducing Light Damage: Wavelength

The range of light we are concerned with includes the visible spectrum (ROYGBIV, as we learned in school: red, orange, yellow, green, blue, indigo, violet) and the segments of invisible light on either end. Just past the red is the infrared, the waves responsible for the transfer of heat, and on the other end, just past the violet, is ultraviolet light. The wavelengths of light are measured in a unit called the nanometer (nm), one billionth of a meter. Visible light ranges approximately from 400 to 700 nm. The ultraviolet range we are most concerned with ranges from 300 to 400 nm. These wavelength figures do not represent sharp cutoff points, but gradual transitions.

Light waves at the ultraviolet and blue end of the spectrum have more energy and are therefore more damaging to objects. Light damage at different wavelengths is on a logarithmic scale, so that the damage doubles for every twenty-eight nm decrease. Since neither ultraviolet nor infrared contribute to viewing conditions, both should be eliminated from exhibition and storage. However, it is an all too common mistake, even among museum professionals, to work to eliminate ultraviolet and ignore the damaging effects of visible light. I have seen grant requests that ask for money for ultraviolet filters so that the highest possible levels of visible light can be used for exhibitions. A review of a major installation in a major museum printed in a major newspaper once claimed that the museum had discovered a way to remove all the harmful rays from the light. Do not make this mistake: the harmful rays *are* the light. Removing ultraviolet is a great help, but it will not protect objects exposed to high levels of visible light.

Recent articles in the conservation field show some pigments and dyes for which UV filtration does not lessen fading rates. It is undoubtedly true that all materials do not share the same relationship between damage from UV and from visible light. These technicalities should not move us to change our policies on light. Proper care of collections requires both removal of ultraviolet and strict control over visible light levels.

There are two major sources of ultraviolet, sunlight and certain fluorescent tubes. This is complicated by the fact that some specially-made fluorescent tubes have less UV output than the average incandescent lamp. The bluer the color of the light, the more UV can be expected. Ordinarily, UV filters are recommended for sunlight and for fluorescent tubes, not for incandescent lamps. The range of lamps available may make this formula too simplistic. To be safe,

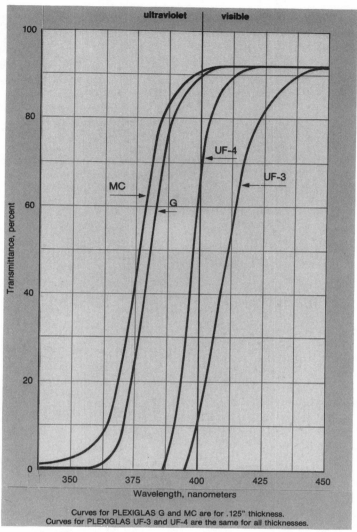

Fig. 6 Transmission spectra of ultraviolet-filtering Plexiglas® UF-3 and UF-4. The other two lines show the spectra of two plastic films used in construction. 400 nm. is the commonly used demarcation line between visible and ultraviolet light. UF-3 transmits much less UV than UF-4, and filters out some blue light, which gives UF-3 its characteristic yellowish tint. Graph courtesy of Rohm and Haas.

the spectrum for each lamp should be evaluated individually.

Removal of ultraviolet entails the use of ultraviolet filters. These consist of certain chemicals which themselves absorb ultraviolet light, embedded in a transparent plastic, either rigid like Plexiglas® or flexible film. Literature from the manufacturer usually gives a percentage of ultraviolet that is cut off at a particular wavelength. The standard in the U.S. is a form of Plexiglas® sheet made by Rohm & Haas designated UF-3. When choosing another kind of filter, manufacturers' specifications should be compared with the figures or with graphs for UF-3 (See Fig. 6). Other companies make acrylic sheet of corresponding filtering power. Some ultraviolet-filtering materials made for architectural purposes give significantly less protection than this; specifications must be checked carefully.

Because of the way filtration is accomplished, the removal of high percentages of near UV also entails the removal of some visible (blue) light. The cause of this can be seen in the graph for UF-3; the small corner of the blue part of the spectrum at the upper left that is cut off shifts the color of the sheet. Ordinarily, UF-3 is used to frame works on paper when they are on exhibition, even though major sources of ultraviolet have already been excluded from the galleries. The loss of some of the blue light provides additional protection for

the paper, since blue is the most damaging color of visible light. The appearance of prints is not changed noticeably by the yellow shift. The human eye is designed to adapt easily to small color shifts like this; that is why we do not think that the color of things changes when the color of daylight changes, as it does constantly through the day and in different weather patterns. Few viewers would notice the difference unless they could compare one portion covered with UF-3 to an uncovered portion. Likewise with windows: if all the windows in a gallery are shielded with a slightly colored plastic sheet, few viewers would notice the difference. In a situation where the yellowing would be objectionable, UF-4 is an acceptable subsitute. It is clear, with only a few percentage points less UV filtration capability than UF-3.

The use of titanium or zinc-containing paints is often recommended as a way of reducing UV because these pigments absorb it. Exact figures on the percentage of these pigments required in paint, and the actual percentage reduction seem to be lacking. This technique should only be relied on as a secondary measure of protection for daylit galleries with other filtering methods in place.

Ultraviolet filters should be used to shield all sources of daylight in a museum. Sheets of rigid filtering material can be laid over interior skylights. Sheets can be screwed onto window frames, or, to avoid condensation between the window and the Plexiglas® and to make cleaning easier, the plastic sheet can simply be hung from small hooks screwed into the window frame. Flexible plastic film with filtration corresponding to that of UF-3 is made by several companies. It is prepared with an adhesive to adhere to glass, but should not be used on historic glass. Films of about the same filtration are manufactured by several companies (See *Sources of Supply:* 3M Energy Control Products, Solar Screen, Madico, Inc.). Although some users have reported difficulty in applying this product to glass without leaving bubbles or wrinkles, others have reported no such problems. With ultraviolet filters as with many other construction matters, it may be best to purchase a small sample from the manufacturer and try it on one window before making a large investment. Users report durability of at least ten years with careful maintenance. These films have one additional advantage: they improve the safety of window glass in case of breakage.

A common type of UV filter is thin plastic sheets sold rolled up to be used around fluorescent tubes. The sleeves should be long enough to cover the ends of the tubes, where UV output is highest. They are easy to use, although there is always the possibility that they will not be re-used when tubes are changed. If this is a real danger, it is possible to use instead acrylic sheet in the covers of fixtures. After a long period of time, the plastic of these sleeves can degrade, losing its curl and falling off the bulbs. However, they are quite inexpensive, so replacement should not be a problem. Experience and manufacturers' guarantees indicate a useful life of about ten years.

Ultraviolet-filtering varnishhas been mentioned several times in the museum literature as an alternative filter that can be applied to glass. The commercial product is not made for permanence and is therefore not appropriate for museum use. It is made for use on boat decks, with the UV-filtering material added to slow deterioration of the varnish itself from high levels of sunlight. It is also difficult to apply evenly to glass. A non-yellowing conservation-grade resin can be mixed with a UV-filtering chemical for application to window glass instead; this would be helpful for uneven or weak historic glass.

It is important for both private collectors and museums without their own framing facilities to specify from commercial framers the use of ultraviolet-filtering acrylic or polycarbonate (e.g. Lexan®) sheet equivalent to Rohm & Haas Plexiglas®. Unfortunately, many framers charge an extra fee for this which can be quite a bit more than even the retail price of the material justifies. A framer who does not have the material in stock and does not want to order it may try to dissuade you, or try to claim a huge mark-up. Be stubborn, or learn to do the framing yourself.

How do we know what ultraviolet levels are? The usual unit for measurement of ultraviolet is microwatts per lumen (μw/l), and the commonly repeated recommendation is that exposure should not exceed 75 μw/l, the output of an average incandescent lamp. Since μw/l is not an absolute measure, this standard can be deceptive. If visible light levels are low, 75 μw/l will be a small amount of ultraviolet. If visible light levels are high, 75 μw/l can add up to a great deal of UV. Again, it is vital in avoiding light damage to collections *both* to filter out ultraviolet and reduce levels of visible light.

In most cases conservators tend to recommend that museums proceed with ultraviolet filtering simply on the facts of the case, that is, in any space with either daylight or fluorescent tubes, without taking measurements of ultraviolet. UV meters are significantly more expensive than visible light meters, and relatively few museums or conservators have them. With the new generation of electronic meters, the situation has changed somewhat, although UV meters are still more expensive than visible light meters. It is probably appropriate for museums working on light control to hire a conservator or engineer to take UV measurements before and after a project is completed to

assure that the filtering materials do what they are supposed to.

To my knowledge, rigid-sheet filters have always proved to be a reliable product. There have been sporadic reports of inconsistency with flexible sheet filters. It is important to stay with manufacturers whose products are well known in the museum market.

How long do UV filtering materials last? Some of the museum literature recommends that new filters be installed every ten years, but there is little data to support this. The ten-year figure probably was derived from data on the loss of physical properties of the flexible sheets rather than on a loss of UV filtration. Common wisdom has been that the filtering chemicals do not deteriorate with time and that the acrylic or other plastic sheets yellow slightly, making the filtering power stronger, since more blue is filtered out. One manufacturer's study[10] showed that 5 mil polyester film with a UV absorber lost ten percent of filtration power after fifteen years' exposure in a greenhouse. Rohm & Haas' technical data shows very little loss of filtration under very high light levels. At our present state of knowledge, replacement every ten years should be considered unnecessary. Since deterioration is undoubtedly linked

---

[10] Bogle, Michael. "Textile Mounting and Framing with an Internally Incorporated Thin-film Ultraviolet Light Barrier" *Textiles and Museum Lighting* p.63 (1980)

to the amount of light exposure of the plastic, sheets laid in skylights will deteriorate faster than those used to frame prints. It would probably make sense in rooms where UV readings have been taken previously for further readings to be taken every few years as a precaution. This is another issue that should be referred to a conservator likely to stay abreast of the most recent data. However, panic is unwarranted; changes that may be occurring involve small percentage shifts, not a massive loss of filtration.

If ultraviolet carries more energy than visible light, then it is also true that blue light carries more than yellow or red. This fact is used in photographic developing rooms: red lights are "safe" for exposure of light-sensitive films. Store-keepers know this also: orange plastic sheets are often used over store windows to reduce the fading of clothing on display. If the color of light is shifted toward the warm end of the spectrum, then damage will be lessened. This is important when choosing lamps. No one would recommend orange lights in museum galleries, but warmer-colored lights are certainly to be preferred where they are appropriate.

This brings up the confusing problem of color temperature. Color temperature is a way of describing the different colors of white light. Although these numbers, expressed in degrees Kelvin, are used to describe incandescent light bulbs, they have nothing to do with the temperature of the bulb. They are derived from a theoretical construct called black body temperature, which refers to the colors produced by a completely colorless (black) object when it is heated to various temperatures. Think of a gas flame: the hotter parts of the flame look blue or white; the cooler parts are yellow and orange. Higher color temperatures apply to light that is bluer; this can be confusing since these colors are referred to as "cooler" than the yellowish light that has a lower color temperature. Different colors of white light can be seen easily in real life: when a brightly lit building is viewed at night from the outside, rooms with fluorescent fixtures look green in comparison to those lit by incandescent lamps.

Just to add to the confusion, color temperature cannot accurately be said to apply to fluorescent tubes. The spectra of fluorescent lights are different from those of incandescent bulbs. Black body temperatures do not apply because the light is not produced from a glowing filament. The specific wavelengths of the light produced by the phosphors in the tubes creates vertical bars in the spectrum. This affects what is the called the "color rendering" capability of the tubes: Because of the distortion of the usual spectrum, light from many fluorescent tubes does not look "natural". Some fluorescent tubes are much better than others (See *Sources of Supply:* Verilux Inc.), but in exhibitions, even the better ones are usually mixed with incandescent lamps to improve their color rendering qualities.

Studies of color temperature and its relation to the lighting of works of art have led to contradictory conclusions. It is often said that at low light levels, people feel more comfortable in light that is yellower (warmer) than seems comfortable at higher levels. In various work involving the lighting of paintings, where art historians are the most fussy, different researchers report different conclusions. Although conservators would prefer yellower over bluer light for preservation reasons, this controversy is a matter of taste rather than scientific fact. Tests carried out to determine people's preferences in viewing paintings have produced contradictory results; there is as yet no "scientific" way to determine in which light colors look "truest".

It is important that those responsible for lighting paintings as well as other works learn to be sensitive to subtleties, look critically at a large number of different exhibition techniques, and find out what they like. There is no substitute for taste developed over long hours of critical viewing, particularly when it is coupled with investigation of the specific lighting equipment and techniques used in each case.

Reducing Light Damage: Oxygen Levels

The use of an inert gas like nitrogen to surround objects has been reported to retard fading as well as other forms of deterioration. This seems to require evacuation of a very large portion of the oxygen before any benefit is reported, so for now this technique is used only for the most precious items and only in technically sophisticated institutions. As usual, there are some complications in this method of reducing deterioration, as the lack of oxygen may actually promote fading of certain dyes, so detailed technical studies must be carried out to assure that a particular object will be helped and not harmed by its new environment.

Reducing Light Damage: Heat and Relative Humidity

Incandescent lamps, sunlight, and the ballast from fluorescent fixtures produce a great deal of heat. Incandescent lamps give out over 90% of their energy as heat. The heat from lights affects objects in two different ways. Direct sunlight and strong beams of light from incandescent lamps produce very sudden increases in the temperature of objects, causing expansion of materials. The stress this causes is compounded by the daily repetition of the expansion and contraction cycle. In rooms with direct sunlight, seasonal shifts in the physical limits of shafts of light must be noted to avoid damage year round.

Another source of local heat on objects is picture lights, the small fixtures using tubular incandescent lamps that are attached to the back of a frame. These are seldom appropriate for museum use, and are often mis-used even in private collections. Picture lights should be pulled as far as possible out away from the picture plane so that they do not heat the painting surface and do not cast shadows from the frame. Pulling them away from the painting surface also widens the area lit by the bulb; many picture lights do little more than create small pools of light at the top of a much larger picture.

Very tall pieces can unwittingly be damaged even where heat and light levels at normal heights are quite low. It is important to remember that the footcandle is a measure of brightness falling on a particular spot, not a measure of light output from a lamp. The inverse square law applies: the light level two feet away from a lamp is one fourth the level one foot away. If a light fixture on a ten-foot ceiling is aimed down along the surface of an eight-foot quilt, light levels along the top could be sixteen times higher than at the bottom, and the heat buildup at the top could be quite dangerous. Dark burn marks have been known to appear on museum textiles under conditions like these.

Objects with heat-sensitive components like oils or fats may be seriously altered by local heating from light sources as the heat liquifies them and brings them to the surface. Animal skin materials originally treated with oil as part of the tanning process and wood coated with oils can both be affected. African objects with oily surfaces can create quite a mess under these conditions. Paradichlorobenzene (moth balls) that has been used to treat objects can be brought to the surface where it crystallizes.

The second way in which light heats objects is by raising the ambient temperature in rooms or in exhibition cases that hold light fixtures. In this case, temperature changes in objects are much slower than when objects are heated directly, but shifts in relative humidity caused by ambient temperature changes can be damaging. When these shifts occur repeatedly, as in day-to-night lighting changes, the results can be extremely damaging, particularly inside cases with little air flow to buffer the changes. Fluctuations in the temperature also cause changes in the air volume as the air inside a case expands and contracts. This forces air through case seams and increases leakage.

Proper museum case design demands that any heat-producing lights be situated above a solid sheet of glass or Plexiglas® so that heat is vented outside the case enclosure. If fluorescent tubes are inside cases, they should be wired with the ballast outside the case. For improved security and convenience, light fixtures should be located in a separate compartment so that the case does not have to be opened in order to change lamps.

Even when light sources are outside a sealed case, the lights can produce heat inside the case much as the sun produces heat in a greenhouse. When case lighting is tested, thermometers inside cases should be used to monitor such effects.

A dichroic reflector is a type of incandescent lamp that will prevent the worst of heat damage to objects. This complicated sounding term means that the front surface of the lamp is coated with a different material than the back. Infrared radiation that comes to the front of the lamp is reflected toward the back and is transmitted by the coating on the back surface of the lamp. Visible light that goes toward the back of the lamp is reflected forward and out the front. Some of the red leaks out the back with the infrared, so that the ceiling behind these lamps has a pinkish glow. Because the heat goes out the back of the bulb, fixtures that accommodate these bulbs have porcelain rather than plastic sockets, and vent holes at the back.

There are two major types of these lamps, PAR lamps (for parabolic aluminized reflector) and MR-16 lamps. PAR lamps are a familiar-looking shape, similar to traditional spot- or floodlights. They come in both types, and in several different wattages. Representative types are Sylvania Cool-lux lamps and GE Cool-beam lamps.

MR-16's are low-voltage (12V) tungsten-halogen lamps, much smaller and more efficient than PAR lamps. Fixtures with a separate transformer in each are available. It is also possible to install a single transformer, so that low-voltage wiring can be used to connect sections of track. The advantages of this set-up are the small size of the fixtures that can be used and the ability to dissipate the heat from the transformer at a remote location.

MR-16 lamps are available in a tightly focussed configuration, so they can be used at a considerable distance from the works to be lit, and their color temperature is closer to that of sunlight. They are, however, deceptively powerful and usually should be filtered or dimmed to keep light at safe levels. Questions have been raised about their output of ultraviolet. Because the lamps are made of quartz rather than glass, the short-wave ultraviolet that is filtered by glass and is therefore not usually a cause for concern is part of the ouput of MR-16's. Fixtures for MR-16's are customarily made with glass fronts as a safety factor, so the UV is filtered out. MR-16 lamps, because of their smaller size and greater efficiency, can make the use of track lighting a much more attractive proposition than the standard PAR lamps, which use fixtures often referred to as "cans" for obvious reasons.

New kinds of low-voltage quartz-halogen lamps frequently come onto the market, and the availability of different fixtures suitable for collection use changes often. It is important to consult someone with up-to-date knowledge in this field before fixtures or lamps are purchased.

For objects which need locally brighter light but are very sensitive to heat, other solutions are available. One is the use of mirrors or fiber-optic cable drawing light away from a small lamp located elsewhere. Another solution is a relatively new technology called light pipes, tubes made of 3M Optical Lighting Film (See *Sources of Supply: 3M*). These are white tubes which have very high internal reflectivity. If a light source is placed at one end, the light bounces back and forth along the length of the tube and out wherever holes are placed. The tubes can be cut lengthwise with scissors and attached behind baffles along the length of cases to provide overall light, or installed to leave a hidden circular opening inside a case. The heat stays near the lamp, and only the light is transported.

Relative humidity levels have some effect on light deterioration rates. Textiles and paper are said to fade more at higher RH levels, higher moisture content in general increasing the rates of reaction in organic materials. However, these effects are of a significantly lower level than the effects of heat. Some research shows that an RH reduction of from 65 to 45% will not reduce fading; reduction from 45 to 25% will, but the reduction in flexibility for many materials would make this low level undesirable.

Reducing Light Damage: Photography

Museum photography of collection material can be quite hazardous, although more from the effects of heat than from light. In photo studios, photographers must be specially instructed when photographing art or other precious material. Lights should only be turned on when absolutely necessary. For long exposures, heat-insulating filters should be used on the lights or fans should be used to blow hot air away from the surfaces of the objects.

Knowledgeable staff should always be present to make sure the pieces being photographed are handled properly, are supported securely, and are not endangered by heavy equipment. When lights are used for a long time, someone should also monitor the ambient temperature of the room, and if it goes up more than about two degrees, work should be stopped temporarily. Television or newspaper photographers should be similarly monitored when working with collections.

The amount of light created during the use of a flash by museum visitors is not harmful. Even though flashes can be very bright, the short time of exposure prevents damage. Many museums prohibit the use of flash because of the possibility of flash bulbs bursting and spraying exhibits with glass splinters and because of the possible disruption to other visitors.

Natural Light

The use of natural light from windows to light exhibitions in museums is usually out of the question for several reasons. There is no control over the angle of light or the amount of light in changing weather conditions. It is impossible to control glare, and the viewing of works hung on walls is almost impossible in any position relative to a bright window. In addition, windows mean security problems and the loss of wall space. If museums are sensitively designed, small sitting areas between galleries or other non-collection spaces can be provided with small windows to give visitors a sense of direction and scale, and a connection with the outside.

Otherwise, natural light in museums usually means skylights or clerestory windows. When natural light from skylights is used in galleries, strict controls are necessary. Not only is it vital to limit light transmission when the light levels are high, but artificial light must be added when the weather is cloudy or when galleries are open at night. In order to avoid unnecessary light exposure, there should be a way of cutting off light entirely when galleries are closed, as in the early morning hours. Even if all this is done, galleries are bathed in an overall haze of light with no capability to direct light at objects. Given all these limitations, we are no longer talking about a technologically simple architectural feature or an inexpensive source of light.

Condensation is a problem common to skylights and clerestory windows, since glass is a very poor insulator and quickly becomes cold in cold weather. In order to avoid condensation, some architects recommend directing warm air along the skylights or strong fans to dissipate any water that accumulates. These are, however, rather expensive and energy-consuming solutions. Leaks are another unfortunate feature of many skylights, and the difficulty of cleaning is another problem. In real life, many museums with skylit galleries simply learn to live with a certain amount of dripping water. Maintenance staffs become quite expert in learning where and when drips will occur, and in the placement of buckets.

In museums, skylights are generally constructed of two sections of glass, one set forming the roof of the building and the other forming part of the gallery ceiling (laylights). This provides a margin of safety against both leaks and condensation, although not completely preventing either. In between is a space big enough for people to walk, where supplementary fixtures, shades, or louvers can be placed. Ultraviolet or visible light filtering plastic sheet can be used for the interior laylights.

Many people love the changing qualities of natural light on paintings, and claim to be repelled by paintings displayed with artificial light alone. The spacious airy quality and gracious proportions of traditional skylit paintings galleries, as well as people's natural attraction for this type of collection, may have more to do with this preference than the actual nature of the light. The problems of natural light can be solved with a combination of filters, shades, and lights, with louvers to direct light at the walls, but by the time daylight is properly "tamed" in this way, much of what is lovely about it may be gone.

Still, in museums with the technological sophistication to use it properly, natural light can be a real asset. The Clore Gallery for the Turner collection at the Tate, for example, was designed specifically to include natural lighting controlled by computer to allow variability but keep annual levels of exposure to about 45,000 fc-hours per year. The construction of a scale model of the building was necessary to test the lighting design. This is far too complicated for most institutions.

Although most of the discussions about natural light relate to paintings, natural light can be attractive in galleries where large stone or metal sculpture is shown, but for smaller objects, the light from skylights is usually too strongly vertical, leaving the faces of sculpture in shadow.

For historic houses and not particularly historic houses (yours), problems with natural light are quite different, and windows need to be dealt with. UV-filtering clear acrylic sheet, or possibly either the gray or copper-colored forms, should be used over all windows.

This method is highly recommended for institutions, but is not very satisfactory for homes, particularly since, whenever windows are open for ventilation, all protection is lost. Any other method which will keep light from getting into windows, like planting more shade trees, should be considered. Any method that keeps out summer sun will both reduce the load on air conditioning equipment, and protect all household belongings from light damage.

The problem of protecting art and household furnishings from light damage is not a new one. In centuries past, fabrics were much more precious than they are now, and protection was vital. Before summertime air conditioning, it was also important to learn to keep houses cool. Traditional and practical methods are too often forgotten in a blitz of high-technology. Heavy shades can be pulled down behind draperies when rooms are not being used. Louvered wooden shutters are a simple way to keep heat and light out and still allow air circulation. Fabric "throws" on any pieces of furniture exposed to direct sun will help. The most light-sensitive material can be hung in corridors, corners of rooms parallel to windows, in dark corners, or in rooms like dining rooms or bedrooms which are more often used at night and can be left dark during the day. Rotating works on paper or textiles, or moving furniture away from windows are other simple ways of avoiding damage.

In wintertime, there is less motivation to keep curtains or drapes drawn, unless drafts are a significant problem. It is important to note that winter light exposures can be almost as high as those in summer, so do not allow the lack of heat to make you complacent.

Conservators will undoubtedly continue to be pessimistic about the use of natural light in museums except in the most exceptional circumstances. There is certainly room for disagreement in this matter, but please do not allow your collection to be the victim of lighting designs that do not take its welfare into account.

Lighting Exhibitions

Before we get into details, it may help to summarize the differences between fluorescent and incandescent lamps, although within each group there is also wide variety:

Fluorescent tubes	120 V Incandescent lamps
minor heat output	major heat output
significant ultraviolet	insignificant UV
overall general light	controllable focus
unattractive fixtures often hidden	wide range of fixtures available
dimmers unusable	dimmers available
long life	relatively short life
short throw	long throw
poor color rendering	better color rendering
efficient energy user	inefficient energy user

Fixtures for tracks generally have small clips in the front that provide a space for the addition of diffusers, neutral-density filters or other special additions; this is another option that makes them advantageous. Because MR-16's show improved efficiency and long life, they have many other advantages over fluorescent tubes or other incandescent lamps.

This is not a textbook for doing exhibition lighting, but a few points should be made here. If done carefully, lighting can be done at safe levels so that objects can be seen in a flattering way. This means first of all eliminating glare,

unwanted reflection. In any room with a bright window and any reflective surface, glare is almost inevitable. Likewise, in any setting with parallel sheets of glass or Plexiglas®, glare is unavoidable. Glass or Plexiglas® that is not kept scrupulously clean makes glare worse. Exhibits must be designed with this in mind to avoid the problem from the beginning. Wall surfaces and the walls of cases should be of low reflection, and high color contrasts should be avoided. In general, background colors similar but slightly lighter and slightly less glossy than the objects displayed will help avoid glare and help in making low light levels work. Objects should be lit somewhat brighter than the surrounding walls. The lack of gross contrasts allows the eyes to adjust to subtleties in color.

This is one reason why modern art is often exhibited against stark white walls, Old Master paintings are traditionally hung against fairly dark textile-covered walls, ethnographic materials are often displayed against matte earth tones, and silver is often shown against gray or gray-blue satin. In good exhibition design, aesthetic, cultural, and technical values coincide.

It is vital that eyes be given a chance to adjust gradually to low levels of light. If at all possible, exhibits within a building should be arranged so that light levels are lower in each successive gallery as someone walks through the building.

The lighting system conservators commonly recommend for gallery spaces where works are hung on walls is low-voltage tracks using MR-16 lamps. (New kinds of lamps and fixtures can be added as they become available.) The standard directions by which everyone seems to install track end up with the track slightly too close to the wall, so that deeply carved frames leave dark shadows along the tops of paintings. It is still possible to cross-light, that is, to aim fixtures from each track at the opposite wall, although this can leave the

angle so low that viewers are staring directly into the lights. Various diffusers are available to attach to the front of the fixtures to keep the angle of light narrow and avoid this.

Once tracks are in place, the process of lighting an exhibit consists of trial and error, using some broader beams as "wall washers" to provide a low level of overall light, and then using smaller spots to highlight exhibits. Light from both sides of an object will emphasize the flatness of a piece; light mostly from the left (the preferred direction) will emphasize texture, a particularly important matter for textiles and bas reliefs. When fixtures are in place, a light meter should be used to check for general levels as well as the presence of undue "hot spots". The effective use of track lighting usually demands a large number of fixtures to provide light exactly where needed. After the fixtures are set in place and aimed, dimmers can be used to bring the whole installation into the proper range.

Small exhibition cases can be lit in a similar manner, but large cases are often fitted with luorescent fixtures inside to provide overall lighting, and then track lighting from outside the case to highlight objects and to improve the color balance.

Although it is vital to know the simple facts before doing museum lighting, words or even photographs cannot convey the look of an exhibit. Anyone responsible for the design of exhibitions must, as was stated above, spend a great deal of time looking, and trying to figure out why certain installations look good, why certain exhibits tend to draw us in and lead us toward the objects and others provoke only a quick and cursory glance. What makes a gallery look dignified? What makes the works look well-cared for? What makes a room look glitzy and superficial? How much flash and glitter is too much? This is a matter of taste, not conservation.

Although museum professionals may argue endlessly about preferred color temperature and the virtues of natural vs. artificial light, it is difficult if not impossible to isolate the effects of light from all other variables in a gallery. For example, the classic skylit gallery, which is what most people think of when debating about the use of natural light, has many advantages other than light. This kind of gallery often consists of beautifully proportioned mansion-like rooms. The paintings, perhaps Dutch domestic interiors or still lives, or lovely portraits, have none of the confusing or upsetting aspects of contemporary art or of earlier religious works. The galleries may have fabric-covered walls, chair rails, and wainscotting, and may be decorated with beautiful old furniture, ceramics, and flower arrangements. Here visitors will feel comfortable in a setting

resembling a grand home. The exact color temperature of the light may be of relatively little importance.

In other kinds of galleries, with low ceilings, flat undecorated walls, and no "period" touches, with abstract paintings with no subject we can relate to, we will never feel as comfortable, no matter what the light.

In more and more situations, museums as well as private collectors are hiring lighting designers as consultants to exhibition design projects. Lighting designers can be of great help, particularly in keeping abreast of the latest available fixtures and lamps. The choice of person is of course vital, particularly since the number of lighting designers specializing in museum work is small. Have the people under consideration done a museum display before? If so, check on their references, speak to the people they worked with, and if possible, go to see the finished job. Ask about conservation issues. How much does he or she know about protecting works against heat build-up and light deterioration? Beware of answers that contain the phrase "Don't worry about it". Be as specific about what you require as you can.

One well-known study of visitor reaction to museums lighting has shown that low levels can be satisfactory if the contrast between the light on the exhibition material and the rest of the space is not too great.[11] Yet, in the same journal (*Museum News*, September, 1972), another author states, "The design of illumination has been established as a minor art form for some time. There is little evidence of its application in most museums."[12] You have a good chance of doing better with some modest application of common sense, careful observation, and trial and error.

---

[11] Kimmel, Peter S., and Maves, Mark J. "Public Reaction to Museum Interiors" *Museum News* Vol.51, p.17-19 (1972)

[12] Russell, George Vernon. "Plain Talk on Renovation" *Museum News* Vol.51, p. 32 (1972)

Where More Lighting may be Better

One problem with the usual footcandle recommendations is that museum workers tend to apply them to storage facilities as well as to exhibitions. In storerooms where people do not usually work, light levels in the "safe" range can be dangerously inadequate. Light levels in exhibition spaces are measured at the surface of the work of art; in storerooms, if readings taken at a normal working height in an aisle or at a work table are in the 5- to 15-footcandle range, the amount of light that reaches an object resting at the back of a shelf can be minimal. This certainly prevents fading but encourages many other problems. Even with white shelves that maximize the reflection of light into their recesses, low light levels make it almost impossible to spot problems without moving objects or using portable lamps. One of the dangers of storage is that minor problems can turn into major ones if not caught in time, and dim storerooms discourage adequate inspection of objects. It is important to be able to see not only into the recesses of shelves, but also into unused corners of rooms and onto ceilings to be able to spot water staining or other signs of leaks, flaking paint on objects or walls, insect or rodent debris, corrosion of metal shelves or metal objects, empty spaces where objects once were, or any other indication of trouble.

If storerooms are used for working, arrangements should be made so that work tables can be well-lit while other lights are off. Storeroom lighting should be designed so that aisles can be lit one at a time and so that lights are not left on by mistake when personnel leave. High light levels for very short periods of time are the ideal for storage. Fluorescent fixtures with light bounced off white ceilings may be the best way at present to provide overall lighting for storerooms.

In exhibition spaces, it is important to have enough light for security personnel to see into all corners at night when normal gallery lighting is turned off. When museums are open, it is important to have enough light so that visitors and staff see ramps and stairs clearly. It should be possible to arrange lighting so that necessary light does not expose collections unnecessarily, although this may require some ingenuity.

Deterioration of objects caused by impurities in the air is difficult for most people to take as seriously as deterioration from other sources, because it is seldom as easy to detect. Deterioration from the numerous substances that appear in air in miniscule amounts may take many different forms, but mostly involve accelerated aging of the same kind that results from excesses of light or from inappropriate relative humidities. From an historic point of view, some pollution-caused problems may be relatively new in the life of old objects, since air pollution has increased so much in the last forty years or so and since so many new chemicals have been added to the pollution pot. Many pathological conditions arise from a combination of factors: for example, corrosion of metals takes place at a lower relative humidity when certain pollutants are present; other pollutants can increase the rate of fading from light. Much of the research on air pollution relates to outdoor conditions; its applicability to indoor conditions is uncertain. For all these reasons, research on air quality in museums is at a rather primitive level compared to that on other conservation topics. Despite haziness in the details, however, the broad outlines of the problem are clear.

Before we discuss the complications, let us list the principle pollutants, their most common sources, and victims.

Sulfur in its various forms: Sulfur dioxide (SO_2), the most abundant pollutant, from the combustion of fossil fuels; a major factor in the deterioration of paper, cotton, leather, alkaline construction materials like concrete, and some stones, contributes to the formation of bloom in paintings. Hydrogen sulfide (H_2S), from rotting vegetation, from protein materials like wool, animal glue and leather, from foam rubber; tarnishes silver and polished copper and blackens lead pigments, produces black spots on bronze.

Chlorides, usually as sodium chloride (NaCl), common salt, from salt air and perspiration, also from burial soils; cause corrosion of copper and silver, accelerate corrosion of other metals.

Nitrogen oxides (NO, NO_2), mainly from traffic exhausts, but also from the deterioration of cellulose nitrate in photographic films and in other products.

Formaldehyde, from foam insulation and boards made from wood chips, from fabric finishes, adhesives, foam rubber; corrodes lead, reacts with cellulose in textiles and paper and increases their acidity, bleaches or discolors paper, causes embrittlement and sometimes color changes in proteins like gelatin, animal glue, leather, and animal tissues, can cause efflorescence on glass. Formaldehyde is classed as a VOS (volatile organic solvent) and is by far the most abundant of these. A large variety of other solvents evaporate into the air from sources including cigarette smoke, plants, and many industrial materials; some are purposely added to the airstream in humidification systems.

Acids created by reactions of each of the above with water, either moisture in the air or condensation on the surface of objects: sulfuric, hydrochloric, nitric, formic and acetic acids. Organic acids are also released during the drying of paints and the deterioration of many organic materials. The organic acids (chiefly acetic and formic) emitted directly from wood are responsible for serious corrosion of lead and the darkening of lead-based pigments. Acid vapors, in general, attack cellulose (paper, cotton, and linen) and to a lesser extent other textile fibers; they attack proteinaceous materials, including paint media, making them structurally weaker and more soluble. Calcium carbonate materials like coral, shells and marble are susceptible to acid attack. Acids accelerate metal corrosion of various kinds. Leather

is also extremely sensitive to acid levels, as is rubber. Formic acid can produce formate crystals on moist glass surfaces and therefore contributes to problems from "weeping" glass.

Ozone, from some electrical devices, like photocopy machines and electrostatic air cleaners; cracks rubber, accelerates fading of some organic dyes and pigments and loss of strength of fabrics, can cause efflorescence on glass. Ozone can also be a byproduct of reactions of other pollutants.

Alkaline aerosols (particles so small as to be equivalent to gases), emitted from new concrete; discolor linseed oil films and some dyes and pigments, attack the strength and luster of silk, alter soluble salts into insoluble ones, cause serious deterioration of murals, produce whitish haze on paintings, and disturb the accuracy of humidity sensors.

Particulates, with particle sizes ranging down to the very small particles of smoke, including greasy soot and a multitude of other materials organic and inorganic; disfigures all objects, is particularly damaging to porous materials like paper, textiles, and baskets, from which it can be difficult to remove. Dust also attracts pests, holds moisture and acids on the surface of objects, and can abrade fragile surfaces.

Indoor Pollution

Harmful materials in the air come from many different sources, but for museums it is useful to divide them into two categories: those which come indoors from the outside, and those which originate from building interiors, from construction materials, paints, and carpets, and in some cases, from the objects themselves. Many contaminants have sources both inside and outside, but the ways we handle them are quite different.

Contamination from materials inside the museum is probably more significant than from outside because the concentration of pollutants can be so much greater. When a source of contamination is sealed inside a container with an object, damage can be quite severe and fast-moving. Visible damage caused by contamination from construction materials has been noted within two weeks of pieces being put into poor quality cases. It is within our power to choose materials that do not harm objects; this job is a much more straightforward one than dealing with the tiny quantities of contaminants in outside air.

The sources of harmful substances are numerous. Rubber in gaskets, in upholstered furniture, and as a padding for carpets, emits sulfur, as do many molding compounds used to make casts of objects, and Plasticine, sometimes used to hold objects securely on shelves. Drying oils in paints and varnishes emit harmful fumes even after they are touch-dry; alkyd paints and polyurethanes also contain drying oils as plasticizers. Curing agents for epoxies or polyester adhesives may be corrosive until they are completely cured. Many synthetic adhesives also emit harmful fumes even after an initial drying time. Polystyrene and polyvinyl chloride, two common plastics, emit corrosive fumes, as do polyurethane foam and styrofoam. The anti-oxidants in drycleaners' bags have been known to cause yellowing in textiles.

Textiles used in cases or for upholstery or draperies can be expected to have been treated with a multitude of chemicals, many of which produce harmful fumes. These include dyes, flame-retardants, finishes (including formaldehyde for permanent press), water-repellents, anti-statics, moth-proofers, softeners, stiffeners, bleaches, fluorescent brighteners, and surfactants, in short, a chemical factory. Cellulose acetate, diacetate and triacetate emit acetic acid, a byproduct of their deterioration. Although natural fiber fabrics tend to have fewer additives, they can have enough to cause problems. Animal fibers contain sulfur. Felt, a common decorative fabric in museum displays, is the worst of all because of the large amount of adhesive used to stick the fibers together.

Wood is the source of harmful acids, mainly acetic and formic. Wood products, like the various chipboards and laminates that have become more and more common because of their lower price, are even more dangerous than lumber, because the wood has been ground up and therefore liberates more volatile chemicals, and because the adhesives used in their manufacture add others. Formaldehyde is a major component of the most common plywood adhesive, urea-formaldehyde resin. Phenolic resin adhesives for wood particle boards emit about ten times less formaldehyde; products manufactured with them should be used in preference to those made with urea adhesives. Other wood-related products like cork and excelsior packing materials are also acidic. If treated with fungicides, insecticides, or flame-retardants, a wood product can give off additional kinds of chemicals.

The manufacturers of plywood and wood-chip boards that are made with urea-formaldehyde resins have claimed that emissions of formaldehyde initially are due to an excess of adhesive used in manufacture, and that after an initial period, emissions are greatly reduced. Unfortunately, it has been shown that reduced emission from manufacturing excess is replaced by emission from deterioration of existing resin. Emission does decrease after the initial period, but does not stop.

Industrial products should always be tested before use because much harmful off-gassing is caused by trace components like opacifiers, plasticizers, fungicides, and stabilizers, rather than from the primary material. The presence or identity of these numerous chemicals is usually impossible to ascertain from product literature. The amounts and identities of additives in different batches may vary significantly. The dyes on textiles may be the critical factor, so every color of a group of fabrics should be considered separately. To complicate matters, synthetic materials may have been manufactured with additives that stabilize them against chemical deterioration, but the additives themselves may be volatile, and the materials therefore become less stable with aging. Testing of a new product may preceed the onset of deterioration and therefore of off-gassing.

Many museum or household activities release fumes into the air. Ammonia or chlorine fumes from glass or Plexiglas® cleaners can harm objects. The volatile components of floor polishes may be harmful. Photocopy machines release solvent vapors, nitrogen oxides and ozone. Workshops, food service facilities, and artists' studios produce both particulates and gaseous pollutants.

Sand or pebbles used in the bottom of cases may contain chlorides from sea salt. Plants are sources of both particulates and gaseous contaminants.

Cigarette smoke contains many different harmful pollutants both gaseous and particulate and leaves a characteristic yellowish layer on surfaces. Smoking should simply not be allowed in rooms with unprotected sensitive materials, and working fireplaces, as lovely as they are, should be strictly forbidden. The greasy dirt from smoke can be difficult to remove, even from objects that can be cleaned with water. Objects like textiles, paper, and basketry that cannot be easily washed may be permanently disfigured from smoke.

Contamination of collections from alkaline aerosols is a different kind of problem. The only known significant sources of alkaline pollutants are newly-poured concrete and new plaster. Even in well-ventilated spaces, concrete has been said to release alkaline material into the air for about two years after it is poured. Alkaline particles in the air can cause a variety of problems, although there have been relatively few reports in the literature of actual damage from this source. It is likely that the time involved in construction makes it rare that collections are moved into spaces with newly-poured concrete. It is just as likely that problems have simply not been identified as coming from this source.

How much pollutant is too much? This is a question almost impossible to answer. Some figures are available: 0.1 ppm (parts per million) is the government limit for human exposure to formaldehyde; concentrations of one tenth of that can corrode metals. Standards for the presence of the most common pollutants in museum air have been set, but they are based largely on the limits of available technology of air cleaning rather than on any hard safety data. It is probably impossible to set safe limits because of the reactions of combinations of pollutants, the wide variety of sensitivities of different materials, the contributions of relative humidity, light, and other factors.

Because of the chemical variety of materials found in collections and because we are committed to work toward providing conditions where no chemical change takes place, any contaminant should be considered a harmful one. Materials used with collections should ideally be completely stable ones themselves, since any chemical reaction inevitably produces gaseous byproducts. Any container that, when opened after a period of being sealed, has a pronounced smell, should be suspect. It is important to remember that objects continue to accumulate toxins throughout their lifetimes, which may be many dozens of human lifetimes; unlike people, they can neither eliminate toxins or regenerate damaged parts, so our goals should be even stricter than those for people.

With such a wide assortment of hazardous materials, what materials are safe for use near collection material?

Archival paper products. These include an ever-widening range of papers and boards, including acid-free corrugated boards, acid-free tissue paper, acid-free glassine, and acid-free kraft paper (brown paper). Although there have been some complaints that materials sold as archival are not always so, the major manufacturers and distributors (See *Sources of Supply*) seem to have done an excellent job in providing the materials that museums need and use, and have regularly come up with new products when conservators set new specifications. In order to be sure of the quality of manufactured products, it may be advisable to have independent tests done before purchasing large quantities of archival paper products. Paper conservators generally keep up to date on problems that have been found with commercial products; don't hesitate to ask.

Traditionally, acid-free papers and boards have been those made from 100% rag, with no wood pulp used. Materials have become available in the last few years which are said to be of archival quality, but are made from trees

with all the acidic materials (primarily lignin) chemically removed. Chemically, then , they are said to be the same as 100% rag products. Conservators remain somewhat wary and continue to consider these chemically-purified pulp papers somewhat inferior in strength to rag, although generally safe.

Many acid-free materials are also buffered. This means that acid-neutralizing materials have been incorporated in the paper so that acid contaminants from the air do not contribute to the acidity of the paper. Under most circumstances buffering is desirable. With certain photographic materials, conservators prefer non-buffered storage containers, since some photographic media are very sensitive to any shift in acidity. The main concerns here lie with albumen prints, a common 19th-century photographic medium, and with cyanotypes. Some modern color dyes are said to be alkaline-sensitive. A few conservators prefer that buffered papers not be used with proteinaceous materials like wool or leather. No actual reports of damage due to alkalinity have been reported in the museum literature to my knowledge, and damage from buffered papers remains solely theoretical. Because of the high reactivity of old photographic images and the complications involved in their treatment, restriction of buffered papers with them is perhaps more warranted than with wool or leather, where damage, if it occurs, is apt to be less critical.

In most cases, it is easy to tell acidic from acid-free boards, as acidic boards are tan or brown color on the inside, with light-colored face papers. Ragboard is always the same color throughout. Acid-free pulp boards are now also the same color throughout. In questionable cases, a simple test can determine the acidity of boards. The archivist pen (See *Sources of Supply:* Talas) is a felt-tipped marker with ink that changes color based on acidity. Although not easily used on dark colors, and not as accurate as laboratory pH meters, it is easy to use and basically reliable.

Readings from an archivist pen or from a pH meter will be affected by the exposure of the paper to acidic air. The pH of acid-free but unbuffered matboards will decrease (that is, the acidity will increase) with long-term exposure to acidic air. Storage of either buffered or unbuffered papers in acidic environments like cardboard boxes or wooden shelves before use with objects will of course shorten their useful life and will use up some of the alkaline reserve in buffered products. Although some conservators recommend changing all ragboard for new after ten years, this is unnecessary. It may be helpful to monitor pH changes, perhaps every five to ten years, but it is difficult to imagine that small shifts would affect collections at all until perhaps twenty to thirty years had elapsed.

Acid-free storage materials are not vital for collections that are themselves acidic. Wrapping baskets, for example, in acid-free paper may seem a waste of money. However, acid-free materials will last much longer than acidic ones, so for long-term use, acid-free materials are preferable, and buffered materials should offer a significantly increased life when used with acidic objects. Acidic papers become brittle and crumbly as they age, and leave a mess; acidic boards become so brittle and weak that they break from any flexing and can therefore cause damage to any object supported by them (See Fig. 7).

Glass and Plexiglas® (acrylic sheet, Rohm & Haas) and its counterparts, and other plastic sheets like Lexan® (polycarbonate) sheet, General Electric). **Some plastics,** including polyester, polyethylene, and polypropylene. Polyethylene and polypropylene may yellow, but this is apparently not indicative of instability. Ethafoam® or Microfoam® (sheets of these may be useful as acid barriers). Mylar® (DuPont). Commercial plastics used to make boxes and bags may be unpredictable because it is often minor components like plasticizers that cause harmful off-gassing. It is best to test plastics before a major investment is made.

Stainless steel, anodized aluminum, enamelled steel. Enamelled steel, a common material of storage furniture, has

Fig. 7 Damage to an old photograph (around 1910) because of the brittleness of its original acidic mounting board. The mount was oversized and was stored without proper support. A rather gentle knock caused a bad break. From the author's collection.

recently proved to be a problem in some institutions. When steel cases are painted and then baked, the baking has to be carried out at a high enough temperature for the proper length of time in order to burn off the organic medium of the paint. Because of the way air circulates inside the cases during baking, the lower portions of the inside of a cabinet may not be at a high enough temperature, and the resulting cabinet may off-gas formaldehyde. In order to bake the hard-to-reach areas enough, some other areas may get small burn marks. Because these burn marks

show more in light colors of paint, white cabinets are most likely to be under-baked.

If you purchase enamelled steel cabinets for collection storage, do not assume they are safe. Properly baked cabinets should have no smell whatsoever when they are opened after being closed for a long time. Test them before use, and write the specifications for purchase so that the manufacturer will re-bake the finishes if they are not satisfactory. Specify also that in the case of re-baking, the manufacturer will pay the freight as well as the refinishing costs.

A new process called powder coating has recently been developed (See *Sources of Supply:* Delta Designs) for the purpose of eliminating volatile emissions in the factory during the manufacturing process; it also eliminates off-gassing from the finished product and produces a very durable surface. Cabinets coated by this process are strongly recommended for use with collections.

Stainless steel and aluminum have not exhibited any problems, and there is no reason to expect that they will, but they can be quite expensive.

Some fabrics, but only if tested first. Cotton, linen, nylon, and polyester fabrics are safe if not contaminated with processing chemicals. Polyester batting is considered safe as a padding material. The less dyeing or finishing a fabric has undergone, the more likely it is to be safe. In some states or cities, flame-retardants may be required for upholstery fabrics; this is likely to off-gas. The harmful minor components of fabrics can be very corrosive; conservators have seen nails and hooks used to hang objects on case walls break off at the point where they penetrate a fabric wall covering after no more than a few months of exhibition time. Washing in hot water without detergent will help get rid of some

impurities; this process should be carried out before testing.

Latex paints, in general, as long as they are thoroughly dry. **Two-component epoxies,** if mixed accurately. **Heat-set melamine chipboard,** probably, but more testing is in order. **Moisture-cure polyurethane.**

This is obviously a very short list, too short to provide us with any materials to make a case with. What do museums do? In many institutions, they have used materials they shouldn't and have had to deal with the consequences later. The classic sad story from one major institution is storage furniture made of the usual combinations of plywood or chipboard, sealed with several coats of polyurethane. Within weeks of the installation of Oriental metal objects, white crystals appeared on their surfaces. Analysis revealed that the crystals were a lead salt formed from reaction with formic acid which was a byproduct of formaldehyde in the adhesives of the wood products. Oriental metal objects are particularly susceptible because they usually have higher lead levels than Western alloys. Aside from damaging the objects, this salt is toxic to humans because of its lead content, and is very light in weight, which results in its being picked up into the air and inhaled.

Because the lead saga has been published, and because of the added dimension of human toxicity, this particular problem has received the rapt attention of museum professionals. It is important to remember that lead salts are only the most obvious manifestation of a common and complex problem. Tarnishing of silver happens anyway; we may not notice that it happens sooner rather than later. Textiles get brittle, paper gets discolored with or without formaldehyde; shifts in the rate of deterioration may be difficult to discern. Few objects, if any, are immune to deterioration from the chemicals that contaminate our air. If we do not see this deterioration, it may only be because we are not looking closely enough or because we do not know what to look for. If it weren't for lead in objects, the museum field would have taken much longer to become aware of the problems from contamination with exhibition materials.

If ideal materials cannot be used, it is still important to keep fumes to a minimum. If plywood must be used, phenol resins rather than urea resins should be specified. Plywood and chipboard stamped by the American Plywood Association are certified as being made with the phenol adhesive. Materials without flame-retardants should be chosen.

When less than ideal materials are used, it will help to use as little of them as possible. For example, bins for paintings can be made using some plywood, but with most of the smaller partitions made from acid-free corrugated boards. This kind of design is an excellent compromise between cost and safety, since the collections in the bins are only moderately sensitive, and there is considerable ventilation in the space to flush out contaminants.

The severity of potential damage from pollutants depends on the proportion of harmful materials to the space, the degree of ventilation, the sensitivity of the objects, the amount of time the objects will be in the space, ambient temperature and relative humidity levels, and the closeness of contact. Higher temperatures and relative humidities both increase the off-gassing rate and the rate of corrosion. It is important to consider all these factors before making a decision that will affect an entire collection. If the more important source of pollution is outside the container, then the best seal possible is beneficial; if pollution sources are within the container, then greater ventilation should be built in.

The better containers are sealed, the more important it is to be absolutely scrupulous about materials. Works on paper sealed in frames must be backed and matted with acid-free materials to prevent discoloration of the paper. However, if a decorated acidic mat is available for re-use, it can be backed with ragboard so that it does not touch the paper. The porous acid-free materials inside the frame will help to soak up the acid fumes so they do not affect the object. The encapsulationof acidic paper in mylar or polyethylene envelopes has been shown to enhance deterioration of the paper because it is stewing in its own acidic juices without any other material to absorb them.

Sealing painted or printed paper or textiles behind Plexiglas® or glass inside frames creates another phenomenon that so far has not been shown to be harmful, but should be anticipated. This is off-setting of an image onto glass. With time, a cloudy image in tiny whitish particles forms on the inside of the glass or Plexiglas®, even when it does not touch the object. This image is probably related to the deterioration products of the organic binder and is sometimes mistaken for mold. Framed pieces should be removed from their frames periodically, perhaps every five to ten years, to clean the glass of this material and to insure the good condition of the piece.

The materials most closely in contact with many objects are the materials of mounts. Particularly where mounts touch objects, they must be of the utmost purity. Plexiglas® is an excellent material for mount-making, since it can be formed in so many ways, and can be painted to look like other materials. Metals covered with surgical rubber or synthetic varnish are generally safe, although it is important that no direct metal-to-metal contact be made with the object. Wood lined with a padding material is good for wooden objects. Molded epoxy or wax are good supports for very fragile items, but they need to be isolated from the surface of the objects.

Plaster can be used, although it should be sealed with a stable resin, because raw plaster holds moisture. Textiles, particularly cotton or polyester, are usually safe for contact with objects. Hollow metal objects should if possible be mounted with some access of air to the inside to avoid moisture buildup.

Since the general nature of the acid deterioration of collections was first identified, many coatings have been used to seal wood surfaces. For a long time, shellac was used in museums as a wood sealer. Shellac in itself is not harmful, but layers of shellac are quite brittle, and crack as the wood expands and contracts, allowing the acidic fumes that the shellac originally sealed in to escape. When problems with shellac became widely known, many people switched to polyurethane, which seemed a more modern material. Polyurethane in itself emits corrosive fumes, and, like shellac, does not provide a permanent seal. The most commonly recommended sealants at present are a two-component epoxy and moisture-cure polyurethane. As stated above, the epoxy must be mixed exactly according to directions, and applied in several layers. Not mixed properly, it can off-gas just the vapors we are trying to avoid. Both of these materials are excellent barriers, but neither are inexpensive or widely available. They both may off-gas solvent vapors (not acids) for up to a year.

Latex paint is generally safe, but is not a good barrier. White or light colors of latex paint generally include a high proportion of calcium carbonate, which neutralizes acid. This should make latex paint an inexpensive, moderately good protection in cases with objects that are not extremely sensitive to acid damage.

The kind of aluminum paint used to prevent rust on iron radiators is an excellent moisture seal, but the drying oils in the medium are harmful. It has been suggested that a latex paint with mica or aluminum flakes mixed in would solve this problem, but so far, no commercial source can be found.

An alternative to coatings, and perhaps a more reliable one, is to use a barrier film to cover the inside surfaces of plywood or chipboards, adhered with the adhesive recommended by the manufacturer. A highly recommended material is a sandwich of aluminum foil, Mylar®, and polyester (Marvelseal® See *Sources of Supply:* Art Preservation Services). This is similar to the thin foils sometimes used in packaging potato chips or breakfast cereals. It is extremely impermeable; the plastic layer helps make it less apt to rip than foils or mylar alone. Unfortunately, this film cannot be painted. Any panels in exhibition cases that would be exposed would have to be covered with fabric.

Sheets of buffered ragboard cut the full size of the sides of a case are also good barriers. Designers may like the appearance of colored ragboards as case interiors. This solution to the problem has the distinct advantage of making use of a material already in common use in museums.

Any wood or plywood sealed on the inside to stop off-gassing of fumes should be coated on the outside only with a permeable layer like latex paint. This will allow gases to escape through the outside and will eliminate a buildup of gas pressure that might contribute to failure of the barrier.

Another way out when less than ideal materials must be used is to employ what is called a pollution scavenger. This is a chemical that picks up gaseous pollutants and either absorbs or adsorbs them onto its surface. (The difference is unimportant for the purposes of consumers, but important to scientists.) The most commonly recommended is a chemical called potassium permanganate, which is deposited on a base of alumina, producing a pebbly substance. Like silica gel, potassium permanganate (See *Sources of Supply:* Purafil, Inc. and Carus Chemical Co.) can be purchased in bulk and used in small trays. The kinds of trays used for storage of tableware have been recommended for this purpose. It is difficult to say how much chemical is needed, or how long it will last, as this will depend on the volume of pollutants and on the exposure of the chemical prior to museum use. The amounts of pollutants generated in museums are far less than those in other industrial applications, so frequent replacement should not be necessary. Potassium permanganate is a purple chemical that turns brown when its reservoir is used up; knowing when to change it is therefore easy, as long as periodic inspections are carried out. Some studies indicate that potassium permanganate is significantly less efficient in removing nitrogen oxides than ozone or sulfur dioxide, but test results vary, perhaps because of differences in air circulation. It is a good idea to place in the tray a note with the date the material was poured.

For convenience, porous polyethylene tubes 10 by 2 3/4 inches containing Purafil® are available (See *Sources of Supply:* Art Preservation Services,

Conservation Materials Ltd.). Although more expensive, there is no risk of messy spills, and no further supplies or staff time is necessary. One unit per shelf must be used in cases where there is no air circulation between shelves.

It is very difficult for non-conservators to have a sense of proportion about the safety of materials used with collections. Containerization can be extremely beneficial to collections in protecting objects from handling, theft, RH changes, dust, and pollutants. It is, however, a form of conservation treatment and can have negative as well as positive consequences when unanticipated problems with materials arise. Before object containers are designed, before any decisions are made that involve large numbers of objects or a large expenditure of money, a conservator should be consulted, and every material used should be investigated carefully.

How Can Air Quality be Tested?

Some simple inexpensive detectors of pollutants are available from scientific supply companies, but these are not recommended for museum use, because they are meant to detect only high levels. A more common detection system is the use of metal samples, one each of lead, polished silver, and copper. These are placed in the environment in question for a period of time of a few weeks to a

few months. If a set is to be put inside an exhibition or storage case, it is important to provide an identical set for comparison placed in the same room as the case. The degree of loss of metallic luster or growth of corrosion products indicates the severity of attack. As a first step, different materials can be compared visually. Corrosion on the samples may be enough to indicate the serious nature of the effects of pollutants on objects. If more precise information on the composition of a pollutant or its source is needed, scientific analysis of the samples may be necessary. Purafil, Inc. provides a kit of metal coupons, and will perform any analysis required (See *Sources of Supply:* Purafil, Inc. and Art Preservation Services).

Commercial laboratories can also be relied on for air sampling and analysis when tests for specific chemicals are required or to answer specific questions such as: Does a particular case off-gas formaldehyde? Are chlorides from a reflecting pool or fountain getting into the museum air? How far from photocopy machines can ozone be detected? Are cooking fumes responsible for specific examples of metal corrosion?

The use of metal coupons is important for assessing the real potential for damage to collections just because it is not specific to any one or number of pollutants. Very minor pollutants may be important in deterioration processes. Figures for sulfur dioxide, the most abundant pollutant in outdoor air, may or may not be representative of the actual potential for damage in an air sample. Tests specifically for formaldehyde in air, for example, may not include amounts of formic acid, and would therefore underestimate the destructive power of the air and the amounts of pollutants in it.

Testing of paints, textiles, or other materials that are being considered for use in storage or exhibition is often done on a similar *ad hoc* basis. It is important to test all materials because of unexpected additives like insecticides in sheet lumber, and because of wide variations among similar products. Samples of the material to be tested are placed in a small container with samples of polished metal, along with damp cotton or another source of moisture that will accelerate the reaction. The container is warmed to further accelerate any reaction. These tests yield results within a few days. So far, there have been no reports that tests like this have produced results inconsistent with the behavior of materials in actual use; such tests are therefore highly recommended.

Outdoor Pollution

The damage to collections from gaseous pollutants in outdoor air is difficult to assess. Other than an increase in the rate of silver tarnishing, it may be difficult to prove real damage, since paper and leather, for example, show acid attack primarily from acids within the objects. Most research on the deterioration of stone and metal has been done on exterior stone and metal which is made worse by the presence of acid rain and by freeze-thaw cycles. The actual amounts of pollution that penetrate to the inside of buildings are very small, and therefore very difficult to study. Measured levels of pollutants indoors show levels in the range of one half to one tenth the outdoor levels, but in some cases, levels higher than those outside have been measured. Because outdoor levels change quickly, the accuracy of these comparative measurements can be called into question.

Amounts of reactive chemicals in the air are reduced inside by either reaction or deposition, particularly on porous materials like woolen carpets, textured fabrics, and matte paints. Without constant replacement by polluted outdoor air, pollution levels are lower inside than out, and lower in cases than in galleries for the same reason. Because light, including ultraviolet, often increases corrosion of metals by pollutants, lower light levels inside may make pollutants less harmful, and lowering of relative humidity has the same effect. The danger from outdoor pollutants is therefore greatly decreased by a proper museum environment. Completely unabsorbent features like glass walls, which are not recommended in museums for other reasons, can actually cause an increase in pollutants from outdoor levels. They do not allow any deposition or absorption of pollutants. The increase of both visible and ultraviolet light multiplies the damage to artifacts and causes chemical changes in pollutants that make them more harmful. Temperature increases caused by sunlight likewise increase the rate of corrosion.

No conservator would say, however, that gaseous pollution from outside is not harmful, particularly when environmental control systems raise the humidity and therefore the reactivity of corrosive materials. Confirmation of a more pessimistic interpretation would seem to be upheld by research on library materials. Several studies using books from the same edition that have been held in libraries in very different environments have shown that the holdings of urban libraries are more acidic than the same books in libraries in relatively unpolluted parts of the country. It is likely that gaseous pollution from outside is a significant contributing factor to deterioration in some materials, but in ways that are difficult to detect. There is no mechanism of deterioration as obvious as the growth of crystals on lead to warn us of damage, and so it is hard for some people to believe that such damage exists. Particularly in buildings with wintertime humidification, this source of deterioration should be taken seriously.

Dust, or Particulate Pollution

Air-borne dust is a more obvious problem for collections because it looks bad and increases the need for housekeeping. Dust creates some less obvious problems too; it is abrasive, holds moisture and gaseous pollution on objects, and attracts insects. It can be very difficult to remove, in some cases entailing major conservation treatments, particularly when it incorporates greasy soot from industrial pollution. Dust is produced both outside and inside, from dirt on people's feet, from cork flooring, lint from carpets, asbestos, chipping plaster and paint, construction (sanding, etc.), silica and other mineral particles from abraded stone or sand, clay, carbon, pollen, mold spores, salts, industrial soot, kitchen grease, cigarette or fireplace smoke, deterioration of objects, hair, insect body parts, frass, etc. Many particles are acidic and therefore, with moisture, act as centers for corrosion and other deterioration.

Static electricity on Plexiglas®, synthetic varnishes, and plastic wrapping materials holds dust and makes its removal difficult, particularly at relative humidities below 40%.

Ducted air handling systems necessitate additional control of pollution-producing activities in a building because of possible spread of dust through ducts. Machine shops, wood-working shops, photo studios and conservation laboratories can produce both dusts and gaseous pollutants that should be kept out of ducts, and should therefore be ducted in separate zones from collections areas. Fumes from nitrate films should also be vented outside of central ductwork. Any areas in the building where smoking is allowed or where cooking takes place (please, not in galleries!) should be isolated.

The use of floormats inside doors, and the use of revolving doors or double doors with a vestibule between will help keep outside dust outside, as will insisting that visitors leave coats, packages, and umbrellas in checkrooms. Cases that are not well-sealed can be fitted with small holes with dust filters so that circulating air will preferentially go through the filtered hole rather than through cracks or gaps in the case. All textiles, baskets, and other hard-to-clean objects should be displayed inside cases or under glass or Plexiglas®.

Filtration

Where centralized environmental control systems are in operation, filtering in the airstream for recirculated as well as make-up air is the way to provide clean air for collections. Gaseous and particulate pollutants require different kinds of filters. Electrostatic air cleaners, either as part of centralized environmental control systems or as local units, are not recommended for use in museums, as they give off ozone and nitrogen oxides. Activated charcoal filters, commonly used for gaseous pollutants, are quite effective, but can become secondary emitters. That means, in common English, that when they have taken up as much pollutant as they can hold, they start to give off the excess. They must be replaced, therefore, *before* this happens, and even in the changing a great deal of pollutants can be accidentally released into the air stream. There does not seem to be a reliable rule of thumb to predict when activated charcoal filters need changing, and since there is no simple way of monitoring pollution levels in buildings, the situation invites disaster. Some engineers recommend water washers, sometimes with alkaline wash water, to clean the air of gases, but these devices are quite complex to run and therefore are inappropriate for most museums where maintenance is a constant problem.

Generally recommended for gaseous filtration in a museum context are filters using potassium permanganate. Potassium permanganate filters consist of a bed of pebbles of activated alumina impregnated with potassium permanganate. These filters, like activated charcoal ones, become "full" sooner or later, but do not become secondary emitters, so at worst they will be inefffective rather than harmful.

Recommended levels of gaseous pollution depend on available technology rather than on actual recommendations for collection safety. As with human toxicity, it is virtually impossible to set a level below which there is no threat to health, although there is a standard, referred to perhaps over-optimistically as "country air" that represents pollutants as they appear naturally. In this standard, sulfur dioxide levels in country air are 50 $\mu g/m^3$. On the other side of the problem, measuring filtration

113

capacity for gases is complicated by the fact that outdoor levels vary quickly as wind directions and weather patterns change, so that both indoor and outdoor levels of each contaminant have to be measured continuously over a period of time to determine filter effectiveness. Some common filtration systems filter out about 60% of sulfur dioxide on each pass, which means that levels in recirculated air are significantly lower than 40% of outside levels. Ozone is effectively dealt with by the same filters that remove sulfur dioxide, but nitrogen oxides may not be.

At present, despite the remaining questions on the efficiency of various media with nitrogen oxides, potassium permanganate is the recommended filtration medium for museums. The design of the system may be the crucial part of the equation, since the contact efficiency, that is, the percentage of pollutant that actually comes in contact with the medium, is obviously as important as the efficiency of the medium.

For particulate filtration, filters usually consist of a series of fibrous mats through which the air is pulled by fans. Coarser filters stop the larger particles, and the smaller particles are removed by finer filters. A series of filters ("balanced" filtration) is needed to prevent the finer filters from getting clogged with large particles. So-called "bag" filters,

which are rolls of filtering material, make filter changing easier. 95% filtration by weight of particles 1 μm. or larger is the recommended level for museums, particularly in urban areas, where finely divided soot is perhaps the most bothersome part of particulate pollution.

Monitoring of pollutant levels in the airstream should be carried out. Rather than laboratory techniques that rely on air sampling, the usual procedure is to place monitors in the ducts. These accumulate gases for a few months, after which they are sent to a laboratory for testing. Although they do not provide the kind of instantaneous monitoring that would show when filters were becoming clogged, they are better than nothing, and will help to avoid the worst mistakes.

Air filtration in ducts slows down the air flow and therefore makes it necessary to install more powerful fans than would be needed otherwise. This, in turn, uses more energy and raises the already steep costs of HVAC systems. For this reason, many museums have installed centralized environmental control systems with relative humidity control but with no filtration. There has been some suggestion that air filtration can make up some of the total cost by allowing less dilution with outside air and thereby lowering heating costs, but data to support this somewhat encouraging suggestion are lacking. The exact nature of the problems encountered by collections in buildings with RH control and no air filtration is as yet undocumented. Unfortunately, because few museums have had complete air filtration systems in operation for substantial periods of time, the practical information available is limited. Experience that would tell us how often filters need to be changed in museum environments or how well recommended systems actually work in practice is lacking.

It is sometimes said that filtration is not needed in rural or suburban settings, but hard data that would substantiate this are also lacking. Some recent research on outdoor pollution levels indicates that polluted urban air masses can move great distances essentially intact. Crop and forest damage from acid rain and ozone have been documented repeatedly. The idea that country air is pollution-free may be no more than nostalgia.

With or without centralized air cleaning, much can be done to prevent pollution damage to collections. First, outside air intakes must be placed in the cleanest location possible, away from congested roads, garages, or the smoke trails of chimneys. Revolving doors work well in keeping out pollution, as well as making any environmental control more efficient. Make-up air levels, the amount of fresh air taken in from outside, can be kept to a minimum. Although some building codes specify minimum levels to avoid what is referred to as the "sick air syndrome" for people, leaks in walls and windows and the opening of doors can account for a great deal of the requirement and 10% make-up air should be sufficient. Polluting activities indoors - cooking, carpentry, painting - can be isolated from gallery spaces. Containerization also helps keep pollution away from objects. Some measurements indicate that any container or limitation on ventilation, like the backing on a painting, will lower pollutant levels by five to eight times.

A poorly monitored and poorly maintained air filtration system may be worse than no air filtration at all. However, air cleaning should be considered a necessary part of any centralized environmental control system, particularly if humidification is part of the package. If the maintenance of filters and the monitoring of pollutant levels are too much for you or your institution to contemplate, take it as a sign that the whole project of ducted air conditioning may be out of your range. Containerize all dust- and pollution-sensitive collections inside cases or boxes made of safe materials, and consider your collections well-protected.

Because the subtle nature of damage from polluted air may be an acceleration of processes already occurring, the lack of data makes it difficult to demonstrate how important air quality control may be for particular collection materials. Information on this important subject will undoubtedly appear in the museum literature in increasing volume over the next few years because of greatly increased interest in pollution inside museums and out. There is, however, no question about the basic issue: the less pollution, the better, for people and for things.

Mold and Pest Control

Actual occurrences of insect or mold damage to collection material are not often publicly discussed by museum professionals, but infestations can cause major disruption in the life of an institution, and can cause significant damage to collections, particularly where a large amount of material is stored away and only infrequently inspected. Damage from insects can proceed to a point where wood pieces are represented by only a crunchy skin of wood, or where feathers have lost all their fuzz. Textiles and paper can be turned to lace. Mold can leave dark stains on paper, textiles, and even ivory.

It has been said a thousand times before, and I repeat: prevention is the best policy. Aside from the damage to objects and buildings, killing insects and mold after the fact has traditionally involved chemical insecticides and fungicides including arsenic, DDT, mercury compounds, strychnine, carbon tetrachloride, cyanide, and a host of other nasty compounds toxic to humans and, in some cases, explosive as well. Most of these chemicals are no longer legal in the United States and are not used in well-regulated museums. Even the small number of compounds still licensed for use in institutions or homes is coming under constantly greater scrutiny as health hazards.

The first thing necessary to understand about pest control, therefore, is the possible human health hazards from pesticides. Common practice and legal restriction in the use of chemicals have changed a great deal, but only recently. This means that many institutions, and probably some exterminators, still have on hand supplies of extremely toxic chemicals they may be tempted to use (and, based on recent surveys, are still using). In addition, many pesticides were intended to have a residual effect. This means that they remain on the object; some, like mercury and arsenic, staying virtually forever. Even if the most dangerous chemicals are not still being applied, we have to deal with objects permeated with them.

Although most fine arts objects are not likely to have been subjected to insecticides, the use of residual fungicides is a possibility on any piece subject to mold growth. Any piece that has traces of mold staining is suspect. Insecticides may have been used on any wooden object that exhibits old insect damage. Woolen textiles may have been treated with residual moth-proofing agents. At least one major conservation laboratory in the midwest used a lining adhesive for paintings that included a poisonous mercury compound as a fungicide. Research on the history of pesticide use and tests of objects in collections have so far revealed widespread patterns of use in natural history and ethnographic collections, but little information on fine arts or decorative arts material has been compiled and many surprises are undoubtedly in store as more collections are tested.

For ethnographic objects or organic natural history specimens, insecticide use is common, if not, as some have claimed, universal. The use of highly toxic materials, like arsenic, is part of taxidermy procedures, although most of the toxins probably remain on the interior surfaces of the skins. Mercuric chloride is still used routinely on herbarium specimens in England.

Spot-testing for the remnants of such chemicals is highly recommended where possible, so that appropriate health precautions can be taken. Although spot tests on objects can be done by people experienced both in doing the tests and interpreting the results, it is easier in many cases to have small samples from suspect objects sent to someone to perform the analysis. A conservator should be hired, either to carry out the tests or to coordinate work with a commercial testing laboratory and then to supervise either cleaning of the objects or the establishment of safe working procedures. Some work has been done in removing insecticides from objects, mainly by removing dust under carefully controlled conditions, and this may become more common in the future.

Short of testing each object, care in handling seems appropriate. Neither food nor smoking belong near collections. Wash hands carefully before and after handling collection material. Do not allow children to play with things that may have been treated. If you are working in dusty storerooms that are repositories for objects treated with toxic chemicals, use at least a particle mask (better a respirator), as powder from deterioration of objects may contaminate the air. Some studies of other toxic dusts have shown health effects in the families of workers, presumably from dusts brought home on workers' clothes, so anyone working with such material should also wear a disposable lab coat. Table tops should be covered with paper that can be replaced every day. If you have been working with pesticides and have health problems that seem inexplicable, consider the possible role of toxic chemicals. Industrial hygeinists are the occupational group trained in this area. Your regular doctor may know little about this field. The Center for Safety in the Arts (See *Sources of Information*) is an excellent group to consult; they have pertinent literature for sale and can answer questions over the telephone. If you are in an institution that will not take your concerns seriously, threaten to call the Occupational Safety and Health Administration (OSHA).

In case these warnings seem extreme, consider this: a recent article quotes a survey of natural history museums in England and Scotland in which 30% of the respondents reported medical ailments related to pesticide use.[13] On the other hand, a study conducted by the Harvard School of Public Health showed no unexpected health problems in pest control operators with long years of work in the field.[14] The contrast betweeen the two studies may point to a difference between educated and uneducated users of pesticides, or between British and American regulations. As with food additives, data on the health implications of small amounts of pesticides are incomplete and difficult to interpret. Only a small minority of licensed pesticides have been thoroughly investigated for their health implications, so do not take any chances. Use as little of any chemical as you can manage. When there is a choice of chemical, use the less toxic alternative. Support all efforts to use non-chemical methods of pest control. Do not follow recommendations in out-of-date literature, particularly recommendations originating in other countries. Avoid liability by

following current federal, state, and local laws. Make sure that all staff authorized to handle objects know of possible hazards.

If you are working in a museum and want to be careful of your health, you may have to upset existing patterns of behavior in the institution. Surveys in 1980 and 1983 of New York State and New York City museums respectively[15,16] indicate continuing use of illegal chemicals with little or no regard for the most elementary safety precautions. Fumigants regulated for use only in a vacuum chamber were reported as being used during working hours in rooms where staff has complete access. Almost half of the museums reporting pesticide use in the latter study reported that the staff's sense of smell was the only detector used to indicate the presence of pesticides - even though methyl bromide, a common fumigant, has little or no smell at toxic concentrations.

Do not forget that pesticides and fungicides have a variety of toxic effects ranging from

---

[13] Child, R. E. "Fumigation in Museums - A Possible Alternative" *Museums Journal* Vol.88, p.191-192 (1989)

[14] Story, Keith O. *Approaches to Pest Management in Museums* Washington, DC, The Smithsonian Institution (1985) p.85-86

[15] Bell, Bruce M. and Stanley, Edith M., "Survey of pest control procedures in museums." In *Pest Control in Museums: a Status Report* (Stephen R. Edwards, Bruce M. Bell, and Mary Elizabeth King, eds.) p. 11-14, Association of Systematics Collections, Lawrence, Kansas (1980)

[16] Peltz, Perri. New York City Museum Survey Results. *Art Hazards News* Vol.6, p.2-3 (1983)

dermatitis, headaches and dizziness to long-term kidney and liver damage. Some are carcinogens and some have been linked to reproductive hazards in both men and women. It is difficult to be a voice crying out in the wilderness when everyone else behaves as if you are crazy for fussing, but an institution is violating its legal, not to mention ethical, responsibilities by not warning all staff of hazardous materials. If you are lucky, others may eventually thank you for speaking out.

The recommended procedure for monitoring health or safety hazards due to pesticides or other toxic chemicals in the workplace is the establishment by the institution's administration of a Health and Safety Committee. This group usually starts with a survey of the building and of possible hazards such as chemicals, power tools, poorly-lit stairways, or the storage of flammable material, and proceeds step-by-step with physical improvements and staff training. The Committee, or in smaller institutions, one person, is also responsible for keeping abreast of current governmental rules and regulations related to health and safety. It has been shown in lawsuits against institutions that the existence of a Health and Safety Committee demonstrates the institution's intent to protect its workers, volunteers, and visitors, and can therefore be some protection against liability actions for negligence. For this reason alone, American museums,

libraries, and other institutions can expect a flurry of activity in the area of health and safety within the next few years.

There are lessons in this besides those of individual health care. One is that it is vital to keep records of pesticide or fungicide use. These should be part of the conservation record accompanying each object, and part of a separate list maintained by either a private owner or a museum staff member. In museums, where maintenance staff tends to have long memories but less paperwork skills, it is particularly important to harvest this information. Interview long-time staff members about their memories of pesticide use. Look in basements and other storage areas for old pesticide containers. Search for purchase orders with information on pesticide purchases.

In all collections, it is worth compiling information about chemical use along with information about past treatments when pieces are acquired. A seller of an object may tell the purchaser that a piece has been fumigated in order to calm the buyer's fears about infestations. If you hear such a vague statement, insist on knowing exactly what was done, when, where, and by whom. It may mean that the seller sprayed the piece with a household-type bug spray two days previously, or that the original maker wiped it with a local oil thought to have insect repellent qualities. Both your health and the safety of the object may be involved, so force yourself to be pushy until you are reasonably assured that you have all the information that can be acquired.

Information on past pesticide use has implications beyond those of human health. The chemical changes wrought by pesticide use may invalidate the results of sophisticated chemical analyses or dating methods. Existing residues may interact with future pesticides.

Treated and untreated pieces may behave differently in their aging patterns or response to conservation treatments. Residual heavy metals (like lead, mercury, or arsenic), for example, may increase light-sensitivity. Compiling a history of pesticide use in a collection and keeping records up to date is therefore important in many phases of collections management.

Common Collection Pests and What They Eat

Elsewhere in this book are descriptions of the kind of changes that occur in old organic objects: drying out, embrittlement, and fading. In the area of insect pests, these changes work to our advantage. The number of insects that are interested in eating old dried out things is substantially fewer than those that eat fresh plant or animal matter. Once these insects get to work, the damage they do is considerable, but the number of different insects we have to learn about is sharply curtailed.

The main categories in temperate climates are carpet beetles and other similar creatures, clothes moths, powderpost beetles, silverfish and cockroaches, and book lice. Although the word "termite" seems to be used by some as a sort of generic term for wood-eaters, actual termites are rare in collections in non-tropical climates.

Carpet Beetles and their Relatives. These include creatures belonging to the family *Dermestidae* called odd beetles, larder beetles, cabinet beetles, and furniture carpet beetles. Members of the *Anobiidae* family, the cigarette and drugstore beetles, have similar habits. Cigarette beetles are also known as herbarium beetles because of their love for dried plant specimens. All carpet beetles are variously colored small insects which specialize in eating proteins like wool, hair, skins, horn, feathers, dead insects, stored drugs, and spices. The larvae do the damage, and the cast-off larval skins found inside drawers or boxes, under rugs, in heating registers, or in cracks and crevices are the most commonly noted signs of infestation. Adults have different food preferences from larvae; many enjoy the pollen and nectar of fresh flowers, and can be found in abandoned nests and hives. Their life cycles and preferred habitats vary somewhat, although many come inside to lay their eggs in dark dusty places. Certain specific types, including the hide beetles that some museums use in captive colonies to clean small skeletons, can do a great deal of damage very quickly, so identification of beetles is important.

Clothes Moths. Although most of us are aware of these insects feeding on woolen sweaters, they also eat other protein like feathers and fur. Like the carpet beetles, it is the larva that does the damage. Moths are usually detected from the holes they leave, from the silky cocoon- or web-like silky fibers they leave behind, or from the presence of the adult moths or caterpillars.

Powderpost and Furniture Beetles. These represent several families of wood-eaters in North America. The insects themselves are rarely seen. Their presence is detected from small round holes in wood surfaces and fine powder ("frass") that pours out of the holes. The adults lay eggs in the wood, and the larvae eat channels in the wood parallel to the grain, but avoiding the surface (See Fig. 8, next page). New adults eat holes in the surface of the wood, fly away, and burrow into another object to lay their eggs, or go back into the same hole. Most become inactive at wood moisture content levels below about 10% (that is, below about 55% RH), and long periods at low RH levels make some unable

to reproduce, thereby making infestation in institutions without wintertime humidification self-limiting. However, eggs can lie dormant for long periods, and the hatched larvae can still eat a great deal.

Silverfish and Cockroaches. Well known to any city dweller, these insects are mainly damaging in the messes they leave, although they do eat starches, sometimes leaving trails on the surface of paper or paperboards with starchy finishes. They also eat the microscopic mold that grows on damp plaster and drywall and feed on broken-down cellulose. Silverfish seem endemic around new construction and are probably interested in new wallboards, although they may also be brought in with cardboard cartons. Large numbers of either of these insects are usually indicative of poor environmental conditions, like dampness and overheating or poor housekeeping practices.

Book Lice. These insects do little real damage to books, but are indicators of poor environmental conditions, since they love the damp. They often appear when a leak or drip has left books or paper wet, or when plaster is damp. They cannot fly, but are carried into buildings and spread when materials they infest are moved, or are moved by air currents.

Although all creatures have their favorite foods, they will eat

Fig. 8 Insect damage on a painted wooden mask from Bali. The nose had been eaten quite hollow. Handling had caused collapse of the thin shell of wood that remained. From the collection of Mr. and Mrs. Jonathan Warner.

other things, particularly to get to their favorites. Some insects will eat through plastic bags adjacent to something more delicious. It is important to remember that if many similar things are kept together, an infestation can do a great deal more damage than if types of materials are mixed. For example, a storeroom full of horsehair-stuffed furniture can breed a huge colony of carpet beetles. Metal storage cabinets filled with a collection of insects or snakeskins can also harbor major infestations because of the amount of similar material so close together. Segregating collections by material is usually the best policy for other reasons, so it is particularly important to be aware of the hazards and provide for periodic inspections of susceptible storerooms or exhibition cases.

Preventing Insect Damage: Stopping Entry

How do harmful insects get to collections in the first place? Entry routes are numerous. Many pests arrive in newly acquired objects, particularly those from tropical climates. Careful inspection and isolation of suspected pieces can prevent a great deal of trouble. For museums, insects can come from objects brought into the building for sale in a gallery shop, inspection by a staff member, decoration of an office, or loan exhibitions. Insects can come from food brought into a restaurant or catering facility. Food used as part of a period room exhibit or as party refreshments can attract insects. They can come in on fireplace logs, in plants or cut flowers, or in building supplies or packing crates. Bird or insect nestsunder eaves or on sills or in the chimneys of unused fireplaces can harbor bugs. Spider webs, with their remnants of insect bodies, can attract other bugs. Dried grasses, dried flowers, and nests used as part of habitat exhibitions are other sources.

Period room settings often have several of the above hazards including fireplace logs, flowers or plants, even food. Rooms with upholstered furniture, fabric bed coverings, heavy draperies and mattresses have many dark and dust-laden spaces that provide happy homes for several different kinds of insects and for mice. If possible, fireplace logs should be fumigated before being brought into a museum building. Artificial flowers and plants should be used, and plastic or plaster foods should replace the real thing. Frequent inspection of dark, dusty corners is vital.

Many museum pests are happiest in the dark, and thrive in moist places like ductwork with pools of stagnant water. They are happy under furniture, in dark dusty corners of storerooms, in crawl-spaces over dropped ceilings, and in voids between walls. In addition, bugs like to eat other bugs, so any dead bugs, whether part of a collection or simply debris, will attract others.

The exclusion of light from areas where collection material is kept is, in the case of pest control, an unfortunate policy. Problems stemming from this must simply be countered by frequent inspection. The use of sticky traps or boards (devices that catch insects and vermin with an extremely sticky material) in exhibition or storage cases can make inspections easier, as the traps can be expected to collect a representative sample of insects in the vicinity. It is easier to inspect the traps than to inspect each object.

Even in brightly lit galleries there are plenty of dark spaces, between objects and walls, under objects, under pedestals; these must be inspected. The undersides of furniture should be inspected carefully, as raw rough wood surfaces are much more attractive to wood-borers than smooth varnished surfaces.

Dust is full of all kinds of nutritious proteins, so good housekeeping is essential. Dust, dirt, and stains on objects can make them more attractive to pests; caterpillars, for example, will not eat much clean wool. Dampness makes some pests happy, so unnoticed leaks can also produce unnoticed infestations in areas of rotting wood or plaster.

Good housekeeping for pest control includes more than inspection of collections and vacuuming (not sweeping!) of all interior spaces including attics and basements. All gutters, downspouts, eaves, and sills should be periodically cleaned out and all debris removed. All windows should be tightly screened, and all other entry points into the building, including doors, air intakes, air conditioners, and openings for utilities should be sealed as well as possible, periodically inspected, and cleaned as necessary. All food service facilities and their garbage should be carefully supervised; food should not be allowed in other parts of the building. Any unwelcome sources of water should be found, stopped immediately, and dried out as quickly as possible; this includes leaky roofs and pipes, condensation on the outside of ducts or inside walls, water infiltration through basement walls, and standing water inside ducts. Exterior drainage may have to be improved so that downspouts from gutters do not deposit water right next to the base of the building. Many experts also recommend that shrubbery or flowers not be planted close to any museum entrances, and organic mulches like those made from bark chips not be used near doorways. Exterior lighting near doors should be of the sodium vapor lamp variety, or at a distance from the doors to avoid attracting insects inside the doors.

Integrated pest management (IPM) is a relatively new term in museums for an approach to pest control that emphasizes preventive methods, and the use of chemicals as a last resort only. In institutions, this generally means naming one staff member as a coordinator who supervises inspections, keeps records, and acts as a liaison with outside experts. This person is also responsible for expressing concerns about pest control when policy related to other collections management issues is formulated, for example, in the planning of building renovations or special exhibitions. In addition, the IPM coordinator is charged with keeping abreast of the literature on health hazards and legal restrictions related to pesticides.

The idea of approaching pest control with the use of chemicals only as a last resort is very helpful in preventing infestations. In the past, those with the greatest professional experience with pest problems were exterminators, who made a living by applying chemicals, and who learned much of what they knew from the pesticide manufactures, who in turn have an obvious interest in seeing that as much as possible of their chemicals is used. Putting the emphasis on the other side of the process, that is, in doing everything possible to keep pests out with only minimal use of chemicals, should prevent a great deal of damage to collections, to personnel, and to the world around us.

Preventing Insect Damage: Case Fumigation

The use of pesticides in low concentrations inside cases or cupboards or other containers to prevent infestation is often referred to as using repellents, even though the chemicals commonly used for this purpose are technically fumigants. The most common one is paradichlorobenzene, otherwise known as PDB, para, or moth balls. PDB is a crystalline solid that vaporizes at room temperature, giving off a characteristic smell. Because the fumes are heavier than air, PDB should be kept at the top of a container, hung in a fabric bag at the top of a wardrobe or laid wrapped in paper or cloth on top of pieces in a trunk, for example. The solids should never touch objects. Once the smell is apparent, no more chemical is needed.

The use of too much PDB in a too-small space may cause the condensation of crystals onto objects. The fumes have a solvent effect on certain materials, primarily plastics or resins. The tarry coating on waterproof paper softens quickly, although most materials that are sensitive to PDB only become slightly sticky. PDB may contribute to the fading of feathers, the deterioration of leather, and to the corrosion of bronze.

Because PDB is such a familiar material, it is difficult for some people to take seriously as a health hazard. However, people who work with it can become sensitized, reacting quickly to any object treated with it, suffering from rashes, nausea, headaches and other symptoms. PDB should be used only in closed cases or boxes, and handled only with gloves. No one should work for long periods where there is any smell in the room. Some sources recommend handling PDB only when wearing a respirator, and certainly this is sensible for those who frequently handle large amounts, but it is difficult to convince the many people who grew up with the smell of PDB in their nostrils that this kind of precaution is advisable. PDB is considered very effective in preventing insect damage, but the changes it can cause in some materials and the lingering nature of the smell can be distinct disadvantages.

Naphthalene is another chemical used for moth flakes. It is a repellent rather than a fumigant, and its effectiveness has been questioned, so its use has generally been discontinued in favor of PDB.

DDVP (short for dimethyl-dichlorovinylphosphate) is another common fumigant used as repellent, sometimes referred to as Vapona or dichlorvos. It is the chemical used in no-pest strips. This is a highly toxic substance, being reviewed by the federal government because of suspected health problems. At the concentrations which result from use of the strips as directed (one strip per 1000 cubic feet), the likelihood of health problems is lessened, and no review is underway for this particular use. However, appropriate precautions including handling the strips only with gloves, and not using in a very small space, should be followed scrupulously. The strips should not come in contact with objects. Fumes may be corrosive to metals at high relative humidities, and some softening of resins has been observed, so use should be restricted to organic materials, and to well-sealed cases or storage containers.

The Shell Oil Company was the major manufacturer of the strips, which are a plastic (polyvinyl chloride) impregnated with liquid DDVP. They no longer make them. Another company took over the manufacture of this product, but at present (late 1989) no longer makes them. Although the manufacture and use of these strips is not prohibited by federal regulations, companies may be unwilling to take the risk of possible liability. The future availability of the product is in doubt.

Repellents are very popular, for obvious reasons. The objects receive a relatively small dose, while the insects are kept away. However, as a sensitive nose will attest, there can be considerable amounts of chemicals left on the objects, which may affect both the object and its human handlers. Do not use more PDB or DDVP than is absolutely necessary. Neither is harmless.

Identifying Insects and their Damage

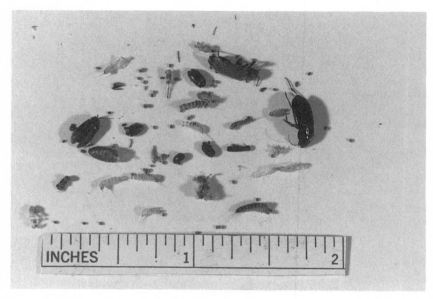

Fig. 9 A collection of assorted collection pests. Note the small size of most of these remains; careful observation may be necessary to spot one on a shelf. The small melon-shaped crumbs are frass. The shrimp-shaped items are cast-off larvae cases from various beetles. Anything of this sort found near collection material warrants immediate investigation. From the author's collection.

The only way to stop insect damage is to find it before it goes too far. This means periodic inspection. Schedules should be set up for this, more often in the spring and summer than the winter, because insects tend to be more active in warm weather. Storerooms and exhibition cases should be arranged if possible with surfaces covered in a smooth white material that will show insect debris. The materials to be looked for include frass, the coarse powder made up of insect excrement and food remains and often referred to incorrectly as sawdust. Any dead body, bit of fluff, crumb, or chip (See Fig. 9) should be collected in a small jar or plastic bag, labelled, and examined carefully. Insect bodies can be preserved in a jar of alcohol or placed in a dry jar for identification as an alternative to squashing. Any little bit that may have fallen off an object, if not a sign of infestation, could be the sign of some other kind of deterioration that should be reported and investigated. A study collection of insects found and identified or photographs of them will help staff learn more about the subject and will keep to a minimum the need for outside consultation.

Any museum staff member or household employee who works near collections should be specifically alerted to the importance of reporting unusual dust or debris under objects. Diligent cleaning personnel who daily or weekly wipe crumbs off shelves or wall moldings without further notice are giving the little creatures extra time to feed undisturbed.

Sticky traps are often used to aid in the detection of insects. Although not foolproof, they help to provide an inventory of species present. In spite of the small number of creatures who actually eat works of art, the insect population of a building may consist of many different species, some of whom live off the dead bodies or partially digested meals of others. If one species, uninterested in eating collection material, finds a good home in the damp insulation of ducts, another more art-loving species may be attracted to the bodies of the first, and then, on to the collections. It is therefore important to follow through on any infestation in a building.

For wooden objects, the flight holes of powderpost beetles (small round holes in the wood surface)

are a sure sign of infestation, although it may be an old one. If the wood that shows inside the flight holes is light-colored and fresh, an active infestation is more likely. If active infestation is suspected, the piece should be bagged in plastic and the bag sealed with tape. It should then be left without being moved for one to two weeks. If there are live insects, more frass will be ejected from the holes; if not, no frass should come out unless the piece is moved. Even if no activity is evident, the piece should be watched carefully, particularly in the spring when eggs may be hatching and new larvae may be present. Inactivity of wood-borers in low relative humidities may make it necessary to extend such tests into damper or warmer weather.

Any object suspected of harboring insects should be isolated in a room with separate ventilation from the rest of the building, so that insects cannot travel to other rooms through ducts.

A good first source for insect identification should be *A Guide to Museum Pest Control* (See *Further Reading*). Another source is a local exterminator, the Cornell University Cooperative Extension (See *Sources of Information*), or the entomology department of a local natural history museum or university. Louis Sorkin, Entomologist at the American Museum of Natural History, is willing to identify samples sent to him there. Send both insect bodies or parts of bodies and any frass available, and information on where the body was found.

The first question after initial identification is whether the creature is one that eats art or whether it simply came inside to get away from the cold. If it is identified as a collection eater, information should be sought on the length of the life cycle, how far the insect travels between generations, what it eats, and what conditions of temperature and relative humidity it prefers, as well as what kills it. This will help to direct the search for further infested pieces. A thorough examination to reveal the complete extent of the infestation is vital. Infested objects should be isolated in plastic or in a separate room until treatment can be carried out.

Institutions with food services usually are required by local laws to have periodic visits from an exterminator. This firm may be a useful source for information if their cooperation is cultivated carefully. Exterminators are licensed by their states as "Certified applicators", but the knowledge or experience required varies widely from one state to the next. Most exterminators will not be familiar with the problems peculiar to collections, but some will be interested in learning more, and others will simply offer the remedies they use habitually. The people who actually come to your building to spray may not know as much as others in the firm; calls for advice or information should start at the top. As with all outside experts, you must judge by personal experience whom to trust with the welfare of your collection. Ask if the firm is a member of the National Pest Control Association and other professional organizations. Find out if they regularly supervise non-chemical monitoring and control methods or just send in workers with cannister sprayers. If possible, find an exterminator interested in collection problems by referral from another museum in your area.

Killing Bugs

Once an infestation is discovered, what can be done to kill the culprits? Identification of the species is important, because information on the life cycle will make it possible to assure that the infestation is stopped permanently. The eggs of most insect species are built to survive highly unfavorable environmental conditions. Eggs have an extremely slow metabolism, so that their intake of air, poisoned or not, is incredibly slow. Eggs can survive through temperatures that would kill all larvae or adults. The difficulty when attempting to halt an infestation is therefore in killing the eggs. Killing everything else will simply provide a false sense of security; after a certain amount of time, the eggs will hatch and restart the infestation. Wood-eaters lay some of their eggs deep within a piece of wood; the difficulty in reaching them with a chemical adds to the problems of stopping infestations.

The traditional method of killing insects that infest an object is fumigation in a vacuum chamber using a gaseous fumigant. The extraction of air assures that the fumigant penetrates the object. Because the fumigant is a gas, it is supposed to have no residual effect, therefore protecting both the object and personnel against toxic effects after the process is complete, although not protecting the object against further infestation. Fumigants are extremely toxic materials which must be used in vacuum chambers designed specifically for this purpose.

Unfortunately, fumigation in a vacuum chamber has turned out to be not quite the panacea hoped for. There are several problems. First, in order to kill everything, the proper concentration of fumigant in the whole chamber must be maintained at the proper temperature and relative humidity and the proper level of vacuum for the required number of hours. Fumigation then becomes a highly technical process. Even then, it is possible that viable eggs remain. Some sources recommend a second fumigation after twenty to thirty days at room temperature when remaining eggs will have hatched,

but before any surviving adults will have laid more eggs. In my experience, the practice of a second fumigation is rare, and re-infestation may therefore remain a danger.

The design of chambers has been reported as a problem. Particular difficulties cited are improper sealing of the doors, permeability of walls, and improper placement of ducts leading into and out of the chamber. Reports have circulated of intakes for fresh air located downwind of the vents leading toxic fumes out of the chamber, thus recirculating the same fumes. Some uncertainties involve the permeability of concrete walls to fumigant vapors. Proper design and installation of a chamber, with whatever redesign and alteration may be necessary, is an expensive and technically demanding process. Proper safety precautions including the monitoring of fumes both inside and outside the chamber, locks and warning lights, and alarms in case of malfunction add to the cost. In-house fumigation will take up a great deal of staff time and space. For these reasons, vacuum fumigation off-site, and only when absolutely necessary, is recommended over in-house treatment.

Other problems with chamber fumigation include possible immediate risk to the object. In one study, the evacuation of air in a vacuum chamber caused a 40% drop in relative humidity within a few minutes.[17] This could be disastrous for many organic objects.

Another problem is the dispersal of fumes. Many concerns have been expressed with regard to avoiding direct contact of people with the vented gas before it is diluted. Given the condition of our surroundings, full of toxic junk from every conceivable source, it is unlikely that society will continue to allow toxic gases to be dumped into the air. Vacuum fumigation chambers are not allowed in New York City because of population density, but the only solution to this has been to site chambers in northern New Jersey. We can only hope that alleged solutions like this will not be allowed to continue much longer. Sooner or later ways will have to be found to neutralize all fumigants chemically before they leave the chamber.

Fumigant gases are theoretically evacuated completely from objects after a suitable period (usually up to a week) of flushing a chamber with fresh air. Unfortunately this has not turned out to be the case. Ethylene oxide, a commonly recommended gas, becomes chemically bound to many materials, dissolving in the fatty or oily components of proteinaceous materials like leather. Not only

does this change the chemistry of the protein, making the results of future technical analyses questionable, but it implies long-term changes in the condition of the object. Ethylene oxide changes the properties of paper, and can make Carbon-14 dating impossible. Residual ethylene oxide is emitted over long periods of time, creating a toxic environment for personnel. Chemical reactions of the fumigant with any chlorine in the object produce a very toxic chemical, ethylene chlorohydrin, which remains in the object for even longer periods, and can be absorbed through the skin of anyone handling the object. The most recent federal regulations (1984) require no more than one part per million of ethylene oxide before an object can be removed from the fumigation chamber. With current technology, this level may be impossible to reach; the object itself may continue to give off more than that for several months. Because of the carcinogenic effects of residual ethylene oxide and its byproducts, ethylene oxide has been virtually removed from use as a fumigant in the last few years, at least by those who are paying attention to current standards.

Unfortunately, articles recommending the use of ethylene oxide in plastic bags cannot be expunged from the literature. This method is probably still being used. If you are working in an institution that uses ethylene oxide in this way, or even in a vacuum chamber, speak up!

---

[17] Arai, and Toishi, Kenzo. "Humidity Control in the Reduced-pressure Fumigation Apparatus for Artistic and Archaeological Objects" *Science for Conservation* Vol.11, p.15-20 (1973) Summarized and translated in *Art and Archaeology Technical Abstracts* Vol.10, p. 12 (1973)

Methyl bromide is the fumigant most commonly used to replace ethylene oxide. Much less problem with residual effect has been noted, although because of its chemical structure, methyl bromide can be expected to leave a nasty smell on objects with sulfur, like wool, leather and rubber. Several conservators have reported no offensive smell after using methyl bromide with sulfur-containing materials, or a two-week period of some smells which then disappear; the reaction is probably related to high relative humidities. Just because there is no smell does not necessarily mean that no reaction is taking place; the potential for chemical changes in proteins, particularly leather and feathers, remain. Some weakening of paper may result from methyl bromide. Problems have also been reported with corrosion of metals.

Sulfuryl fluoride (Vikane®, Dow Chemical) is another fumigant that appears to be suitable for use on collection material. Vikane® is not a good killer of eggs; when used for infested objects, two fumigation cycles are necessary. Most industrial experience with this chemical is in the fumigation of whole buildings. The museum field has relatively little experience with Vikane® in a vacuum chamber. It is known as a fast disperser, so no problems with residual gas on objects should be anticipated. Tests to date with Vikane® reveal increases in the acidity of paper so small that only the most stringent tests show them.

The changes may be due to chloride impurities in the fumigant.

It is unlikely that a search for a better fumigant will result in the adoption of a chemical of proven toxicity against pests combined with low risk to human beings and no measurable changes in objects. It is, after all, the reactivity of the chemical with proteins in the insects that produces toxic effects, and the same chemicals can be expected to react with proteins in objects and in people.

For infested textiles and other objects like baskets, where penetration is not a problem, many conservators recommend fumigation with PDB or DDVP in a well-sealed box, perhaps a metal-lined lockable wooden box with a tightly fitting gasketed cover. Some institutions with experience in this area use such homemade chambers for infested wood as well. When done correctly, this kind of homemade solution to insect problems is appropriate, but undertaking such a construction is more complex and time-consuming than it may seem. Fumigation of wood may take at least a month in the chamber. Disposal of the fumes and protection of personnel when the box is opened must be carefully planned. Do not undertake a project like this if you are not willing to do all the necessary research and take all necessary precautions for the safety of the object and personnel as well.

Some anecdotal evidence indicates that the time periods needed for a complete kill in this kind of fumigation may allow an unacceptable amount of material to be destroyed even as the fumigation proceeds. For very active infestations, quick treatment in a vacuum chamber may save the object.

Clothes moths and beetles in textiles can be eliminated by dry cleaning or washing. These are potentially damaging conservation treatments that should be undertaken only by a professional. Such treatments may be impossible for extremely deteriorated textiles.

For reasons that should be obvious by now, any chemical with a residual effect, no matter how desirable the effect might seem, is simply not recommended except in the most extreme conditions. Residual moth-proofing agents and common disinfecting agents like thymol and pentachlorophenol, even in small amounts, may have slow-working damaging effects over long periods of time, and are, therefore, not allowed to be used on exposed wood in living quarters. The presence of chlorine, a chemical characterized as a common harmful pollutant, is often a clue pointing to possible problems of deterioration, and chlorine is present in many pesticides. (paradi*chloro*benzene, di*chloro*diphenyl. . ., etc.)

There remain serious questions on the long-term effect of all pesticides on objects. Some testing has been done, and it is possible to identify particular pigments, for example, that react with certain pesticides. However, since almost never would a piece needing fumigation have had extensive analysis, it would be impossible to assure that the piece was safe. Many pieces have, in addition to their original materials, repair materials like synthetic varnishes or adhesives which may be sensitive to the action of fumigants that would otherwise be safe for the object.

Obvious and immediate effects, like color change of dyes or pigments, may not be the only or most significant alterations to an object. To use the analogy of human health, long-term health effects are difficult enough to predict over a life span of eighty years. With objects that we are trying to keep forever, even a small change in the rate of deterioration could, over 500 years, have major consequences.

Some problems have been noted with the reaction of one pesticide with the remnants of another. Given the lack of record-keeping in many collections, this could be an additional problem.

Tests done with pure pesticides may not produce data relevant to real fumigation, since it may be impurities in commercial insecticide formulations rather than the pesticide itself that are the source of the problem. In order to make better predictions in the future, better records should be kept on the use of pesticides. For chamber fumigation, records should include temperature and relative humidity in the chamber as well as the manufacturer of the pesticide, time of fumigation, concentration of fumigant, and results. ICOM (The International Council on Museums) Committee on Conservation, Working Group on Biodeterioration has recently begun a registry to pool museums' experience in dealing with infestation, and this will be a great help. However, in order to pool information, we will need to have documented such experiences precisely.

Other methods of applying pesticides to kill insects in a building rather than individual objects are often recommended, but may not be suitable for museums. Chemical "bombs", for example, have been used in storerooms. These will, however, only kill insects they contact directly, and the solvents that carry the pesticide can stain objects they land on. In order for the fine sprays to have any effect, all containers need to be open during the activity time of the bomb. In my experience, this method of application has been used carelessly, with personnel setting off the bomb while holding their breath, and running out of the room, performing this feat on a Friday night so that staff will not be exposed to the fumes over the weekend. Bombs have very specific uses, but must be used with appropriate precautions.

Solvent-based sprays such as those used in homes generally have oily carriers that can stain textiles or paper, and lack sufficient penetration to produce the desired result. Chemical dusts made up largely of finely powdered silica gel are sometimes recommended as safe insecticides. The powder abrades the waxy coatings of insect bodies and kills by dehydration. Some doubts have been expressed about the possible effects of the desiccant on objects. Various powder and liquid pesticides are suitable for application to baseboards, crevices in walls, and small spaces under storage furniture, for example, but must be chosen and applied by professionals. More work needs to be done on the effects of different delivery systems on both pests and collections, but any application of pesticides without proper supervision can be both dangerous for personnel and possibly ineffective in its outcome.

Anyone responsible for overseeing a pest control program must assess the attitudes and practices of staff in either a museum or household before allowing any use of toxic chemicals. If you think some staff members will only obey safety precautions when a supervisor is watching, do not let them deal with pesticides. Do not deal with any infestation without expert advice: someone who knows about the insects, the chemicals, the safety of the objects, and the safety of personnel. If you can find one person to address all these concerns, fine. If not, call as many people as necessary. On top of your responsibility to your collections and to staff, legal liabilities are involved.

For all these reasons, the current trend is to look for non-chemical methods of killing insects, and although these have clear advantages, the long-term effects on objects and the certainty of a complete kill have not been adequately researched for a wide range of objects. Experts in pest control are actively investigating new methods, including sex lures, pheromones, and glue traps. It is widely hoped that new developments in this area will make the use of toxic chemicals less and less necessary.

To discourage cockroaches, silverfish, and book lice as well as carpet beetles, alteration of the environment is a more effective long-term strategy than any chemical treatment. When objects are infested, fumigation may be necessary, but a change in the conditions that provoked the infestation remains just as important after fumigation takes place, since fumigation leaves objects with no residual protection. Temperatures around 50° F. will halt feeding, even though they will not kill. If there is any possibility of cold storage, objects suspected of being infested can be kept there until other methods have been investigated and a decision has been made. Roach control systems like Combat® made by American

Cyanamid Company are extremely effective for cockroaches.

One promising non-chemical technology is the use of microwaves (ionizing radiation). The heat generated inside objects can kill, although this type of radiation cannot be used with objects with any metal components. Composite objects like books can be damaged because of steam generated inside objects that have been kept at a high moisture content. For textiles or paper, the attraction of this technique is its speed and the ease of use of a microwave oven.

Freezing temperatures will kill most insect pests. This generally requires two applications, with a proper warming time between to give the viable eggs time to hatch. The time required for a complete kill depends on the speed with which temperature can be lowered. Additional complications to this technique are the need to mitigate drastic RH changes during treatment and to avoid condensation when cold objects are brought back into warm surroundings.

Other promising non-chemical treatments include the use of heat produced by infrared, or simply by normal heating plants or ovens. A few hours at 130° F can kill most pests. Again, problems with changing RH levels may appear in sensitive objects.

The use of a chamber that can withdraw oxygen and replace it with carbon dioxide is a promising technique where equipment is available. Another technique that holds promise, but requires equipment not readily available, is gamma radiation. Gamma radiation has the advantage of penetrating materials so well that objects can be treated without being removed from their containers, thus sparing the dangers of handling.

Under proper conditions, with the appropriate objects and appropriate insect victims, non-chemical insecticidal measures can have very satisfactory results, but few have been widely used or tested on a variety of objects. Do not attempt any insecticidal procedure without consultation with one or more conservators or other experts familiar with its use.

Flies

In most surroundings, flies are simply a nuisance, but fly specks (excrement) are highly acidic and produce permanent damage on collection material. For some reason, eighteenth-century American paintings often show terrible disfigurement from fly specks, which erode small pits in the paint surface and leave circles of brown discoloration. Paper also suffers from fly specks (See Figs. 10 and 11 on pages 122-123.) Even if sophisticated environmental control systems are out of reach for many collections, window screens should not be!

Mice

Mice are established inhabitants of many old buildings. A common treatment for mice is grain impregnated or mixed with poison. This should not be used in museums. The grain stays attractive to insects, who are not killed by the same poison that kills mammals, and the little dishes of grain that many exterminators put down have a habit of spilling, leaving the grain under shelves and in deserted corners. Meanwhile, if mice eat it, they retreat into unreachable parts of the building to die, leaving a carcass that is food for carpet beetles. Good hygiene, sealing openings into the building, and the use of sticky traps, multiple-catch traps, or snap traps should help deal with mice. Do not forget to keep a record of where all traps are placed, and check them frequently.

Mold

Mold is a kind of fungus whose spores are ever-present in air-borne dust. In any environment hospitable to the particular kind of mold, the spores will settle and germinate into tiny plants with recognizable parts analagous to stems, flowers, and roots. Under slight magnification, the "stems" with small round "flowers" on the end can be seen easily. The "roots", thread-like filaments, stretch between one plant and the next, creating a small colony (See Fig. 12). When the colony starts, it is often quite perfectly round and appears fuzzy when viewed with the unaided eye.

Many other phenomena are often mistaken for mold. These include: off-setting of a design on the inside of glass in a frame; efflorescence of soluble salts; lactate crystals on leather book covers from an excess of potassium lactate used in treatment; DDT or PDB crystallized on the surface of treated objects by over-heating; altered residues of oil on West African wooden objects (See Fig. 13); paint splatters; and natural efflorescence on red-bud twigs used in California baskets.

Examination with magnification will help in identification. Because alcohol kills mold, a small drop of isopropanol (rubbing alcohol) or ethanol (denatured alcohol) applied to a suspect spot will help to distinguish it from other spots; if it is mold, it should disappear and not come back. Careful testing is required to assure that alcohol will not affect the object adversely.

Mold most commonly appears where there is poor air circulation combined with high humidities and temperatures. The figures commonly given for mold growth are over 70° F. and over 70% RH. These figures are relevant for paper and books; many types of mold will grow at significantly lower temperatures and relative humidities if the medium is nutritious enough, as you know if you leave leftovers too long in your refrigerator. Once spores germinate, a mold colony will continue to grow at RH levels lower than those required for germination, and colonies have been see growing over long periods at below 60%.

Mold is most often seen on books and paper, on glue- or

Fig. 10. The effects of fly specks on paper. This photograph shows the front of a drawing badly stained by fly specks. The verso of this drawing can be seen on the next page.

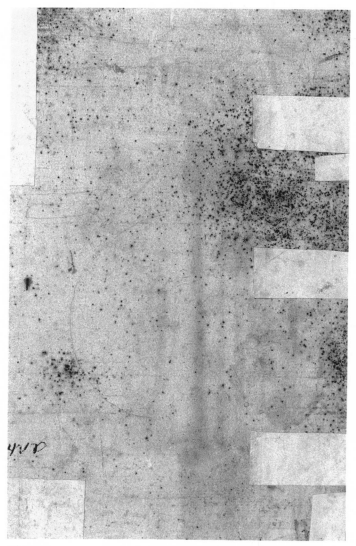

Fig. 11. The effects of fly specks on paper. This photograph shows the verso of the drawing from Fig. 10. Note that the acids from the fly specks on the verso have penetrated the paper and stained the front. Photographs courtesy Paul Himmelstein Collection.

Fig. 12 Mold growing on a sheet of glass. Mold has grown around body parts of insects that infested a hair wreath framed behind the glass.

gum-rich paints like those in miniatures and pastels, and on dirty objects like baskets and gourds. In bad enough conditions, mold can be seen growing on small amounts of dirt present on glass or Plexiglas®. Mold contributes to the breakdown of the material it grows on, and leaves stains of various colors on paper, textiles, and ivory.

The least dangerous treatment for mold is the use of alcohol or the ultraviolet in sunlight. When these cannot be used, moldy objects are often fumigated in home-made chambers using thymol. Thymol is a fairly toxic crystalline material that is vaporized, usually with a small light bulb, in a chamber holding the object. Proper precautions are often not used with thymol chambers, and the chambers are simply opened to room air to vent the gases at the end of treatment. This practice should be discontinued. PDB fumes also kill mold; PDB is probably safer and easier for most institutions to handle than thymol.

In general, the practice of fumigation with toxic fungicides is probably overdone; such treatments should not be necessary very often. The idea

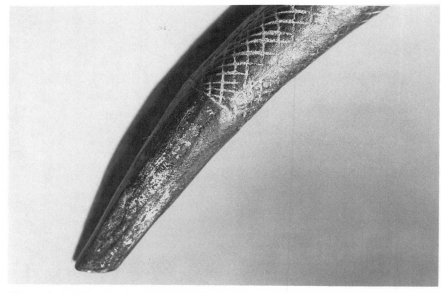

Fig. 13 Oily residue on the horn of a Bambara Tyiwara. White crystalline materials like this are often mistaken for mold. Courtesy Drs. Lois and Georges de Menil Collection.

that an object is sterilized by such treatment is ludicrous, since mold spores are everywhere. Frequent inspections will catch outbreaks in their early stages, when only a few pieces are affected. Treatment of individual objects by brushing the mold off and killing the colonies with local application of alcohol will stop the growth. Changing the environmental conditions that favored the germination of the mold will radically reduce the possibility of future outbreaks. Improved air circulation may be the only change that is required to encourage evaporation and to discourage spores from settling on objects.

There may be a traceable source for a heavy infestation of mold; this possibility should be investigated if the cause of the outbreak is otherwise not apparent. Heat-exchange coils in air conditioning equipment have been cited as the source for some infestations. Stagnant water in ducts may also spread an unusual volume of spores into rooms. The dead leaves of plants may get sucked into air vents, providing a good home for mold, and soggy spots on carpets under planters can also harbor mold growth.

For serious infestations, more serious measures may need to be taken, particularly since high levels of some species of mold are associated with human health problems. Vacuuming the mold off objects with a wet/dry vacuum cleaner with 10% sodium hypochlorite (liquid bleach) in the tank is sometimes recommended to prevent spread of the mold. If rags wet with alcohol are used to rub down affected objects, these should be washed with bleach to kill spores present.

The use of residual fungicides is not recommended, since these represent potential danger to staff in handling objects, the possibility of incompatability with other pesticides, the possibility of bad effects on objects and on conservation materials used on them, and possible odor retention. Except perhaps in tropical climates, residual fungicides should be unnecessary.

Preventing Physical Damage

The safe handling of fragile objects is best learned from watching someone else, because handling collection objects can be an entirely different matter from handling their real-life counterparts; it is an attitude as much as a technique. If an object looks like a teapot, for example, it may be a teapot but it may not behave like a teapot. Picking it up by the handle is an act you may regret.

One of the main problems here is psychological. As we have said before, old things, even if their appearance is unchanged, can have very different physical properties from when they were new. They are usually not only weaker, but more brittle. Mechanical damage from handling is often due to the unexpected embrittlement of materials; textiles, paper, leather, baskets, even oil paintings on canvas and some metals, can lose their ability to bend or flex without harm. Either temporary or permanent embrittlement can cause damage, because the piece cannot be handled in familiar ways. In a museum setting, the differences in handling, once learned, are easier to keep in mind, because the setting is a constant reminder that the objects are special in some way. In our homes,

this can be harder to remember, and guests who wish to touch and feel may be quite annoyed by our insistence on what may seem like ridiculous precaution.

It is difficult to give specific rules for handling all the different shapes and sizes of objects that one is apt to come across, other than to say that it is always best to handle every object as if it were fragile, whether it is or not. It is easy to say what not to do. Do not pick up anything until you know you have a place to put it down. Do not pick up an object by the handles or by other projections. Do not put your thumb over the rim of a piece to pick it up. Do not grab paintings in your fist with fingers curled behind the stretcher bars. Do not slide heavy pieces across the floor. If any object is heavy or awkward to carry alone, don't. Do not carry more than one object at a time - just think what you would do if a swinging door came in your direction! The best policy is, in fact, not to touch pieces at all. Hold paintings with your hands flat, on either side of the frame or stretcher so that you do not touch either the front or back of the canvas. Put objects on a rolling cart or in a padded basket. Carry paper and textiles only on a support, like a sheet of cardboard. If you must pick up an object that sits happily on a shelf, think of your hands as a substitute shelf: slip one hand beneath and use the other hand on the side for balance.

Carry large flat pieces, like marble tabletops, stained glass panels, or framed paintings or paper vertically. For large things, watch out for doorways; many large sculptures already have a series of nicks at door-frame height. Watch out for your own clothing - rings that can catch and necklaces that can drag and buttons that can scratch.

Learn to anticipate problems. Everyone seems to realize that glass and porcelain are fragile, but these are not the only objects damaged from handling. People seem to forget that wooden objects also break if dropped, and the breaks can be very nasty to repair because of ragged splintering of the wood. Any kind of bump can cause chips and nicks and scratches (See Fig. 14), and bumps into painted walls can transfer streaks of paint to the object. Knocks to a canvas painting can result in a series of circular cracks that may take years to develop. Rough handling can put holes in textiles, and can cause paint loss on pieces where the paint is not strongly attached. Picking up an object with unattached parts can cause breakage when the pieces come apart in your hands and fall.

Fig. 14 Southwest Native American ceramic damaged from abrasion. This piece was kept on a bookshelf for almost fifty years, and has scratches at the widest part of the shoulder, where it rubbed against other things on the shelf. Courtesy Leo and Blanch Appelbaum Collection.

Taking a moment to familiarize yourself with the condition and structure of an object before you pick it up will help avoid disasters. Think about how it is most vulnerable: is it hard and brittle and subject to breakage from shock, or is it soft and subject to scratching? Is there a piece sticking out that might bump against a wall? If you are picking up an object to examine it, do so over a soft surface, not over a concrete floor. Anticipate the worst, and you can avoid it. And when someone else less familiar with the objects than you is handling them, explain precautions specifically. Telling people to be careful is meaningless without some knowledge of what to be careful of!

Age-embrittlement occurs in many traditional restoration materials as well as in the objects themselves, making old repairs more and more susceptible to failure. Animal glue and shellac, two traditional adhesives for mending ceramics, are both very prone to this. Damage to breakable objects often occurs when unrecognized repairs give way during handling and the pieces fall on the floor, breaking again. Generally weaker parts of objects - handles, ankles and necks of figures, must be protected, both because they are in danger of breakage and because they are likely to have been broken and repaired before. It may be comforting when an object breaks in your hands to look for shiny spots of adhesive along the break, a sign that the break was there before.

Another problem in handling is the bare hands issue. Most manuals recommend that no object be touched with the skin unless gloves would make it too slippery to hold safely. Let us be frank. Conservators don't mind making this recommendation because they get to touch things all the time! Use your common sense. Polished silver and bronze and other metals, as well as the surface of photographs, will show fingerprints, and the fingerprints may well become engraved in the surface, thanks to the acids and salt in perspiration. Bronze disease in the shape of the whorls of fingerprints can sometimes be seen on smoothly patinated bronzes: don't let them be yours! Porous white things like plaster, ivory, marble, and paper can easily become stained from the dirt or grease on fingers, or from the dirt that later will cling to spots where fingerprints have left a slight stickiness. Removal of the stains or dirt can be difficult or impossible, and may entail major conservation treatment. There should be very few times when paper objects need to be handled directly; they should almost always be mounted and matted or encapsulated so that they can be viewed without touching. Many wooden objects, dark-colored stone pieces, sound glass and ceramics, will not be harmed by occasional handling with clean hands.

In a home, part of the pleasure in owning objects lies in being able to handle them, to share at least a part of the experience that the maker had as he gave life to the raw materials. In a museum, feeling the weight and texture of objects is a real part of studying them. It is pointless to recommend that curators or owners never touch original objects. It is on the other hand not unreasonable to demand clean hands, and only when the tactile experience is important. When handling a large quantity of material, use white cotton gloves or thin surgical gloves; when not wearing gloves, use tissue paper or clean cloth. The "no touching" rule must, of course, apply to all objects on museum exhibition because of the number of people involved, the lack of supervision, and risks to security.

In a museum, it is important that policies on handling be enforced consistently. If it is the policy that a technician use white gloves, everyone else must too, including the Director and members of the Board of Trustees. When an exception is made, it should be clearly stated as an exception, and for a particular reason. If this is not done, technicians and other staff quickly get the idea that care must be taken, but only when someone is watching!

Perspiration from handling is a definite danger to certain objects, since it contains acids, moisture, and salts and is therefore extremely corrosive, particularly in hot weather, but there are many other materials that can cause harm from contact. Adhesive tape, sticky labels, rubber bands, pins, nails and paper clips head the list. The adhesive tape can pull off bits of original surface. Labels should never be adhered to the reverse of paintings on canvas. Metal fasteners can rust, fusing the metal to a textile or paper, and leaving nasty stains. The sulfur in rubber bands can leave stains and localized spots of deterioration. Molding compounds are another hazard; before you give permission for casts to be made, find out exactly what materials will come in contact with the piece and check with a conservator. Do not, please, use original objects as containers for food or wine or candles or flower arrangements. Oily material or colored fluids can penetrate the cracks of porcelain or small pits in glass, leaving stains. Algae in flower water or mold on food can stain.

In any setting, coffee cups, peanut butter sandwiches, ballpoint pens and the like do not belong near objects. Being careful only goes so far; it is more prudent to set up the situation so that care is not needed. There is a modern technique in the teaching of safe driving that calls for establishing a maximum "cushion" of space around the car on the road. This could be adapted for the care of objects. Make sure that there is nothing close enough to an object to damage it in the case of an accident.

The placement of objects should also minimize environmental damage. Do not hang pieces on walls near heating ducts or over working fireplaces. Do not place moisture-sensitive pieces in bathrooms, particularly those with showers or tubs. Do not hang anything on walls subject to vibration from elevators or banging doors or large equipment. A great deal of smoking will deposit yellowish greasy dirt on everything. Do not hang paintings over buffets or anywhere near possible food splashes.

If you own lovely candlesticks or vases or fruit bowls, use them. But try somehow to keep this group of household items separate from what in a museum would be collection material. The term "object d'art" becomes useful here. Either what you have is a vase, a bowl, a plate, cup, or candlestick, or what you have is an "object d'art". Use the first group with pride and pleasure; put the second in the China cabinet and leave it there (See Fig. 15).

Fig. 15 Broken fan. This is an example of an inherently weak object which may be impossible to repair by ordinary means. If repaired, it would never be strong enough to handle, and would probably require a supportive mount to hold the fragments in position. Of no intrinsic value, this kind of piece would best be discarded once it is broken. Courtesy Julia Mae Rosen Collection.

Common Causes of Damage

Much breakage occurs not when pieces are being handled, but after they are placed on precarious perches. The classic case in private collections is an object displayed on a bookshelf. When the book-end slips and the row of books slides down, the Mexican figurine lands on the floor. Object conservators have a steady supply of these objects - and don't need to see any more. Inspect the area around all your pieces to make sure that this kind of thing cannot happen. No object should have parts projecting over the edge of a table, shelf, or pedestal. None should rest on a support that can be bumped by passers-by.

Another common cause of breakage is dusting. Housekeepers cannot be blamed for damage when they are being asked to dust around fragile objects, particularly when they are precariously perched on high shelves, or when these objects do not sit solidly on the shelf. Few objects are flat on the bottom, either because of their design or because the bottoms have been damaged previously. You have a choice: either do the dusting yourself and move the objects somewhere else as you do it, learn to live with a little dust, or put the objects in a case of some kind, so that dusting does not have to be done very often. As for dusting the objects themselves, usually a soft brush will do the job, but if you live in a place where objects need frequent cleaning, it would be best to consult a conservator about the problem.

In museums, the problem of dealing with dust is not necessarily much easier. Who cleans the storerooms in museums, and who dusts around objects on exhibition? Who cleans dusty objects? In my experience, few museums have answered this question satisfactorily; in general, any cleaning of objects is left to a conservator or experienced technician, and the dusting of shelves is perhaps not done as often as one would like. The possibility of breakage when shelves are being dusted and the difficulty of cleaning dust off many kinds of objects should underscore the need for providing a relatively dust-free environment for collections.

Even floor- and window-cleaning can be a source of danger when there is collection material in a room. Vacuum cleaner wands and mop handles can knock objects off shelves or dent paintings. Cleaning solutions on mops can (and often do) splash onto the bottoms of large contemporary paintings. The fumes from ammonia in glass-cleaning solutions can cause corrosion on metals. Wet-mopping can create difficulties for a humidity-control system.

Pieces that usually hang on a wall are commonly damaged when they are taken down for some reason - often when rooms are being painted or other renovation is being done. At times like this, in museums or private collections, always anticipate the worst. If framed pieces are to be leaned against a wall, place large sheets of cardboard between them. Make sure that they are resting on something that will not slide, and cover the whole pile with a sheet of plastic to make sure nothing spills on them. If there is space, put everything of value in a room where there will be no work done, but follow the same precautions anyway. I remember a collector who very carefully put a painting face down on a bed to keep it safe from the painters, but the painters stood a table on top of it, leaving four holes! Every conservator of my acquaintance has treated paintings that have been leaned against the corner of a coffee table or piano stool, or that have dents from the corner of another painting. Whenever a painting is off the wall, there should *always* be cardboard over the face (and the reverse also if there is no backing). Sheets and towels do not prevent this kind of damage.

In case you are not convinced, please remember that few paintings can safely be patched; the repair of a hole or rip in a painting often entails major treatment, and that means major expenditure! If you can, keep sheets of cardboard just larger than the outside dimensions of the frames of your paintings in storage, so they can be available whenever needed. This is just as important for pieces framed behind glass. If the glass breaks, you will be left not only with a mess of broken glass but probably a scratched or ripped object as well.

I will not make myself popular with pet-owners, but do not forget to pet-proof any at-home collection. Cat urine does not enhance contemporary art, and cats curling up in Indian baskets do them no good at all.

Making a Collection Damage-Proof

There are many steps that can be taken to eliminate the possibility of damage. For paintings, these include proper framing, backings, and secure hanging hardware. Frames are a traditional means of protecting paintings. A frame should be strong enough so that the frame helps to hold the painting together, not the other way around. Strip-moldings do little to protect paintings, but if they are the frame of choice, then make sure they are screwed into the sides of the stretcher, not nailed, as nails eventually work loose. The stripping should protrude forward at least one quarter inch past the painting surface so that when the painting is leaned against a wall, for example, the surface is protected.

Frames are important enough for both aesthetic and physical reasons that an examination of the frames should be included in a conservator's examination of the paintings. When paintings are being examined for possible treatment, some judgment should be made on the condition and appropriateness of the frames so that repair or replacement can be done during the treatment of the painting. For museums seeking grants to fund the treatment of paintings, attempts should be made to include work on the frame as part of the treatment cost if at all allowable by the granting body. Good-quality frames are extremely valuable; they should be treated by trained personnel. Original frames should be treated by conservators who specialize in gilded and joined objects, not by a local fix-it shop.

Many conservators like to pad the rabbet of the frame with strips of felt or flannel before the painting is secured. (The rabbet is the little ledge that the painting rests on.) In many cases, conservators attach stripping to the edges of the stretcher before it goes into the frame. Either of these methods prevents abrasion of the edges of the painting by the frame.

Paintings should be secured in their frames with metal straps held with screws, not with nails. Many conservators insist that one screw on each strap goes into the stretcher of the painting to avoid shifting of the painting in the frame. This is a good idea, particularly when a painting is travelling. Panel paintings must be framed in a way that holds them securely but allows for movement during changes in relative humidity.

All paintings on canvas should have light-weight rigid backings screwed into the reverse of the stretchers. Backings should have no gaps or air holes cut in them; paintings do not breathe (See Fig. 16). Most conservators use Fome-cor®, but there are other suitable materials. The only possible exception to this is in environments where mold is a common occurrence (although dealing with the environmental cause of the mold is of course a better idea). Backings provide a great deal of protection from fluctuations in relative humidity and from air pollution as well as from sloppy handling and balled-up hanging wires. They provide a place for the attachment of labels. (Never attach labels to the back of the canvas!) They prevent the accumulation of debris in the pocket between the painting and stretcher, where generations of pine needles, hardware, dust and bug body parts are commonly found. This debris often causes lumps in the canvas and increases the likelihood of paint loss along the bottom of canvas paintings, partly because of the moisture it can hold. When paintings are off the wall, backings make stacking paintings against a wall easier.

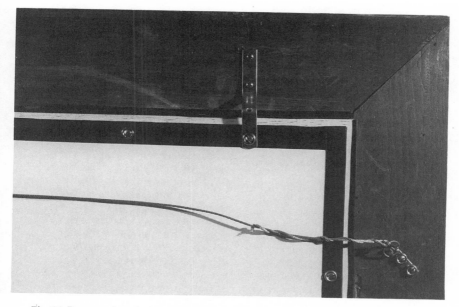

Fig. 16 Reverse of a painting. This painting is properly secured in its frame with straps and screws. A Fome-cor® backing protects the canvas, and mirror plates attached with two screws hold the braided wire. The black line around the edge of the stretcher is polyethylene stripping, which protects the edges of the painting from abrasion by the frame.

Paintings very sensitive to light damage, like contemporary paintings with exposed raw canvas, should, if possible, be displayed under ultraviolet-filtering Plexiglas®. These paintings are also extremely difficult to clean without altering their surface characteristics. Plexiglas® will keep them clean. Paintings in museums with subjects that invite vandalism should also be covered.

One of the jobs a consulting conservator can, and should do, for any painting collection is to resecure every painting in its frame, with a backing, or to teach someone else to do this. It is difficult to describe how to do these tasks in general terms. Every painting and frame are different, and every conservator has his habits and favorite materials. If you wish to try this job on your own, be warned: the job is tedious and extremely time-consuming, and proper materials are expensive.

Proper hanging hardware is a vital protection for a painting. Screw-eyes often work themselves loose. Use instead flat mirror hangers, with two screws on each for the average painting. Use braided wire for hanging. If a painting is particularly heavy, hang it from two wire loops. Do not use nylon monofilament (fishing line) to hang paintings. It stretches and abrades, and is so slippery that knots can work themselves loose. Test wall hooks well, and check them periodically. You would be surprised how often paintings fall off the wall!

Works on paper framed behind glass or Plexiglas® need some special treatment. Cleaning of the front while something is in the frame should be carried out with a cloth that has been sprayed with a small amount of cleaning solution; cleaners should never be sprayed on the glass or Plexiglas®, or they will drip down behind the frame molding and possibly water-stain the mat. Glass should be criss-crossed with adhesive tape on the front before packing; care must be taken that the tape does not touch a gilded frame.

It is important that objects be mounted properly to avoid damage of various kinds. Good mounting accomplishes several different objectives. It enhances the aesthetics of an object. For pieces like masks, it holds them in the proper position and at the proper angle for viewing. It provides a means of safe handling. It can make top-heavy pieces or pieces without a flat bottom secure. It can provide a "cushion of safety" by protruding out past any projections

on the piece and therefore preventing other objects from hitting it. It can provide a psychological reminder that the object has a special significance and should not be picked up mindlessly.

Objects which come into a collection in relatively good condition may become brittle while in a distorted position. The original object, a leather boot, for example, may have been quite flexible. If stored in a "flopped-over" position, it may become stiffened that way, and become extremely difficult to restore to a proper form. As the process of embrittlement progresses, the object may crack at creases. Pieces like fans, parasols, trousers or table linens with pressed-in creases, or any textile that has been sharply folded, are extremely sensitive to this kind of damage. It is vital to consider in what form these pieces should be stored or displayed, and, when they are handled, the potential for these problems must be kept in mind.

Mounts for oddly shaped objects can be a kind of treatment, providing overall support for a weakened object without having to alter the object with treatment. Objects like bags should not be hung from original straps; cleverly designed mounts can provide a stress-free way of hanging the object while having it appear to be hanging from the strap. Muslin "pillows" filled with polyester batting can be made to fit inside shoes, boots, or purses. Plexiglas®

easels can be made to support jewelry or small plaques. For semi-rigid shaped objects like thin metal or papier-mache masks, supports can be carved or molded to support the reverse.

Proper mounting is a job for someone with excellent design skills, excellent crafts skills, and supervised experience in handling museum-quality objects. Stands must not be nailed, screwed, or glued onto objects. Nylon monofilament (fishing line) should not be used to hold pieces to mounts because it is abrasive; as it expands and contracts it can cut through soft materials or leave a polished line of abrasion. Objects should not be drilled to insert dowels. Only the most stable materials should be used. If these restrictions make the job sound impossible, you know why I said that good mount-makers need experience in a museum setting. In general, good mount-makers stick to a very few materials to come into direct contact with objects - Plexiglas® or its equivalent, brass, padded or coated with stable materials, Ethafoam®, unbleached muslin, etc. Stands must be fitted

to objects with great care to avoid putting stress on the object, to allow for any movement in the piece, and to avoid abrasion. Any mount-maker must know when to tell a client to bring the object to a conservator before mounting can be done.

Some traditional mounts, like plate hangers, cause damage unless the hooks are specially padded with small pieces of ragboard, fabric, or plastic tubing. Decorative plates almost inevitably have small chips around the edges caused by the metal prongs of plate hangers.

Good mount-makers are perhaps even more difficult to find than conservators. There is no professional organization; there are no formal training courses. Do not assume that a mount-maker who works for an art dealer is schooled in the kind of long-range concerns that we are discussing. Do not assume this even with a museum staff member. Look for yourself, discuss your concerns, and make sure that they are taken seriously.

What to do When Damage Occurs

Even in the best-controlled collections, something will break sooner or later. Your reaction might be to run for the glue bottle because you can't stand the sight of a disaster. Even experienced conservators sometimes have to

fight this feeling. Calm down first, leave the room if it would help, and get everyone out of the way so that no fragments are crushed. Then pick up *all* the pieces. This is harder than you might think, as fragments fly quite a distance. Get a dust pan and brush and sweep up everything - it is better to include dust balls than miss a fragment. Do not throw the fragments together into a bag where they may abrade each other. Lay them flat on a tray or in a box so that will stay separate.

Find out if your insurance coverage includes breakage or devaluation from accidents. Hope that you have a photograph of the piece whole; you may want to find out the appraised value of the piece before damage and what it would be after repair before you decide on treatment.

There are two kinds of damage that should not wait; either should be followed immediately with a telephone call to a conservator. One is vandalism with lipstick, ballpoint pen, or markers. These materials seep into porous surfaces gradually, and can be much harder to remove later. The other kind of damage that can create a disaster is water damage. Depending on the kind of object and the severity of the wetting, some objects should be dried quickly, while others should be protected from fast drying. Some pieces should be frozen to prevent mold growth.

Loaning Objects

This is a difficult time for all kinds of objects. Particularly with travelling exhibitions, your piece will be packed and unpacked perhaps half a dozen times, installed and de-installed, perhaps attached to a mount and taken off again repeatedly, handled by perhaps dozens of people you will have no contact with, photographed by TV crews, shipped in trucks and planes and ships in all kinds of weather through all kinds of climates. It will undoubtedly gain in market value from all the exposure, and therein lies the problem. How can you resist?

Please, please do not send pastels and charcoals, or Oriental lacquer, or panel paintings with a history of problems. If climate

control is a real necessity, insist on particular levels of temperature and RH, but do not expect that every institution that says it will provide those conditions actually can, or will; don't expect any institution to tell you that it can't. If the climatic changes that seem to be inevitable given the location and time of year seem harsh, particularly if the piece has had humidity-related problems in the past, consider just saying no.

Ask where the piece will be kept when it is not on exhibition. Pieces are particularly at risk when they are out of their crates but not in an exhibition case or on a wall. Long periods of time before or after exhibitions can be a cause for concern. Find out the whole itinerary for the exhibition.

A one-stop, four-month loan exhibition is bound to be safer than a long tour with as many as five or six different venues.

If possible, have a conservator examine the piece before you approve the loan; ask if it can be made any stronger, or if there are any specific instructions on packing or handling that would help. If treatment is needed, try to get the borrower to pay for it, or at least split the cost. Be willing to make a few phone calls to try to find out something about the reputation of the borrowing institution or the organizer of the show. Make sure the piece is well photographed before it leaves your hands. Ask if the institution responsible for the exhibition has a conservator in charge of examining the pieces regularly. Make sure that the contract you sign specifies that no one may do anything to your piece without your permission — no pins or screws or nails or staples in it, no cleaning or conservation treatment, no new mounting or frames, and that you will be notified immediately if any change is noted in the condition. A painting or print should not be taken out of the frame without your permission, and no scientific tests should be done on it without your permission. The time to be tough is before you sign the papers; if the borrower does not respect your caution, or soft-pedals your concerns, think again.

Inorganic Materials

Objects made of inorganic materials (metals, stone, ceramics, plaster, and glass) seem like the most permanent of things. Common expressions like "hard as rock" or "tough as nails" are not without a basis in fact. Even stone, however, the most "natural" of these materials, has been removed from its original environment and placed in an alien one, and is subject to new environmental stresses. Natural forces may work more slowly here than with organic materials, but permanence is still an elusive goal.

Metals

Major environmentally-connected condition problems with metals in museum objects concern unwanted corrosion. Whether tarnishing of silver, rusting of iron, loss of sheen of aluminum, or bronze disease, the environmental contributions to this unwanted corrosion are similar. Oxygen and moisture are both necessary, and corrosive impurities make a major contribution. Metal objects are generally immune to damage from light; heat, because of its effect on moisture content, can only be said to assist in preserving metal objects unaltered.

The exact role of specific pollutants has not been well-defined, although the rule of thumb is that the major constituents of such corrosion are chlorides for copper and copper alloys, sulfur for silver, and organic acids for lead. Minor constituents, however, seem to play an important role. Laboratory tests attempting to duplicate outdoor corrosion using only variations in temperature, relative humidity, and sulfur dioxide, the major pollutant in our air, have failed to reproduce corrosion layers similar to those formed in "real life"; very small amounts of many different pollutants undoubtedly play complex roles. The lack of precise data to describe the contribution of different pollutants to metal corrosion creates practical problems in setting standards for safe RH levels, since corrosion rates in clean air may be very different than those for polluted air, and different kinds of polluted air may produce different results.

The role of environmental impurities in the corrosion of metals can be seen in coins. Examination of a pocketful of change will reveal a variety of colors of corrosion, particularly in pennies. They are various shades of brown, some with turquoise blue or whitish hazes. Virtually identical to start with, only their environments vary.

It is impossible to predict how low an RH would be required to stop corrosion completely. 30 or 40% is often recommended as a safe upper limit, but many factors will influence this. Stagnant air, which may have a higher RH than the rest of the room, the presence of a hygroscopic dust or dirt layer on the object, and pollutants in the air will all lower the safe RH limit. Safe levels may be substantially higher under optimal conditions of clean, well-circulated air and clean objects. One conservator has observed a collection of well-cared-for archaeological bronzes that are stable at RH levels as high as 50%. Only direct and repeated inspection will reveal whether existing conditions are safe for a particular collection. In general, frequent inspections in heated but un-humidified spaces in winter will be unnecessary, but collections should be inspected for loose powder, flaking, or any changes in appearance about every month during the summer.

The sources for contamination are numerous. For archaeological pieces, chlorides may be in place from burial. Dirt layers on the surface are very hygroscopic and can raise the moisture content of the piece even in a relatively dry environment. They can also hide problems as they begin and prevent detection and early treatment. The presence of salts in clay cores of cast pieces is another source of corrosion. Casting flaws may incorporate impurities. The permeability of existing surface layers of stable corrosion may encourage corrosion in layers beneath. Chemicals used during the application of foundry patinas may also introduce corrosive elements. Oils applied to ethnographic metals can promote corrosion. Perspiration from skin contact either from ethnographic use or from subsequent handlingcan cause problems, since it is a source of acids, chlorides, and moisture; all fingerprints should therefore be cleaned carefully from object surfaces before exhibition or storage. Acids from construction materials are one more source. Any of these factors can change the level at which a piece is safe from corrosion.

For pieces made of more than one metal, extremely low RH levels are vital, since contact accelerates corrosion of the less stable metal. Copper alloy pieces with iron additions show this problem; the iron is generally badly corroded, while the copper remains sound. Pieces like this should probably be among the first groups to be referred to conservators for preventive or interventive treatment.

Despite some inability to state an exact figure for recommended RH levels, it is clear that storage or exhibition at low RH is vital, and lower-than-needed levels will not cause harm. Fluctuations in RH are not deleterious for metals, so the provision of proper levels is not as complex as providing proper levels for hygroscopic items. Dry silica gel or heat can be used for this purpose inside containers. Cleaning of ambient air may be impossible, but it should be possible to eliminate all sources of acids, chlorides, and sulfur from contact with objects or from the containers that house them. Pollution scavengers like Carusorb® or Purafil® (See *Sources of Supply:* Carus Chemical Co. and Purafil, Inc.) should be used when other remedies are impossible. Commercial products like 3M Silver Protector Strips® are an easy-to-use form of sulfur scavenger (See *Sources of Supply:* Silver Care Products).

For polished metal objects in storage, various kinds of wrappings can protect objects. Pacific cloth (available in department and houseware stores), a flannel fabric impregnated with corrosion inhibitors, works well, although the pieces wrapped in it are out of sight. Pacific cloth cannot be washed without removing the useful chemicals, so in a dirty space, the cloth wrappings should be rewrapped in something else. Some conservators recommend that silver be stored in sealable polyethylene bags for protection. Kitchen-type plastic wrap is used in many households for this purpose, but it is a chloride-containing plastic and can therefore be expected to off-gas acids; for this reason it is not recommended for long-term use.

The application of coatings by brush is a traditional way to protect metals from undesirable corrosion. Traditional coatings, however, have numerous drawbacks. Because coating materials are fairly transparent when applied, it is very easy to miss spots. As time goes by, the uncoated areas corrode much faster than coated ones, leaving small dark spaces with sharp borders. If left long enough, these spots are almost impossible to polish away. The same kind of reaction can be promoted by coatings of uneven thickness, some leaving parallel stripes of corrosion in thinner parts of a brushstroke. Rough handling of coated metals may scratch the coatings, producing similar dark spots of corrosion.

Traditional coating materials like linseed oil films, dammar, and shellac become embrittled and crack, allowing corrosion along the cracks. They discolor with time and become more and more difficult to remove. The discoloration in silver coatings can be so bad that it makes silver look like brass. Linseed oil coatings, or varnishes that contain linseed oil as a plasticizer, can promote copper corrosion.

On archaeological material wax is a common coating. Tinted waxes are sometimes used for this purpose; they can greatly improve the appearance of a dull or uneven surface. Tinted waxes are particularly damaging over the long term. They do not entirely prevent moisture from collecting at the metal surface, but do not allow the moisture to evaporate away. They hide early signs of harmful corrosion, collect dirt, and obscure details of the original surface.

Modern non-yellowing synthetic coatings applied by spray can provide significant protection, particularly in collections where conservators can monitor any possible problems due to flaws in the coating and correct them before they proceed very far. Some conservators who deal with polished metals prefer as a coating cellulose nitrate-based lacquers for their appearance, impermeability, and ease of application; other conservators feel that even for this purpose cellulose nitrate is inappropriate. The application of either type of coating so that it changes the appearance of the metal as little as possible is a technically demanding process, and should be carried out by, or under the direct supervision of, a conservator, and only after careful preparation of the metal surface. Because of the potential for damage, the application of coatings should be considered part of a conservation treatment, not merely a maintenance procedure. Detailed records on the date and type of coating and the means of application must be kept; this will make future treatment easier, and should assure that there are no attempts to polish a coated object. Polishing silver and brass is more like routine maintenance than a conservation treatment, but for collection material should be done as infrequently as possible, since all polishing entails the removal of metal from the surface and the gradual erosion of design elements. Traditional routines of polishing assume periodic use and repeated washing and polishing. Over years and decades, these activities will produce the characteristic soft sheen of old metals. This traditional maintenance probably worked well in times and places where air was cleaner than in modern cities, and where household help was easier to find.

There are other reasons why polishing of collection material is considered inadvisable. The residue from polishes that stays in the cracks and hollows of a design becomes the focus for more corrosion. In order for them to clean quickly, commercial solutions are formulated with strong reagents like acids or ammonia which "eat through" corrosion layers. Residues may be very difficult to remove, and will continue to react with the uncorroded silver. Polishes that are protective over periods of up to about six months will create more problems than they will solve if they are not washed off and the piece is not repolished. If we wish to bring a piece to a stable condition, the cycle of tarnishing and repolishing must be broken by protecting the pieces against the environmental elements that cause the tarnish.

For metal parts on other kinds of pieces, like the hardware on furniture or metal eyes in African sculpture, it is particularly important to avoid the need for polishing, since silver or brass polishes leave such a messy residue. The residue can stain the surrounding wood and abrade the surface finish.

One additional problem with chemical polishes is that sometimes a metal object turns out not to be what it is thought to be. It may be plated rather than solid. It may have an original tinted coating or later coating. It may be an alloy that responds badly to a polish designed for a different metal.

For collection material, polishing metals should be seen as a conservation treatment, something done only once at a point in an object's life when further corrosion will be prevented by other measures.

Copper and Copper Alloys

Bronze disease is one of the most misunderstood terms in the field of conservation. I have heard well-educated people in the arts talk about "quarantining" objects with bronze disease as though it is contagious, or claiming that "no one knows" what it is. Neither are true. Bronze disease is a particular mineral that contains in its molecule copper, chlorides, and water. Any copper-containing metal can "grow" bronze disease if the other components are present.

Chlorides in copper alloys can come from several sources. Archaeological bronzes usually have a layer of a different chloride mineral sealed under other layers which can turn into bronze disease if moisture reaches it. Tiny pits or cracks in the overlayers can allow moist air in, and the light green bronze disease can be seen erupting out of little pits. Some foundry bronzes have salts as impurities in clay cores. Flaws in the metal can allow these salts access to moisture. Fingerprints or other skin contact can deposit chlorides, as can sandy dirt clinging from burial.

Unlike the various hard crusts that "grow" slowly on copper alloys during burial, bronze diseaseis a soft powdery mineral that forms rapidly when conditions are favorable. The color varies somewhat, but is generally a light bright green. With admixtures of organic salts, the result of contamination from organic acids, the crystals can be turquoise blue. Probing with a needle or other sharp instrument will reveal the soft texture. A chemical test for chlorides is the usual confirmation, but will not rule out organic components.

The rate at which copper is transformed into soft powder makes bronze disease extremely destructive. The mineral is said to stop "growing" below 38% RH, but in practice, the cutoff point is not so definite.

Black spots on copper alloys appear to represent a reaction with hydrogen sulfide either from bacteria or from fossil fuels; the exact origin of this phenomenon remains a source of disagreement. White feathery crystals are usually organic salts.

The growth of any soft corrosion on a copper alloy should be reason to place the piece in an especially dry uncontaminated atmosphere and to call a conservator. Typical treatment involves mechanical removal of the bronze disease and stabilization with a chemical that helps to prevent further outbreaks by chemically tying up the copper (benzotriazole). Removal of hard corrosion layers to expose the original surface of an object is sometimes recommended.

Special Problems: Bronzes

Because copper is so often alloyed with other metals, corrosion problems involving the other components may complicate an object's treatment. Oriental bronzes, with their high lead content, often exhibit lead corrosion long before the copper shows signs of corrosion.

African "bronzes" or "brasses" may present particularly difficult corrosion problems because bubbles in the original casting may hold salty soil that can cause bronze disease where it cannot be easily seen. Chlorides from skin contact during original use can contaminate the reverse of pieces and build up in casting flaws, and original surface treatments can hide outbreaks. Oils originally applied to the surface of ethnographic bronzes can promote deterioration because of acidic components of the oil.

In objects with mixed metals, like bronze masks with iron eyes, the less noble metal, in this case iron, will be preferentially corroded. These objects should be examined by a conservator very experienced in metals conservation to see if this corrosion can be checked.

Silver

It is important to differentiate between the silver of decorative objects and silver in archaeological pieces. The latter may be riddled by corrosion products that make it very brittle and weak. This material may require major conservation treatment to make it either presentable or physically stable.

Fig. 17 A badly tarnished silver trophy dated 1876. The unevenness of the tarnish is due to the fact that only part of the old coating remains. Tarnish in the pattern of fingerprints is visible at the top. Because this was not household silver, it was not routinely washed and polished. Courtesy an anonymous institution.

Decorative silver is of course a fairly strong material, but the desirable nature of the silver surface can be quickly ruined by tarnish. Studies have not untangled the relative importance of hydrogen sulfide, sulfur dioxide, and relative humidity in the rate of tarnishing, but there is evidence that the presence of chlorides promotes silver corrosion.

Prevention luckily does not wait for exact data. Keeping sulfur-containing materials away from silver is the best method, but completely sulfur-free air may be difficult to achieve. Low relative humidity will slow down all corrosive reactions including silver tarnish and is therefore the next least harmful method of protection. Barrier methods like coatings or wrappings will keep contaminants away from the silver surface and slow tarnishing, and sulfur scavengers will clean air that cannot be cleaned in other ways.

Light rubbing of a silver object with a soft cloth will rub off very thin layers of tarnish; some collections of uncoated silver have been maintained simply by daily rubbing by someone wearing cotton gloves. This procedure is obviously prohibitively labor-intensive for most collections. In order to evaluate the hazards of a particular environment to silver, it is necessary to evaluate the rate of tarnishing. Visual inspection will not usually work because all the silver in a case is likely to darken at the same rate. It may be necessary to set up a schedule of monitoring with test polishing of small areas on a few pieces in order to determine the rate of tarnishing. The results of such monitoring should help to determine whether changes in environment are necessary or are worth doing.

If polishing becomes necessary, a commercial liquid or paste polish can be used if followed by careful rinsing. Do not use silver dips, as they are extremely corrosive.

Given the variety of methods possible for protecting silver from tarnishing, there is no reason why silver in collections should require repeated polishing. Where silver is not in enclosed cases, coating should be considered. Possibly because silver tarnish is not regarded as as damaging a type of corrosion as bronze disease or iron rust, many collection managers may not regard its prevention with the same level of seriousness. Silver that is extremely tarnished has not only lost its intended appearance but may actually be damaged and may require much more than a gentle cleaning to restore to a respectable condition (See Fig. 17). This is harmful to the silver, and a real time-waster.

Gold

Modern gold requires little or no maintenance. As with other metals, ancient gold may be quite different. Pre-Columbian gold is a particular problem. Because original techniques of surface enrichment make it appear to be of higher gold content than it is, its corrosion patterns may be more like those of copper alloys or archaeological silver than of gold.

Burial under acid conditions may have leached out some of the copper or silver, leaving a somewhat spongy and brittle metal. Further corrosion can be both unsightly and weakening to the structure of the piece. Pre-Columbian gold should be handled, stored, and exhibited under the best possible conditions.

Lead

Even though few museum objects may be composed solely of lead, lead has played an important role in the growth of awareness of the danger of pollutants in the museum. Formic acid, a derivative of formaldehyde, reacts with lead to form feathery white crystals of lead formate. This is easily observed, and has been noted as occurring within two weeks of exposure. Lead formate crystals are very light-weight, and therefore fly into the air where they can be inhaled. The presence of lead in any chemical

form has the same kind of toxic affect on people as lead metal. The formation of lead formate on objects has therefore received prompt attention from museum personnel.

Because lead tends to be porous, contamination with organic acids can persist even after the source of contamination, and the crystals, are removed, resulting in repeated crystal growth. Special treatments may have to be designed to draw the acids out of the lead.

Iron

Iron occurs in a host of objects, from handguns and cannonballs to shop-signs and architectural hardware. Rusty iron is one of the most difficult problems conservators have to face, particularly when, as with iron

from shipwrecks, the pieces are permeated with chlorides from sea water Storage and exhibition of iron in dry environments is therefore particularly important. The commonness of iron objects in some collections may lead people to be relatively careless in the handling of this un-noble metal, but as with other relatively unremarkable collection material, treatment can be just as complex and expensive as for valuable objects, so prevention of problems is still vital.

Special Problems: Coins and Medals

Coins and medals throughout history have contained a wide variety of metals and alloys. Because much of the value of numismatic collections rests in the clarity of the inscriptions, the avoidance of tarnishing and all other kinds of corrosion and the resulting polishing will help these objects retain their value.

Storage containers for coins have been a problem in the past, as coin collectors have not necessarily been aware of the need for chemical purity to avoid corrosion. Polyvinyl chloride, although it has convenient working qualities, should not be used for coin storage because of its tendency to off-gas acidic fumes. Some other plastics have additives that may be harmful. Polyesters, including mylar, and acrylics are considered safe. Conservators should be consulted when there are any questions about storage containers. For exhibition, Plexiglas® is an excellent material for making mounts for coins. If possible, coins should be containerized to avoid exposure to air-borne contaminants.

Special Problems: Toleware and other Painted or Gilded Metals

Painted or gilded metal objects present special difficulties because corrosion of the substrate metal produces crystals that grow beneath the decorative layer, pushing it off. Some of these objects represent household or folk pieces that have been poorly taken care of, complicating their care and treatment. These objects should be placed in a high priority group for attention by a conservator and for a dry and uncontaminated environment.

The use of commercial metal polishes or abrasives on gilded objects may result in unwitting removal of the gold. The possibility that an object that appears to be gold or brass may be another metal gilded or tinted with a yellowish coating is a good reason for leaving the treatment of metals to experts.

Special Problems: Soft Silver-colored Alloys

Objects commonly called pewter or Britannia metal can include some very different alloys. They are usually tin with admixtures of antimony, copper, zinc, lead, or bismuth. These alloys are quite soft, easily bent, dented, and abraded, and require special handling. Do not use ordinary metal polishes on these things. Conservators use the least abrasive polishes, typically a mixture of alcohol and whiting, with no chemical reagents.

Ceramics

Ceramics represent a wide variety of materials from porcelain to objects fired at such a low temperature that too much water can turn them back to mud. Well-fired ceramic is one of the most durable of materials, unresponsive to changes in relative humidity, to high light levels, to insect damage, or gaseous air pollution.

Particulate pollution, that is, dust, can be a problem with ceramics. The possibility of flaking glazes or unrecognized repairs on ceramics makes it necessary to inspect each piece carefully before even the most simple cleaning procedure is contemplated. Hard-bodied ceramics like porcelain can usually be washed with warm water or wiped with a damp cloth. Gilding on porcelain can be easily abraded, so particular care should be taken with gilded pieces. Undecorated soft ceramics ("earthenware") can be harmed by prolonged contact with water or by wiping when wet. The porous nature of their surfaces can trap dust and make it difficult to remove. Very dusty pieces should be dusted with a soft brush into the mouth of a vacuum cleaner before any other cleaning method is attempted, as wiping, or even handling with the fingers, can push dirt further into the surface. Problems related to the porosity of ceramics are more serious with low-fired undecorated pieces, but even glazed porcelain can be susceptible to staining, for example, when liquids seep into the cracks in the glaze.

Breakage is usually the biggest problem faced in managing a ceramic collection. Handling ceramics must involve the greatest care to avoid wholesale breakage and also chipping or scratching. Decorative ceramics in a home are often damaged by bumping against other objects. Decorative plates are often chipped by the prongs of plate hangers. Before handling ceramics, it is important to note old repairs, as they can represent areas of weakness.

The repair of broken ceramics is something that non-conservators often want to carry out without professional help, and conservators are often asked what adhesive they recommend for this purpose. It is difficult to make such a recommendation. Epoxy should *never* be used by amateurs because of the difficulty of their removal and because they tend to discolor strongly with age. Instant glues (like "Crazy Glue") are likewise not recommended because of difficulty in controlling their application and removal and because their behavior with ceramics can be unpredictable. The liquid can penetrate into porous ceramics, leaving a stain around the break. Emulsion adhesives (white glues) are often used, but once in place, they can also be extremely difficult to remove. They can be softened but not easily removed from the edges of breaks without scraping some of the original surface off. Resin cements like Duco®, even though they discolor, remain among the easiest to dissolve and are therefore the most foolproof, although they should not be used on very soft ceramics.

Most conservators make their own adhesives from the dry resins they get directly from chemical companies. These resins have handling properties which make their use difficult, but conservators learn to deal with them because of their superior aging characteristics. If you undertake the repair of a ceramic object, decide in advance what you will do if you are not satisfied with the results. Do not forget that treatment by a conservator will cost significantly

more if it includes undoing your work as well as redoing the repair, and the results may be inferior.

Although the vast majority of ceramic objects are healthy specimens, porous ceramics can suffer from changes in relative humidity if the pores are permeated with hygroscopic salts. Such soluble salts leach into objects during burial. When the piece is removed from the ground and exposed to high relative humidities, the salts dissolve in the water that penetrates into the pores of the ceramic. When the relative humidity drops, the water moves toward the surface of the piece where it evaporates, leaving the salts behind to crystallize. Normally the surface of a ceramic is not as permeable as the body of the piece, whether because of the application of a glaze or slip, or because of the slight compacting of the surface during its shaping. The crystals tend therefore to form just below the surface and, as they grow, to push the surface layers outward, causing various forms of flaking and loss. Soft ceramic pieces can be turned into collections of flakes by the action of soluble salts, although milder cases can be recognized by a few conical losses.

Pieces afflicted with soluble salts can be stabilized in an environment with strictly controlled RH, preferably at a level below 40%, but conservation treatment is strongly recommended. By the time soluble salts are visible, they have caused a problem. Loose flakes of the ceramic surface can sometimes be reattached with suitable treatment, so prompt attention is warranted. Conservators who treat pieces with soluble salts note that some pieces can simply be treated by brushing away the salts and consolidating whatever weakness resulted from their growth. In these pieces, the crystals do not recur. Other pieces may sprout salts repeatedly; such cases may call for major interventive treatments including prolonged soaking in water to remove the salts or impregnation of the material with suitable resins. Such treatments should be left to conservators well experienced in doing them and should be considered something of a last resort, but any occurrence of soluble salts should be examined by a conservator, since damage can be quick and can entail the complete destruction of the substance of an object.

Glass

Most glass is chemically extremely stable, mainly at risk from careless handling. In some kinds of glass, ultraviolet light can cause color shifts, so light should be controlled. Some glass has an inherent chemical weakness known by the term "glass disease" or "sick glass". This is caused by an original formula deficient in lime, leaving the alkali (sodium or potassium) water soluble, and therefore subject to leaching out. Although glasses afflicted with this problem are usually 17th or 18th century, later and earlier pieces have also been affected. It is perhaps difficult to know how much glass in collections has a potential for disease, since rapid changes between extremes of relative humidity might create a problem in a piece which would have remained sound for long periods of time in a stable environment.

Sick glass is similar in behavior to ceramics with soluble salts. High relative humidities or exposure to water causes hydration of the salts, which then migrate out at low RH. The leaching out of the alkali causes small-scale cracking of the glass ("crizzling") which can be seen in mild cases only under low-power magnification. More serious cracking in a piece acclimated to a high RH can be brought on within only months in very dry conditions, or from spot heating with exhibition lights. Worst cases are brought on by full hydration at a very high RH followed by exposure to very low RH levels.

In European collections, where average relative humidity levels are generally higher than in the United States, a more common form of glass disease is indicated by glass surfaces that are slimy to the touch. This is a result of water held by the hygroscopic salts on the glass surface and is referred to as "weeping" glass.

Various suggestions have been made about the desirable RH for unstable glass. Fully hydrated glass can crizzle even at a 40-60% RH range, but few pieces are apt to be in this extreme condition. For weeping glass, an RH below 42% has been recommended, because below this level, potassium carbonate, the most common form of alkali salts in glass, is no longer hygroscopic. A medium range of relative humidity has also been recommended. Only informed observation of collections will provide an answer to this question. Certainly, it is important to avoid rapid or wide fluctuations of either temperature or RH for collections of glass with the potential for crizzling.

Painted glass or archaeological glass with weathering crusts should be displayed so as to avoid heating. Both require careful handling to avoid abrasion or flaking of surface elements.

The need to avoid local heating of glass makes careful exhibition vital, since many kinds of lighting used for glass will create heat. Glass lit from behind through frosted glass can be attractive, but any heat generated from the lights has the potential to cause damage, particularly from the cycling of temperature and RH caused by turning the lights on and off. Light pipes may provide a technology useful for this purpose.

Stone

Many kinds of indoor stone objects are indeed almost indestructable. However, some kinds of stone can suffer from soluble salts; these should be stabilized at fairly low RH levels to avoid trouble. All calcium carbonate stones like marble or limestone are susceptible to acid attack from environmental pollutants. All porous light-colored stones are subject to staining and dirt deposit; complete cleaning of these materials is not always possible. As with ceramics, chipping and scratching as well as breakage are common, and many forms of sandstone and limestone are quite soft. Conservators who treat stone keep themselves quite busy even with this durable material.

Large stone pieces represent a host of difficulties due to their weight. Moving such pieces at all, not to mention packing and shipping them, can prove to be hazardous for both object and personnel. Even table-top size stone pieces can be surprisingly heavy. The sheer bulk of heavy stone does not make it immune from breakage, both major and minor.

Argillite, a soft stone used by Northwest Coast Indians for the manufacture of items for sale, is more fragile than most other stones. Because of the presence of small amount of clay minerals that remain hygroscopic, argillite undergoes dimensional changes from changes in RH, and is quite susceptible to cracking and chipping. Local heating can be quite damaging, since the dark color of argillite absorbs heat readily.

Plaster

Plaster objects are difficult to care for safely because they are soft and easily scratched; porous and easily stained; brittle and easily broken; moisture-sensitive and easily water-damaged. Since many plaster casts have been painted to look like marble, they are sometimes mistaken for marble in collections of busts or other sculpture. Because plaster casts are historically inexpensive art, they have often been neglected and stored carelessly, or repainted repeatedly every time the surface gets dirty or the previous paint layer flakes. The treatment of plaster is, for all these reasons, often difficult and expensive. If you have neglected plasters in your collection, try to rescue them from the worst abuse before their condition gets even worse. Do not try to treat these things without a conservator; brushing dirt off the surface into the hose of a vacuum cleaner is as much as you should do. Do not, ever, use water to wash down the surface of a plaster, as the water combined with abrasion will cut into the surface. Plaster sculptures with wire armatures inside are particularly at risk from rough handling, and should be protected from any movement or vibration.

Mineral Specimens

Because the environments in which minerals were formed are very diverse, but very stable, each mineral has its own tolerance for environmental factors. Some are light-sensitive, and some are affected by rapid temperature changes. Rapid RH changes can sometimes cause shrinkage cracks, while loss or uptake of moisture can cause recrystallization or decomposition to powder. It is important to learn the individual susceptibilities of specific minerals in a collection to provide for their individual needs. People who handle mineral collections should be aware that some individual specimens may be poisonous if particles are ingested.

Special Problems: Pyrite

Pyrite disease is an alteration of pyrite, a long-term decay marked by the growth of white powdery crystals. Oxygen and moisture are required for the growth of pyrite disease, so storage below 50% is recommended to prevent this problem. Pyrite grains can be inclusions in sedimentary rocks like shale, sandstone, or limestone, so fairly low RH levels may be prudent for these stones also.

Fossils

Many fossils are incompletely fossilized; small spots of organic remains (collagen) in the structure stay hygroscopic. This can cause cracking, splitting, or delamination of the stone matrix if the pieces are exposed to widely fluctuating RH levels. Fossils used as decorative objects are often mounted in a way that causes scratching of the surface; mounts like this should be replaced. Recently, substantial emissions of radon have been detected from some fossils in museum collections.

Organic Materials

Organic materials (wood, paper, textiles, and other materials of animal or plant origin) are more difficult objects to preserve than inorganic ones. In nature, the sources from which these materials are derived have a limited life span. During the lifetime of the plant or animal, the materials are renewed or maintained by the life processes of the organism. Once the materials are removed from the organism, the natural process of decay begins. Throughout history, special processes have been developed to forestall this natural deterioration and make the materials suitable for use.

Utilitarian and ethnographic objects were often not made to last. The objects themselves were seen as having a natural lifetime after which it was expected that they would be discarded and replaced. A modern example of this is the American flag. Federal regulations instruct us to dispose of a flag in a dignified manner when its condition makes it no longer suitable for public display. Yet historical societies, governmental institutions and armories all over the country are preserving flags in miserable condition because of their historical associations. Custodians of collections are fighting both nature and the wisdom of the people who made these things while knowing that irreversible deterioration was inevitable.

Wood and Wood Products

The major problem in the preservation of wood relates to its dimensional change in response to changes in relative humidity. Cracking and warping of wood are familiar to us all; the dynamics of the changes are not as familiar. Wood expands and contracts differently in different grain directions. The greatest changes occur in the tangential direction, that is, around the circumference of the log. When a full log dries and shrinks, a familiar wedge-shaped crack opens up in the log; theoretically, if the RH increased to what it was, the crack would close up. However, few cracks close up completely; the reason lies in what happens if the moisture content of the log increases first. As the cells swell around the circumference, they have no room to expand and therefore get crushed. Once this happens, if the RH drops to initial levels, the wood would crack, because the cells have shrunk.

Other kinds of so-called compression set occur when one part of a piece of wood swells but is restrained by another part. This is the cause of warping of panel paintings: because the uncoated reverse is more quickly affected by changes in RH than the painted front, the swelling of the reverse is inhibited and the wood undergoes compression. Compression in the back of the panel causes an overall contraction of the back of the panel which leaves the panel convex at the front. The shapes created by warping of wood are complicated by the angle of the grain in relation to the faces of the piece of wood and by knots and other irregularities in the grain.

Misunderstanding of the concept of compression set makes people believe that dryness is responsible for the cracking of wood. In fact, the damage occurs during periods of high RH, but only becomes visible during dry periods.

Many people also become confused by the claims made by manufacturers of wood-care products and by the obvious improvement in the appearance of wood when it is waxed or oiled. These coatings make the surface of wood appear less dry, but the phenomenon involves only cosmetic change and does not relate to the moisture content of the wood. "Feeding" wood surfaces with oily or waxy polishes does

little or nothing to slow down moisture exchange with the air or to stop cracking.

Because of the relation between grain and the direction of shrinkage, pieces that include the center of a log, like most sculptures carved out of single pieces of wood, always have a tendency to crack, whereas pieces that do not include the center will expand and contract but seldom crack. Painted wood pieces have additional problems, since expansion and contraction of the wood will eventually result in cracking, cleavage, and flaking of the paint. Painted wooden objects made in tropical parts of the world include a large portion of the world's artistic heritage. When these objects meet the low relative humidities of northern winters, the paint can end up as a halo of flakes on the table around the piece. Conservators can judge the onset of cold weather by the number of inquiries they receive every fall about flaking paint on wood sculpture. Unfortunately, the treatment of flaking paint involves readhering each loose area separately, a time-consuming process that costs more than the price of many objects.

The forces involved in dimensional changes of wood are incredibly strong, conquering even the most ingenious attempts to stop them. Nails, battens, cradles (See Figs. 18, 19 on next page), glue, and all other physical restraints are doomed if the wood is kept in widely fluctuating relative

Figs. 18, 19 These photographs show the front and reverse of Maurice Courant's *Marine* 1881, an oil painting on wood panel. The cradle on the reverse was a common treatment meant to allow a panel to expand and contract across the grain while preventing warping. The vertical members in this photograph are set into slots in the horizontal members so that they can slide as the panel moves. However, slight pressure causes them to stick; almost no cradles have members that still slide. Unfortunately, the theory of the cradle is mistaken. Nothing will stop warping except environmental control. The result of cradling is eventually the pattern of cracking and warping shown here, sometimes called a "corduroy effect". Any cradled panel painting should be examined by a conservator to determine if the cradle is causing structural problems. Courtesy Mr. James McNamara Collection.

humidities. To the extent that they succeed in holding even part of the wood still, they cause cracking while inhibiting warping, a bad trade-off. Filling of cracks in wood is likewise doomed: if the filling material is hard, swelling of the wood will cause breaks and additional compression set; if soft, the filling will be pushed out of the crack. Shrinkage will increase the size of the crack and therefore leave the crack only partially filled.

Other attempts at reducing dimensional change in wood involve coating the wood to slow down moisture exchange with the air. These fail mainly because no visually satisfactory coating is impermeable enough to stop movement completely. Small dimensional changes eventually cause cracking or delamination of the coating. "Eventual" is important here, since the responsiveness of wood does not slow down with age.

It should be clear by now that the only hope of stabilizing wood is by control of relative humidity in the environment. Many objects made of a single piece of unpainted wood can safely be left to expand and contract with RH changes, as unsightly as that might be, but any joined object or any wooden object with paint or veneer will be subject to continuing damage as long as it is subject to RH changes.

The influence of light on wood is often underestimated. Certain kinds of wood are much more susceptible to fading than others because of the chemistry of the natural dyes that color them, and a certain amount of color change in wooden surfaces is sometimes considered part of the object's patina. Light fades or discolors wood, depending on the wavelength. As with other objects worth preserving, any change in color is undesirable. Light also causes some chemical deterioration of the wood surface, and damages coatings.

Insect pests are of course problems with wood, particularly in pieces from tropical climates. Many wooden objects have been infested in the past. Because dryness will halt the reproduction of wood-eating insects, most objects that exhibit signs of insect damage no longer are infested. It is obviously vital to identify pieces with active infestations to avoid spreading the problem to uninfested pieces and to note the extent of wood damage in formerly infested pieces. Since wood-eating insects avoid the surfaces of objects in order to avoid the light, the extent of damage below the surface may not be obvious, and careless handling may cause cave-ins of portions of the object's surface.

Baskets

Baskets are made of various parts of trees and other plants. These materials include roots, twigs, grasses and strips of bark as well as seed pods and thin splints of wood. The variety of materials used represents a variety of anatomical structures and chemical types. Some basketry materials, for example, are naturally coated with waxy materials which are soluble in organic solvents. Others are gummy materials, with components soluble in water.

Because of the complexities of basketry structure, dimensional changes due to RH changes are seldom apparent, but baskets do suffer from embrittlement and discoloration due to a combination of dryness and heat, light, and their own acidity. This brittleness coupled with sloppy handling often leaves baskets ripped and broken, and the gums and waxes which give them their unique colors and textures, lost or denatured. Certain basketry types which are originally quite flexible are subject to breaks and distortion as they become more brittle, so care in handling and storage is imperative.

Unsealed plastic bags are often recommended for storage (left unsealed to prevent condensation). Plastic bags keep dust off the baskets and avoid abrasion between baskets as they sit together on a shelf. For flexible baskets that may be subject to pressure, wads of tissue paper or plastic bags filled with foam packing pellets can be placed inside.

Although light is certainly an important factor in the deterioration of natural basketry materials, its effects are more easily seen on baskets with dyed fibers. Examination of the insides of these pieces will show a major difference between the colors inside and out, and often a difference between one side and the other.

Possibly because of the high incidence of dirt and food residues on baskets, they are subject to mold in high relative humidities. Attacks of insects in baskets are not unknown. It may be important to keep on baskets any remains of food or other material that indicate original use. However, so-called ethnographic remains should not be confused with plain old dirt. Dusty baskets are unsightly, and the dust undoubtedly contributes to mold, pests, and acidic deterioration. Compressed air blown at a basket often removes dirt, but can be overly stressful to very weak baskets. A combination of dusting and vacuuming can sometimes help. But do not ever wash baskets in water. Many basketry fibers swell in water. Baskets with fat coils of grasses can be destroyed by water washing. The coils swell and when they start to dry out, the wrappings of the coils shrink while the insides of the coils are still swollen. This results in the breaking of the wrapping fibers.

Although the results of washing may be less spectacular on other kinds of baskets, the process is still very harmful, and may not even get ingrained dirt out from between the fibers.

The care of basketry is getting to be of more and more interest as the monetary value of baskets soars. Unfortunately, dirt and wear on baskets from original use has left many baskets in collections weak and far from their original appearance. Because of their relative low value until recently, many have not been well cared for. In addition, treatments like impregnation with wax or unsightly repairs have left many pieces in poor condition. Cleaning of dirt and removal of previous treatments are difficult and complicated by the chemical sensitivities of the materials. However, if not roughly handled, baskets, even those in poor condition, will not deteriorate rapidly. Their treatment does not have to be high on a treatment priority list in a mixed collection; treatment of baskets should wait for a conservator well-trained in this field.

Barkcloth

Museum people often disagree about whether barkcloth (tapa) is more properly categorized as paper or textile. Barkcloth is a paper-like material, made of felted vegetable fibers. Objects made of barkcloth are used like textiles, draped and used as clothing. The dispute over the "real" nature of barkcloth sometimes involves which museum department should collect it or whether a paper conservator or textile conservator should treat it, and which methods should be used - those derived from paper conservation or textile conservation.

In fact, barkcloth may be a little of both, but the methods of neither are very appropriate, because most barkcloth is not flat. It was not made flat, and cannot be forced flat. The natural ripples and undulations of barkcloth are not due to dimensional changes from changes in relative humidity; they are a direct result of the production technique. Because barkcloth is not flat, it cannot easily be mounted like a textile or lined like paper. It often cannot be rolled like large textiles. The large size of most tapas makes them a very difficult category of object to handle, to store, and to exhibit.

Objects made of barkcloth often exhibit problems of delamination of the layers, and can be acidic. Their dyes are sometimes water-sensitive, and they sometimes have serious insect damage. If you have a collection of these objects, it is important to anticipate and avoid damage. Many conservators who are not trained or experienced in treating barkcloth can still help you in storing or exhibiting it safely.

Bark Paintings

Both Australian and New Guinea bark paintings can be difficult to handle and display because of their uneven shapes and their flexibility. New Guinea pieces have a tendency toward paint cleavage because the surface of the bark is slick. Australian paintings have a tendency toward powdering of the paint. Both problems are made worse by the responsivenes of these objects to changes in relative humidity.

Some people have subjected bark paintings to flattening procedures and then glued these pieces to boards. This should not be done. It violates the original appearance of the pieces. Attempts like this to keep a piece from responding to changes in relative humidity are doomed from the start; pieces have been known to pull themselves apart after being glued to a board.

Much better is a semi-rigid support that will move with the piece as necessary together with in something that will buffer RH changes.

Bark Objects

Objects made of bark are very sensitive to RH changes, tending to curl, twist and delaminate. Flat pieces of bark like incised scrolls are often encapsulated between glass to allow for easy handling and visibility. For these pieces, careful monitoring is important. Curling of the bark may cause cracking or condensation where the piece touches the glass. The inclusion of some buffering materials like ragboard and perhaps a spacer to allow for some natural curl would probably provide a helpful margin of safety.

Bark baskets should be kept in well-sealed cases to protect them from RH changes and from dust.

Fayum Portraits

Fayum portraits are a good example of how the thickness of wood can be a factor in preservation. These portraits are painted on very thin wood panels that assume their natural curved shape as they cover the face of a mummy. They are quite sensitive to RH changes. Because of the brittleness of the paint, some have severe flaking problems. As with bark paintings, Fayum portraits are commonly flattened and mounted onto a solid support.

As with bark paintings, this is inadvisable both from an historic and conservation point of view.

Ivory

True ivory, that is, elephant tusk, like wood, expands and contracts with changes in relative humidity and can warp because of its grain structure. It tends to develop radial cracks, but also delaminates in layers parallel to the original surface of the tusk. This latter condition may be aggravated by the presence of soluble salts in objects that have been buried. Objects made from whole tusks are very susceptible to damage from changes in RH because of the intersecting pattern of cracks. As ivory ages, the organic components deteriorate, leaving it more brittle. This brittleness, when accompanied by cracking, can leave old ivory pieces quite fragile (See Fig. 20, next page).

Small ivory sculptures like *netsuke* are less likely to have structural problems, because they generally are carved out of the sides of a tusk, not including the central part of the grain structure. They shrink in one direction, but have little tendency to crack. Billiard balls, traditionally made from ivory, are made with this characteristic in mind; they are, or were, made somewhat longer in the grain direction to allow for shrinkage to produce a round ball. Although extremes of RH and rapid changes should certainly be avoided, RH stability is much less crucial for pieces like this than for pieces made of a whole tusk or sculptures that include the center of the tusk.

Ivory, because of its light color, porosity, and because of its chemistry, is very susceptible to staining. Very disfiguring stains can set in from contact with rubber bands, green stains from contact with copper, and rust stains from contact with iron. Ivory can mold if kept in very damp environments; this will likewise leave disfiguring stains.

Ivory can be cleaned of surface dirt with a soft clean brush; additional cleaning may be done on

Fig. 20 Detail of the reverse of an ancient ivory plaque. This piece shows the typical delamination of ancient ivory, aggravated by soluble salts, which tend to force the tiny splinters of material apart. Courtesy Mr. Bernard Selz Collection.

strong objects with small cotton swabs that are just slightly damp with a mixture of water and alcohol. The removal of stains is better left to the professional. Any ivory that shows signs of flaking should be examined and probably treated by a conservator; one sign of trouble is if you can poke a small flake of ivory (gently please) with something not too scratchy (a pointy fingernail or a toothpick) and make it bounce up and down.

For ivory, as for any other material intended to last, do not follow any advice that involves putting stuff on it. Do not coat with baby oil, soak in a cup of warm gelatin, varnish, wax, freeze, or bake in your oven.

Because of their fragility, medieval or ancient ivory plaques should be mounted carefully with only the most stable materials in a way that does not put pressure on them or attempt to flatten any warp they may have taken on. Although mounts covered with a fabric like velvet may seem attractive, they are best avoided because of possible problems with bleeding of dyes. Plexiglas® clips holding them on a Plexiglas® easel may be the safest type of mount. This will allow viewing of both sides and will allow the piece to be picked up without being touched.

Decorative objects imitating ivory have long been made from cellulose nitrate. Any collection that includes nineteenth or twentieth century ivory pieces should be inspected carefully to check for this possibility.

Special Problems: Miniatures on Ivory

Miniatures painted on ivory, on the other hand, are incredibly sensitive to RH changes. The slices of ivory that are used for painting miniatures are so thin as to be translucent; the moisture from the touch of a finger can cause warping. If warping of the ivory occurs inside a tightly-fitting case, the pressure of the case can cause breakage of the ivory.

Ivory miniatures can suffer from several other problems. The extra gum used to create a glossy surface on dark colors and the sugar often added to the medium as a plasticizer make the paint very susceptible to mold growth. The gum can exert strong contractile forces on the paint beneath, causing small-scale flaking of the paint. Some pigments, particularly reds and yellows, are extremely sensitive to light, and the sulfur in air pollution can darken white pigments. In addition, weeping glass has sometimes been seen on miniatures. We can therefore have within a tightly sealed small container an extremely humidity-sensitive piece of ivory, drops of water from the glass, mold growth, flaking paint, and sometimes acidity from cardboard cards used to back the painting. Mold may grow on the locks of hair that are placed in cases with miniatures. These factors put miniatures into a high-priority group for examination by a conservator.

Most conservators are qualified to examine cased miniatures for signs of trouble; few are qualified to treat them, or even remove them from their cases. You should never open a cased miniature; I would even hesitate to do so myself. The few conservators who specialize in miniatures, aside from understanding the problems of the miniatures themselves, understand the structure of the cases, which can be extremely difficult to open without damaging them or their contents.

Leather and other Skin Materials

The term "leather" actually includes two types of material which differ chemically. One is fully tanned leather like that of shoes, purses, and book bindings; the other is usually called "semi-tanned" leather, and includes buckskin, rawhide, and parchment. Tanned leather emerges from its preparation in an acidic condition; semi-tanned leathers do not, and parchment is quite alkaline after processing. The differences in their aging qualities are therefore analagous to those of rag paper vs. wood pulp papers. The "disease" that afflicts acidic leathers is called "red rot". It is characterized by a soft felt-like consistency, powdering, weakness, and loss of surface finish (See Fig. 21). Any abrasion will rub off a characteristic red powder from a piece of red-rotted leather. Red rot is aggravated by high temperatures and relative humidities, by acidic air, and by flexing of the leather. Unfortunately, many leather objects are made to take advantage of the strength and flexibility of new leather; the areas where book bindings, luggage, gun holsters, and the like, flex are the areas where red rot is first apparent. Once red rot begins, the damage it causes is irreversible.

Tanned leather is much more slowly responsive to changes in relative humidity than semi-tanned leather, but all kinds of skin materials may be sensitive to liquid water, although the reactivity of any one object is unpredictable. Parchment is easily soluble in water; much buckskin and tanned leather stains, stiffens, or darkens irreversibly when wet. All skin materials should be well-protected against leaks or drips of water (See Fig. 22, p.168). Desiccation of leather in long periods at relative humidities below about 40% involves irreversible changes in the fibrous structure of leather, and the recommended RH is generally given as 50-55%. It is likely that

Fig. 21 Red rot in a 1920's decorative book binding. The piece of leather covering the spine of the book originally had a rather shiny black surface, which only remains where the tacks kept the leather from flexing. The rest of the leather is soft and spongy in consistency, and has very little strength. Courtesy Mr. and Mrs. Leo Rosen Collection.

Fig. 22 Native American buckskin jacket stained by water. This piece was damaged by a spray of water from firefighters. The spots are actually crusts of dissolved leather. Courtesy the Port Huron Museum of Arts and History.

colder temperatures will provide some protection against acid deterioration, but little museum-quality work has been done to study the long-term effects of cold on this or any other properties of leather.

The application of leather dressings made from various mixtures of oils, waxes, and solvents has been long recommended for stiffened or red-rotted leather. There is probably no other treatment of any kind of object that has fewer advantages and more drawbacks than this. Dressings are intended to slow deterioration by keeping out environmental pollution, to improve the appearance of dull or powdery leather surfaces, and to restore strength and flexibility. Research and simple observation have both concluded no improvement in aging. Leather stiffened from heat or water damage will not be softened by dressings; temporary improvements in flexibility for leather in fairly good condition are of no importance if the piece is not in use. Since leather dressings are designed to impregnate the structure of the leather, they cannot be removed, so they inhibit any future treatment, including repairs of breaks or other structural treatment. Many ingredients in leather dressings increase the oxidation of the leather, increase its acidity, and encourage mold growth. In addition, most dressings stay sticky, making their handling, storage and exhibition difficult, since they stain other objects and attract dirt. These problems occur on the kinds of tanned leather for which the dressings are designed; if dressings are applied to semi-tanned pieces like buckskin, they immediately change the appearance radically. In short, if you are tempted to apply leather dressing to an object, sit down until the urge goes away.

For all kinds of leather, proper storage and exhibition are vital, mainly in the area of proper physical support. Leather objects are easily distorted and torn by long-term hanging, even for pieces which appear to be strong enough to withstand such treatment. The same precautions should be taken with leather as with textiles for physical support, pest control and light.

Parchment is extremely susceptible to changes in relative humidity. Restraining parchment by stretching on a stretcher or attaching to a solid support is completely misguided and will cause more problems than it prevents. Immobilizing parchment by controlling its environment is vital, since buckling can cause losses in any painted design. Because parchment is alkaline, it is a very permanent material, surviving in the proper environment for long periods virtually unchanged. Valuable parchment objects should be carefully containerized in an additionally climate-controlled environment.

Furs are quite difficult to maintain in a museum environment. Very attractive to pests, bulky to store, difficult to clean, furs are best kept in cold storage. Some conservators think that the loss of hair is all but inevitable as the proteins that hold the hair in place age and loosen their grip; whether or not it is inevitable, cold will undoubtedly slow its progress.

Paper

Paper is a fascinating material. Susceptible to damage from virtually everything, easily destroyed by fire and flood, easily ripped to shreds, paper-based objects have survived in large numbers and in excellent condition from every period since paper was first made.

The most potent chronic enemy of paper is acid. Acids in paper contribute to discoloration, brittleness, and eventual powdering to dust. Since the mid-nineteenth century, when attempts were first made to manufacture paper cheaper and cheaper and in larger and larger quantities, acidic materials have been part of most papers. Whether part of the wood pulp or part of the sizing of the paper, these acidic papers have significantly different aging characteristics from the 100% rag paper that has proved through the years to be such an admirable material for works of art and permanent documents.

Some paper objects have other sources of what conservators call "inherent vice". Iron gall inks and certain copper pigments have their own corrosive qualities, and increase the sensitivity of the paper to light, humidity and pollutants, sometimes eating through the paper they touch. Acidity in paper can come from other sources, from the air, from backings, from frames and storage containers, but they can be much more easily dealt with than the acidity that is part of the object. Poor quality paper is one of the major headaches in the field of preservation in art museums, but even more so in libraries and archives.

Because poor aging qualities are so closely tied to acidity, an archivist pen (See *Sources of Supply:* Talas) is a useful tool for anyone dealing with paper collections. An archivist pen is filled with "ink" that is an indicator for pH, the scientific measure of acidity. A small dot of the ink applied to a piece of paper will change to a color that is keyed to a chart that comes with the pen. Although certainly not a hugely accurate instrument, the archivist pen gives a non-conservator some way of classifying objects and planning for their future. (On works of art, only a very small dot of the pen should be used at the reverse corner.)

Another clear indication of the condition of a piece of paper is the presence of foxing, brownish spots that are related to mold growth and/or metallic impurities in the paper. Foxing is increased by high relative humidities, light, and acid surroundings. There are different kinds of foxing, and the causes for different kinds are under debate at present, but any kind of foxing is a sign of a less than optimal environment, as are other kinds of stains and discolorations.

Paper is very sensitive to relative humidity. At different levels of equilibrium moisture content (EMC), paper has quite different properties. It is strongest at about 5-7% EMC (40-50% RH). At higher humidities, it is softer and more easily torn. At very high levels, the surface texture can change, and coated papers stick together. At low relative humidities, paper is more brittle and more easily ripped from flexing. These qualities are mostly recoverable when the changes in RH are reversed.

RH levels have another competing effect on the aging of paper. Because the deterioration of paper is correlated with acidity, higher RH increases the rate of deterioration. In general, the rate of reaction of any organic material can be said to be cut in half for every 10°C. (18° F.) decrease. For paper the rate is considerably higher. Some research has shown that, because of the reduction in acid-related damage from the lowering of both temperature and relative humidity, a change from about 70° F., 50% RH to 40° F., 5% RH will result in an extension of the usable life of alkaline paper of five hundred times, and of acid paper, one thousand times.

If colder and/or drier conditions for the storage of paper are possible, if, for example, a facility for cold storage of photographic materials is available,

it should certainly be considered for long-term storage of paper. Because of the brittleness of paper at low RH, it must be stored so as not to be flexed or folded. The transition to different RH or temperature levels must be accomplished gradually in either direction. If cold storage for books is to be attempted, the books should probably be fanned open while the changes are taking place to minimize stress from uneven dimensional changes. Cold storage is certainly not in the near future going to be a common tactic for the preservation of any organic material, but the realities of life cannot be denied. A very long-term cold facility would be a kind of time capsule for propelling a select group of objects relatively unchanged into the distant future.

Real cold storage is not a likely circumstance, but if indoor wintertime temperatures are 75 to 80°, consider lowering them to 70° or 68° or 65° if you can stand it. Doubling the life of a valuable item is quite an accomplishment, particularly if you can do it while saving energy.

Changes in relative humidity put paper through quick dimensional changes. Because the paper reacts all at once as long as the whole sheet is exposed, the mechanical stresses on the material are not as destructive as changes to wood, for example, but frequent cycling undoubtedly takes its toll on the strength of a leaf of paper. In cases where the paper is restrained in some way, dimensional changes can be very damaging. Paper that has been stretched can rip. Rippling of a sheet of paper can cause powdering or flaking of thick pigment layers. In tightly closed books, where RH changes affect the paper very slowly, distortions of the whole structure of the book can be caused by drastic RH changes.

Light is a major cause of the deterioration of both paper and the media used on it. Acidic paper is even more sensitive to light than alkaline or neutral papers, but all will discolor and become more brittle and weak from light exposure, both visible and ultraviolet. Watercolors are very susceptible to fading, pastels somewhat less so, charcoals even less. The dyes and pigments used in hand-colored prints of the nineteenth century are quite fugitive. Inks vary greatly in their light resistance. Even within one document, different batches or slightly different formulations of ink can show differences in response to light fading. Some carbon inks are quite resistant to light, but because of the sensitivity of the paper and the difficulty of routine chemical identification of inks, this should not be an excuse to subject anything on paper to higher light levels than are otherwise recommended.

Although, as has been discussed above, museums commonly exhibit prints and drawings under reasonably proper conditions, many museum exhibitions of other kinds include one or more objects on paper,

either art or archival material. Many historic house museums have paper objects on permanent exhibition. In these cases, consideration should be given to the display of photocopies or photographs of the original. Exhibition must not become the justification for certain destruction of the items in our care. Acute damage - rips and holes and stains - can usually be repaired; fading and soiling and discoloration from environmental causes cannot. In the case of paper more than any other kind of object, the discoloration and embrittlement of the support coupled with the fading of the medium will leave us eventually and inevitably with a symphony of brown on brown, an unrecoverable image on an irredeemable support.

Air pollution is a major source of paper deterioration, sulfur dioxide being the most important culprit. Ozone has also been implicated in dark fading of watercolor pigments. Paper acts as a kind of filter for air pollution as air passes through it, so pollutants build up in the structure of the paper, adding to the internal acidity. Dust and soot are extremely disfiguring, damaging, and difficult to remove. Containerization of paper is therefore vital. The worse the air, the more important a tightly sealed container is. If more of the acidity source is internal, the container should be vented, or alkaline buffers should be included in the package.

Acidic framing or backing materials cause serious damage to paper. Many prints and drawings are permanently disfigured by brown stains from adhesive tapes or so-called mat burns - brown areas where an acidic mat has touched the object. Many objects have brown designs on the reverse that are imprints of acid mounts - stripes from corrugated cardboard or stripes and swirls from the grain of a wood backing. The materials causing these problems must be removed as soon as possible. Additional treatment to remove adhesive residues or stains should be carried out by an experienced conservator. Washing and bleaching can generally reduce if not completely eliminate the stains, but bleaching can weaken the structure of the paper and leave the overall color too white, so conservators would rather keep bleaching to a minimum.

Infestation of either insects or mold on paper are signs of poor environmental conditions, improper framing in which the paper touches the glass, or something else almost always correctable at the source. Monitoring of paper, particularly when it is in long-term storage, is still important. Schedules for random opening of boxes or other containers for paper are vital in checking for infestation or for any other kind of unexpected condition change.

Sloppy handling is another major enemy of paper. Rips, folds, bashed-in corners, grease stains, and other unsightly messes are usually avoidable. Proper matting, framing, or other kinds of containerization should virtually eliminate even the need to be careful, which is the only certain way to avoid damage. Paper clips, tape, pins, glue, staples, ink, and stickers are all potential sources of damage; do not allow any of them to touch paper you are trying to preserve.

Containerization, either in storage or on exhibition, is clearly the one tactic that will help to avoid damage from almost all of the hazards that await works on paper: relative humidity changes, light, gaseous and particulate pollution, pests, and sloppy handling. It is vital, of course, that all materials making up a container be of the highest archival quality, with no acids, dyes or adhesives that might bleed, or rough edges that might scratch. Acidic paper objects should be interleaved with alkaline paper like buffered tissue to avoid having acid fumes accumulate and accelerate deterioration.

The typical containerization for works of art, either prints or drawings, is for each work to be mounted onto a backing board of four-ply ragboard with two hinges made of Japanese tissue adhered with pure starch paste. A window mat hinged to the side of the backing board provides some protection to the front and offers a safe place for labelling. For storage, a piece of thin paper, usually acid-free glassine or buffered tissue, is placed over the object and under the mat. The package is made in standard sizes so that uniform stacks of matted and mounted works can be stored together in boxes. The standard container is called a Solander box and is in itself excellent environmental protection. Solander boxes in large sizes are not as rigid as would be desirable for easy handling; some other forms of boxes are sold for the same purpose.

When matted and mounted works are needed for exhibition, the slip sheet is pulled out, and the work in its mat is put directly into a standard-size frame. A stiff board, often Fome-cor® is added at the back, and the package is secured in the frame with brads or metal straps and screws. All handling of the paper is avoided, and the whole process is simple and quick.

For works to be exhibited in very polluted environments, many conservators recommend further sealing the frame. This can be done in several different ways. One is to tape the edges of the glass or Plexiglas® to the frame with Scotch Magic® Tape, place the object in the frame, add a backing board, and then tape mylar over the reverse. Some people report problems of dirt accumulating on walls behind the mylar because of static electricity. An alternative is to make a sandwich of the Fome-cor®, the matted and mounted object, and the Plexiglas®, and wrap the edges with the same tape.

This whole pre-sealed package can then be secured in the frame.

Radical changes in relative humidity will affect pieces in even the best-sealed frame. Paper under these conditions can be expected to ripple in the frame. This is not a cause for concern unless the ripples touch the Plexiglas® or the edge of the paper catches on the inside edge of the mat.

For frames backed with mylar or for pictures hung against a cold exterior wall, small separators of about 1/4 inch between the back of the frame and the wall can be used. Squares of Fome-cor® or small corks can be glued to the reverse of the frame to provide this separation.

Framing for works on paper is usually done with Plexiglas® UF-3 (Rohm and Haas) or its equivalent, with the exception of charcoals, pastels, and chalk drawings, where the static charge on the plastic can be a hazard. Glass is therefore recommended for these media. It is important that no paper object touch the glass or Plexiglas®, so for large pieces, or pieces that for some other reason might ripple or belly out, thicker layers of matting should be provided.

For archival rather than art materials, matting and mounting onto ragboard is prohibitively labor-intensive, the cost of materials is too high, and the space required for the final package is too great. For archival materials, other formats are customary. Acid-free folders, various kinds of envelopes, and plastic sleeves are all possibilities. Although lamination, that is, adhesion to a plastic support, has been common in the past, many pieces have been damaged by harmful adhesives, so the process has been largely discredited. The alternative to lamination is encapsulation between two pieces of fairly stiff plastic film (mylar or polyethylene) which are adhered only to each other around all four edges. Encapsulated paper can be handled fairly safely, and this process is often done in collections where documents are handled by researchers. Acidic paper should not, however, be encapsulated without deacidification.

The choices of formats, materials, and housings (file cabinets, shelves, boxes) are so numerous that an experienced archivist should be consulted before any large project is undertaken. Condition of the collection, patterns of use and exhibition, access to conservation professionals, environmental conditions, staffing levels, and the availability of funds are all important factors in these decisions.

Because paper is so sensitive to its surroundings, surveys of the general environment and of the housings of each piece of paper are both vital in preservation efforts. For collections that have not been professionally supervised, a technician trained and supervised by a conservator should be able to survey a collection one piece at a time and remove all acidic backings that are not glued to the reverse. Objects adhered all over to an acid backing should be set aside for a conservator. These objects should be attended to without too much delay, as the acid backings create a great deal of both chemical damage from acidity and physical danger to the paper object from embrittlement and breaking of the board. Loose tapes can be removed, but any tape stuck to the object or adhesive residue should be looked at by a conservator. Framed pieces that you are not certain have been framed with acid-free materials should be removed from their frames. The mounts, mats and backing should be checked for the presence of acidic materials, and the pieces should be examined. It is an unfortunate fact that no dealer or framer can be relied on to provide acid-free mats and backings unless specifically instructed to do so. Even with instructions, periodic checks of work done by an outside contractor should be made with an archivist pen to assure that instructions are always being followed.

For pieces that have been framed to your direct knowledge with proper materials, the frames should be opened perhaps every ten years and the glass or Plexiglas® cleaned, the piece examined and resealed. It is surprising how dirty the inside of a frame can get, partially with particles from the object itself.

Special Problems: Contemporary Paper Objects

Contemporary works on paper pose some special problems because of the use of non-traditional materials. Construction paper, newsprint, translucent papers like tracing paper and other unorthodox supports are very light-sensitive and acidic. Media like markers, colored inks, or "Day-glo" paints are sensitive to light. Oil paint used on paper causes oil stains around the painted areas and accelerates aging of the paper. Works made with these factors of "inherent vice" should be protected with the most stringent measures possible. Even the finest conservation treatments and the most careful environmental protection may not preserve the intended appearance of these pieces, or their monetary value, for very long. Collecting pieces with this kind of inherent vice is a decision that should not be made lightly. If at all possible, a conservator should examine such pieces before acquisition to give a likely prognosis. Any living artist should be asked for a list of materials used, as this will aid both in the purchase decision and in any future conservation treatments.

Many contemporary artists work in very large formats, which create serious problems in mounting, storage, and exhibition. Providing a rigid support for large pieces can entail major expense. Most sheet materials, even acidic ones, are available in four-by-eight-foot sheets; larger pieces have to be special-ordered. Panels fabricated with thin skins of ragboard or Fibreglas® around a layer of honeycomb (a construction like that of hollow-core doors) are sometimes the only way to provide a rigid support for framing oversized works. These are excellent ways to solve the problem, but cost about $25 per square foot. Plan ahead: do not acquire oversized paper without consulting a conservator first. The conservator can provide specifications for a framer based on the size and materials of the object so that you can estimate the possible costs that lie ahead. Acquiring oversized paper without providing foolproof protection is inviting disaster. It is a particular shame to expose a new and pristine object to almost inevitable damage because of a lack of planning.

Collages are a mainly twentieth-century art form that present enormous problems of preservation because of the ephemeral nature of the papers and other materials often used in their construction. Adhesives used are seldom archival ones, and either come loose easily or leave stains on the collage. These objects can become a conservator's nightmare. If you are considering acquiring one, think long and hard first. If you are in charge of a collection with collages, put them first on your list for the highest quality framing or storage, and for the most stringent environmental protection.

Special Problems: Oriental Paper

Oriental scrolls have some special requirements that make them quite different from Western works on paper. Because scrolls are usually kept rolled and exhibited only rarely, they are protected to a great extent from light. Traditional Japanese practice puts them into an inner box of uncoated wood and an outer box of lacquered wood. They are thereby protected against extreme climatic fluctuations. However, they are not protected from very low relative humidities. Although it is true that low RH in itself does not cause damage to paper, it does result in brittleness, and brittleness is a serious problem for multi-layer pieces which are periodically rolled and unrolled. Scrolls kept in dry environments are therefore very subject to damaging cracks and creases parallel to the rollers, accompanied by separations of the painting from the mounting layers of paper and silk. The adhesive used, starch paste, is quite hygroscopic; this is another reason why RH control is important. In some Western collections, scrolls are stored flat to avoid this problem, but this is awkward to manage, and subjects the pieces to damage they would not be exposed to if kept rolled.

Humidity in Japan is high all year round. The system of rolled paintings and traditional storage is designed for this environment where materials are at maximum flexibility. For Oriental scrolls, therefore, RH levels of 55-60% are recommended, with 50% as perhaps the lower limit.

Oriental screens represent another set of problems. Because the paper is under tension, low RH levels may lead to cracking, and very high levels may cause rippling. Pigments are often thickly applied; dimensional changes in the paper may result in flaking of paint layers. Screens are traditionally stored in wooden boxes which buffer them against quick changes in relative humidity, but as with scrolls, will not protect them against long periods of low relative humidity.

Japanese prints are more commonly collected by private individuals or modest museums than screens and scrolls. When matted and framed properly they are not very sensitive to RH changes, but unfortunately the most common pigments used in Japanese prints are very light-sensitive. Some research indicates that common colors of Japanese prints would fade noticeably in ten years at 5,000 footcandle-hours per year, or in one year of constant exhibition at 5 footcandles. Because some colors fade faster than others, fading throws off the color balance of Japanese prints. The printing processes, media, and paper of Japanese prints make the kinds of treatment customary on Western pieces inappropriate. When these objects need treatment, be especially careful to find a conservator who is experienced in this branch of the field.

Indian miniatures often are painted with thick layers of pigments that become quite brittle. RH control is therefore important to avoid rippling of the paper and consequent flaking of the paint, and careful handling and mounting are necessary to help avoid any flexing.

Special Problems: Pastels and Charcoals

Pastels and charcoals present special problems because they consist of dry pigments clinging to paper mainly by friction. Vibration is a major enemy of pastels and charcoals; loans of this materials should never even be considered. Pastels and charcoals should not be hung on the kind of rolling screens commonly used in museums for storage of framed paintings. Plexiglas® or similar material should never be used to frame pastels or charcoals because the static electricity can pull the pigments off the paper.

Pastels are subject to mold growth and should be framed well away from glass to prevent even the slightest possibility of the paper touching the glass. In fact, all possible arrangements should be made so that nothing touches the surface of a charcoal or pastel. Proper framing is probably the safest way to protect these objects from abrasion; they should never be stored like prints or drawings. Pastels and charcoals are less sensitive to light than water colors, but still should be exhibited with the same precautions as any other work on paper.

Special Problems: Stamps

As with coins, major problems with stamps can be prevented by proper housing. Polyester (mylar) enclosures are preferred over vinyl because the plasticizers in vinyl can cause off-setting of the inks onto the plastic. Stamps, like any paper, are responsive to changes in relative humidity. Unused stamps, with their layer of hygroscopic adhesive, are more responsive than used stamps, but proper housing should help to avoid condition problems in all but the most extreme environments. Conservators have seldom become involved with stamp collections, and few if any have experience in the treatment of stamps. The field of philately likewise has little or no experience in dealing with questions of what conservation treatments would do to the value of stamps. Problems like bent corners due to careless handling are of course best avoided altogether, and the small size of stamps makes treatment difficult, but not impossible. If you wish to get a conservator involved in the care of a stamp collection, be prepared to educate them as they educate you. The collaboration might turn out to be extremely productive.

Photographic Materials

Photographic prints and negatives consist of several extremely sensitive materials like paper, gelatin, finely divided silver, and dyes in thin layers that have been flooded with extremely strong chemicals. Collections of historical photographs may also include supports of glass, darkened iron, porcelain, and a variety of plastics, and image layers of collodion (related to cellulose nitrate) and albumen. Many old photographs were originally mounted all over onto acidic boards, sources of both chemical and physical damage. Some of the processing chemicals make the prints and negatives incredibly sensitive to light, and although most of the chemicals are washed out in later steps of processing, enough remain in most cases to continue to influence the behavior of the print. Photographs and negatives are sensitive to moisture, changes in RH, acidity, temperature, pollutants, light, and fungus growth. Negatives and certain other media are also extremely sensitive to abrasion. At the same time, the more finished appearance of fine art photographs is due to extremely subtle characteristics of tones, surface texture, and gloss.

Damaged photographs are very difficult to treat, and there are very few conservators specializing in this field. Serious research on the physical properties of photographs has been going on for a relatively short time; there is a great deal that is not known about the reactions of photographs to their surroundings. Detailed documentation of photographs on exhibition, for example, has shown that they change in ways that are difficult to understand and predict. Silver images have been seen to get darker during storage at low relative humidities, and reactions of photographs to different storage enclosures has been somewhat inexplicable. For all these reasons, the prevention of damage and the slowing of deterioration are vital for photograph collections. In general, collections of old photographs should be among the first in a collection to be examined by a conservator.

Physical difficulties are compounded by theoretical ones. Twentieth century photographs made by artists, or people who thought of themselves as artists, should be handled like other art objects. The actual vintage print is to be considered the legitimate artistic output of the artist, and a later posthumous print made from the artist's original negative by another photographer is often regarded in the same way as a re-strike from a printer's plate — a possibly accurate reproduction but not the same as the original work of art. Historical photographs, either family portraits or photographs made for journalistic purposes or those meant to be sold as souvenirs of particular places, are usually not in the same category. In these cases, is it more important to preserve the negative (if it still exists) or the actual historic print? If the original vintage print were in terrible condition, would a new print from the same negative be a reasonable stand-in? How do we decide if a print is more a work of art or more an archival object that is mainly important for the information it contains?

Uncertainties aside, virtually all of what should be done to care for photographic collections is clear. Light exposure is particularly harmful to photographs; exhibition should be minimal. If possible copy prints rather than originals should be exhibited. Do not drymount prints; do not use rubber cement or adhesive tape. Containerization in the highest-quality materials will protect against air pollution, sudden RH changes, and handling. High temperatures and extremes of relative humidity should be avoided; very low temperatures (probably the lower the better) in moderate to low relative humidities are recommended. Protection against water damage is vital.

For more detailed recommendations, much more must be known about the collection in question. A host of techniques (many not including paper at all), materials, and formats have been used since the invention of photography and will have to be identified before further steps can be taken.

As with general paper collections, containerization is the major issue in photograph conservation. As with archival storage, there are several choices within the range of proper materials (and many harmful choices too). The catalogues (and the staffs) of companies specializing in archival products are a great help, because they generally manufacture to the most up-to-date standards published by conservators. Even collections of photographs that have as yet no historic value will probably be highly treasured by family members in the future, so the use of archival materials should not be limited to museums. Color photographs are probably the only medium that fades in the dark, and even ten-year-old snapshots are quite a different color than when they were new. If you are not interested in taking black-and-white archivally proper photos of your children or your dog, it is still worth something to buy an archivally safe scrapbook to put your best photos in.

Color photographs as art should be kept in cold storage. Artists who work in this medium should be encouraged by their collectors to make color separations, which will provide unfaded prints in the future. RH levels around 30-35% are probably best.

Special Problems: Cellulose Nitrate

Cellulose nitrate is a major headache in photograph conservation. Cellulose nitrate was the first plastic, used through the 1930's in several formats, and until 1951 for motion picture film. Still used for many purposes, it is quite inexpensive to produce and has many desirable properties. Unfortunately, it has a major very undesirable property. Cellulose nitrate has a pattern of deterioration that ends in complete destruction. After proceeding through stages of being discolored, sticky, bubbly, distorted, brittle, and crumbly, it ends up as powder. As it deteriorates, it gives off nitric acid fumes, and it become more and more flammable and explosive. Light speeds up the deterioration of cellulose nitrate, as does continued exposure to its own fumes. Small amounts are not dangerous, but create a harmful environment for objects nearby. Even in buffered paperenvelopes, the fumes get into the air of drawers or boxes, and cause deterioration of the paper and of non-nitrate (safety) films.

Because of differences in initial chemistry, processing, and previous history, different films deteriorate at different rates, and the times of onset vary widely too. Many films will appear completely un-deteriorated, but will be substantially damaged one year later. Uncertainty as to when the process will start makes managing a collection difficult.

The fire hazard is enormous; nitrate fires have occurred in more than one motion picture film repository. In fires, cellulose nitrate emits enormous amounts of lethal gases and commonly causes explosions. Regular methods of fire control are ineffective, because the exclusion of oxygen does not stop a sizeable nitrate fire. Institutions with a large volume of nitrate film should inform their local firefighters of the exact location of the films. Some insurance policies are written to exclude coverage in the presence of nitrate film. The consequences of dealing with cellulose nitrate involve much more than the future of a few artifacts. If you think you have substantial amounts of nitrate film and cannot provide proper storage, either give it away or bring it to your local fire station to have it destroyed.

A preferable alternative includes copying the negatives before disposing of them. For large collections, this is a massive job, but a vital one. Given any mixed collection, the safe care of cellulose nitrate films should be a number one priority.

Cold storage will greatly slow deterioration and will certainly lessen the danger of fire. The National Fire Protection Assocation (See *Sources of Information:* NFPA) code for motion picture film is 35° F. at 50% RH, but a strictly legal vault includes fume venting, pressure valves, and fire extinguishing equipment, something not within many museums' range. Cold storage in water-proof containers to avoid condensation and to protect against malfunctions, should be a short-term solution until copying can be carried out.

Special Problems: Diacetate Films

Diacetate, the successor to nitrate, is dimensionally unstable. Although not a safety hazard, in later stages of deterioration, it shrinks so much that the emulsion layer is tented away from the surface. This process results in the film becoming useless for printing. Historic photograph collections should be surveyed as early as possible. Diacetate negatives, like nitrate ones, should be copied before it becomes impossible.

Textiles

Textiles are a very difficult type of object to handle properly. Textiles, like paper, are very susceptible to all kinds of damage. At the same time, it is hard for people to treat textiles like other works of art because they are so familiar. They do not engender the kind of reverence that paintings or exotic materials do, and they rarely have the monetary value of other kinds of objects. It is difficult for any person in today's society to appreciate the incredible amount of effort required in the production of textiles before the industrial revolution. The importance of textiles in other cultures has been difficult for traditional art historians to understand, partly because in contemporary society textiles have to do with fashion, not high art. In addition, historic textiles are almost all anonymous productions, and throughout history have been largely women's work.   The poor condition of many old textiles makes them shadows of their true selves, faded, brittle, creased, broken along fold lines (See Fig. 23), all sheen gone, unable to be draped or handled or worn as they were. In order for most textiles to be stored or exhibited safely, they must be mounted flat, thereby in many cases obliterating any traces of their original function or appearance.

To add to the problems of caring for textile collections, many collections that have any textiles at all have dozens or even hundreds of similar items. Textiles have been made all over the world, and are possibly among the most varied groups of objects, coming in all sizes and shapes. This makes storage and exhibition, as well as treatment, difficult. Textiles commonly must be treated to be exhibitable, and treatments are usually very time-consuming, not unusually costing more than the market value of the object.

Because textiles seem like such familiar objects, old textiles are often treated by owners as they would treat expensive clothes. Many people wash old textiles in a "mild" detergent, mend rips, darn holes, and line textiles by sewing. Unfortunately, all these procedures can be quite harmful. Old textiles have been altered so much that they may have little in common with new textiles and cannot be treated in the same ways. Old silk in particular can sometimes have more in common with brittle old newsprint than new silk.

Even professional conservators have not taken the field of textile conservation seriously. It is still not uncommon for museum conservation departments to have lower professional standards for textile conservators than for conservators in other fields. Volunteers are still by far more commonly accepted in textile laboratories than in others.

Fig. 23 Japanese silk *obi* damaged at an old crease. Although this piece was probably not used after the silk along the crease became worn, it was undoubtedly stored still folded. Stress from the fold line accelerates chemical damage to the fibers. Courtesy Sandra and Michael Saltzman Collection.

The intrinsic properties of textiles depend on the type of fibers used to make them. The cellulose fibers (linen, cotton) have a different chemistry from the protein fibers (wool, silk), but the differences in response of these fibers to their environment is not so great as to affect recommendations for their care. Other things about textiles, their condition, their size, or their original function, are more relevant reasons to adjust the methods with which we store, exhibit, or treat them.

The effects of temperature and relative humidity on textiles are similar to those on paper. RH levels have an effect on the brittleness of the individual fibers, and cycling of relative humidity results over the long term in weakening of the fibers. Low humidity levels over long periods can, similar to leather, result in desiccated fibers that turn to powder with even slight handling or vibration. Wool that has been removed from Andean tombs is the classic example of desiccation. Powder seems to be created even when these pieces are not moved. Silk is said to be strongest at low relative humidities (ca. 20%) and to deteriorate faster at higher RH levels, but this figure is so much lower than that regarded as safe for other fibers that I have never seen an institution attempt to store silk at this level. Cold storage, although largely untested for textiles, would undoubtedly improve the long-term preservation of all textiles.

Light is of course an enemy of textiles, damaging both the fibers and dyes. Silk is the most sensitive fiber, wool the least. Cellulose tends to be more sensitive to ultraviolet light, and dyes, more sensitive to visible light. Many natural dyes undergo noticeable fading in one year of minimal light exposure. At very low (about 25%) RH, a significant reduction in fading has been reported, but the same study showed no difference betwen fading rates at 45 and 65%. In general, the rate of fading can be expected to increase with higher RH, but the data on specific fibers and dyes is incomplete, and fiber deterioration at an RH as low as 25% rules out this level for preservation.

Following the five-footcandle, four-month-per-year rule for textiles is much more difficult than observing the same rule for paper-based pieces. Textiles are often exhibited with many other kinds of objects from a single culture. Japanese ceramics and textiles, for example, might be mixed with lacquer and wooden or stone sculpture and Japanese prints. The prints could easily be rotated with other prints of about the same size and subject matter, but because of the varying sizes of textiles and the amount of work that goes into their mounting, it is much less likely that the textiles can be rotated. There is no good way to ameliorate the harmful effects of light under these conditions except to stress that pieces be taken off exhibition when at all possible. Permanent exhibition of textiles should not be allowed under any circumstances, but undoubtedly will continue in some otherwise careful institutions. The lowest feasible light levels should be maintained.

The effects of air pollution are also similar to those on paper. All the air that circulates through textiles leaves its legacy of both gaseous and particulate pollution. Acids are harmful to all textiles, and dust, particularly if sooty, is very difficult if not impossible to wash out of fragile textiles. The effects of particular pollutants on particular fibers vary, but no fiber is immune to their effects. Silver and copper-alloy threads on textiles are particularly sensitive to pollutants. Acidic mounts should be removed from textiles both because of acidic contamination and because of the possibility of breakage. Gases from cardboard boxes cause deterioration, and various anti-oxidants in plastics, particularly the thin plastics used in drycleaners' bags, have been implicated in yellowing of textiles. Any wrappings or containerization of textiles must involve only archival-quality materials.

Textiles are well-known victims of insect infestation. Moths and other insects tend to go for dirty textiles, so cleanliness is a must. Frequent inspection is likewise vital. Textiles must be protected against staining, spills, abrasion, and sharp folds. Any piece that must be folded should be folded in a different place than it had been - folding a piece into thirds instead of in two is often helpful. Rolls of tissue paper inside the folds will help avoid creases and eventual breaks at the fold.

Handling of textiles is a major hazard. Textiles weakened by age must not be stressed in any way. This means virtually no handling of the textile itself. Textiles should almost always be laid on ragboard or other solid supports. For small pieces, containers like those for paper, with a backing, a mat, and a cover sheet can be used. Thicker containers that many conservators affectionately refer to as pizza boxes can be made out of archival materials. These provide easy access with protection from shifting temperature and relative humidity, protection from insects, sloppy handling, and light. The boxes can be stacked on shelves for storage.

Some museums have devised methods where the boxes can be opened and used for exhibition displayed on the diagonal or, with some sewing, in a frame.

Designs for containerization must be quite flexible to provide for very long narrow things like sashes that can be partially rolled in the container, or to allow for three-dimensional pieces. It is sometimes difficult to make containers that are rigid enough in larger sizes. However, the idea of containerizing textiles is the only practical way of providing for sizeable textile collections. Various kinds of mounting methods used for exhibition are incredibly time-consuming to do and very expensive in terms of materials. The finished pieces take up a great deal of space and can be quite heavy. In addition, most traditional mounting methods involve sewing or adhering a textile to a colored backing fabric. The color schemes and textures of mounting fabrics chosen do not always stand the test of time, leaving a mounted piece looking its age - not the age of the piece, but rather the age of the mounting fabric.

Samplers and other embroidered pictures are often found nailed around a wooden stretcher and framed directly against glass. This raises the possibility of mold where the piece touches the glass. Stretching the textile on a stretcher puts tremendous stress on the textile and tends to pull open small rips or holes. The textile is rarely protected at the back from dirt, and backings are usually acidic. The opening of framed textiles should be done as early as possible. The pieces, once removed from their frames, can be laid on ragboard and covered with buffered tissue or containerized with a mat and a cover sheet.

Minimal sewing done for exhibition often involves stitches placed only around the edges of a textile. With time, the textile stretches under its own weight and "bellies out". On the other hand, extensive sewing is extremely time-consuming, sometimes hard on the piece, and can be almost impossible to remove. For these reasons, more and more textile conservators are recommending that pieces be shown on a slanted fabric-covered board. The use of fabrics with some "tooth" like cotton velvet provides overall support without any of the hazards of more permanent mounting techniques.

Large textiles like flags, quilts, Navajo blankets and carpets present more difficult problems. For exhibition, strong textiles can be hung from a strip of Velcro® across the top. Textiles not strong enough may require major treatment before exhibition is possible. For storage, thin textiles like flags, if they are strong, can be rolled onto a large-diameter cardboard (acid-free or covered with barrier paper) roller interleaved with tissue paper or other material. Rugs can also be rolled. Such rolled pieces should not be stored lying on a shelf but rather suspended using a chain or rod through the center of the roller. Thick textiles like quilts or embroideries cannot be rolled safely, but can be accordion-pleated on a shelf or in a storage box with padding in the folds. Weak or brittle large textiles like old silk flags may require storage in large flat archival boxes as an alternative to extensive treatment.

Major projects involving the rehousing of textile collections in drawers, on slide-out shelves in cabinets, or in acid-free cardboard boxes would be a major improvement for virtually every textile collection that has not been so treated within the last ten years. Such projects commonly involve both conservators and non-conservators and provide a rare opportunity to examine, catalogue, and condition a whole collection, and to make a major contribution to its survival without the risks or costs of intensive conservation treatment.

Costumes and Costume Accessories

Costumes compound the problems of textiles by not allowing the simple solution of storing them flat. Makers of costumes and costume accessories were unconcerned with permanence, and often made them of incompatible materials which are very light-sensitive. Costumes are often contaminated from use, which leaves behind acidic soiling. The loss of original properties of the textile can be disastrous here. Usual storage and exhibition procedures involve hanging costumes on padded hangers perhaps with additional support at the hips or dressing specially-prepared mannequins. Even the most cautious use of either of these methods cannot protect a costume that rips along crease lines or cannot support its own weight. Heavily beaded dresses and knit dresses that cannot be hung safely should be laid flat with as few folds as possible, and with all folds padded, on a shelf or in a box, but this requires a great deal of storage space.

The care of costume collections is a complex task best left to those specializing in it, but many small institutions have a small number of costumes that need care if they are not to lose their value. Many collections have holdings of fans, parasols, shoes, or other costume accessories. The mixed materials that form these items make the most stringent precautions necessary.

Fans and parasols need to be padded so that they are under no stress. Shoes should be stuffed with acid-free tissue to avoid distortion. Hats may need interior supports that assure no pressure on their rims.

Collections of twentieth century costumes and accessories most likely will include plastic buttons, jewelry, or imitation tortoise shell or ivory made of cellulose nitrate. This is the same material that makes photographic collections so dangerous. In small lumps isolated with other materials and with plenty of ventilation, fire is an unlikely hazard, but the fumes of deterioration can cause serious deterioration in objects in contact with it. Cellulose nitrate belts, buttons, purse handles, etc., should be isolated from other objects, photographed, and wrapped in buffered paper. Once deterioration has begun, pieces should be discarded.

Miscellaneous Organic Materials

Lacquer

Oriental lacquer (urushi) is the resin from a particular tree that dries by chemical reaction rather than by evaporation from a solution. (Many objects referred to as being lacquer are actually other materials made in imitation of the real thing.) Real lacquer is a very tough material that is unfortunately susceptible to damage from light. Light damage involves both fading of colors and chemical changes that make the lacquer more soluble. Light-damaged lacquer objects may therefore be damaged by cleaning solutions that would otherwise have been safe.

Many lacquer pieces have substrates of wood, paper pulp or cloth, and many objects also have elaborate inlays of metals, mother-of-pearl, or other materials. Because of the reactivity of the substrate to changes in relative humidity and the brittleness of the lacquer and most of the inlays, lacquer objects are at the top of conservators' lists of troublesome pieces. Treatment of lacquer is extremely difficult because of the brittleness of the lacquer layers and the unpredictability of its behavior with solvents and heat. Lacquer should join the objects that receive the best environmental control any owner can muster.

Shells

Shells (including egg shells) are calcium carbonate objects very susceptible to acid damage. The white or gray water-soluble salts that form on shells from acids in their surroundings are called Byne's disease, after the person who first described it. These salts are organic crystals from organic acids like those from cardboard boxes and oak cabinets. Byne's disease, if allowed to persist, will turn shells to powder. Coatings slow down the growth of Byne's disease, but are not recommended as they constitute both aesthetic

and chemical alteration of the original. Hygroscopic salts in the shells may aggravate the problem, so washing of shells in water may be helpful. Shells stored in cardboard boxes should be removed as soon as possible. With collections like these that may not be receiving first class attention, it is all the more important to avoid problems that might decimate a collection or necessitate the expenditure of money for treatment. If a shell collection is not worth keeping properly, give it away.

Feathers

Feathers are usually part of complex objects made of many different materials. Feathers suffer mainly from rough handling and from the accumulation of dirt. Long periods of exposure to high light levels cause fading in many kinds of feathers. Feathers often protrude from objects in ways that make them easily damaged. Many such objects can barely be put down on a table without ruffling the feathers. Mounting methods that support the whole object and that protect any protruding parts are vital.

Amber

Amber is not a major component in many collections, but it is very susceptible to damage from many different kinds of fumes: pesticides, solvents, and pollutants can all be absorbed by amber and, when they evaporate, leave the surface crizzled. Another problem with amber is the difficulty in identifying real amber from various copies. Chemical analysis appears to be the only way to do this. Some amber in a collection may be cellulose nitrate, so sudden condition changes should be monitored carefully.

Special Problems: Natural History Specimens

Conservation problems with organic natural history specimens have come under professional consideration only recently, because in previous generations most animal and plant specimens were considered replaceable. With extinction close for many species and with laws against collecting of specimens, the specimens already in museums have taken on an importance that they never had before. Animal and plant specimens on exhibition are subject to fading and accelerated aging from light exposure; in dark storage they are subject to insect infestation. Typical storage for hide collections has consisted of hanging hides from strings threaded through the eyes or ear holes, ripping the hides and causing distortion. Herbarium specimens were routinely glued to acidic boards with adhesives that darkened and became brittle with age. Museums can no longer afford these kinds of deterioration of specimens that may already be, or may soon be, rare sources of information on their species.

Systematics collections of organics are subject to extreme damage from insects when they are put away in cabinets and left for long periods without inspection. Once an infestation starts, it can proceed quickly, because there is so much similar material in close proximity. The fact that such collections may in the past have been impregnated with pesticides may not prevent infestation, because insects have to eat a great deal before they die from the poison.

Among feathers and hides, bones and horn, flowers and bug bodies, organic natural history specimens are subject to deterioration from light, heat, changes in relative humidity, insects and mold, rough handling, and all the other ills flesh is heir to. Containerization of specimens equivalent to what is done with works of art of similar material is not often feasible because of the huge numbers of specimens involved. Money is seldom available for major rehousing projects or for sophisticated environmental control, and in some natural history collections, the collections themselves have low priority compared to other matters like research or field work. At the same time, little organized effort has gone into attempts to treat damaged or deteriorated specimens.

The physical needs of such collections are no mystery: RH levels ideally between 40 and 50%, temperatures below 70° F., lower if possible, clean well-circulated air, and physical support for specimens to avoid distortions and damage from handling would all be very nice. How to see that these collections receive even a nod in this direction is more difficult.

Objects of Mixed Materials

Paintings

It may seem disrespectful to refer to paintings as "objects of mixed materials", but from a technical point of view, that is what they are. An understanding of their behavior and patterns of deterioration depends on an understanding of their composite nature and the interaction among their different parts.

A typical oil painting on canvas has several layers. From the bottom up, the first is a wooden stretcher. Proper stretchers have the capability of being "keyed out", that is, made somewhat larger by adjustment of the corners in order to make the canvas tighter when it becomes slack; they also have enough cross-bars (pieces of wood used to give additional strength to the stretcher) so that the the four sides of the stretcher do not bow inward from the stress of the stretched canvas. A proper stretcher is beveled away from the canvas on its interior face so the inside edges do not touch the fabric. For larger paintings, the stretcher bars should be made from thicker pieces of wood.

The second layer is the canvas, usually made of linen. Linen is more responsive to changes in relative humidity than cotton, but it is stronger. Because of the complex relationships among the layers of a painting, different paintings respond differently to changes in relative humidity. Within one collection, some paintings are tighter in the winter and some are tighter in the summer.

Like any textile, the fabric support of paintings becomes dry, brittle, and weak as it ages. The canvas around the tacks tends to rip, so that the canvas starts to pull off the stretcher and cannot be kept tightly stretched. Sometimes the canvas rips at the front edge of the stretcher or at the corners. The health of a painting on canvas obviously depends on maintaining the strength of the support, and linen is subject to the same aging factors as other textiles. Tests carried out on raw canvas exposed to a maximum of 20 fc (normal gallery lighting) for twenty-four years showed a loss of about 60 to 70% of its original strength. Samples enclosed under Plexiglas® (not UV-filtered), which would have protected the canvas from air pollution and RH shifts, showed only about half the loss of strength, and enclosure in the dark reduced the rate by half again. The exposed samples became more acidic and discolored, mostly from sulfur.[18]

It is interesting to note that this study showed no difference in aging between 35 and 60% RH. This reinforces the theory that actual RH levels, within reasonable limits, do not influence the aging of paintings. Changes in RH are important, and quick cycling of RH, even of small changes, has an extremely deleterious effect on the condition of paintings.

The third layer, sizing, is usually a layer of thinned gelatin. It helps to prevent the oil in the painting and ground from rotting the fibers, stiffens the fabric somewhat, and helps the next layers to stick to the canvas. Because gelatin is so hygroscopic, the amount of gelatin used on a painting seems to have a major influence on its moisture response and therefore its long-term aging properties.

The fourth layer is a ground layer, either of oil paint or gesso, usually a mixture of gelatin and white pigment (sometimes with color added). Gesso grounds are extremely brittle.

The fifth layer is the paint, which may be a thin single layer or a complex layered structure. The surface of the paint may be relatively flat or it may be very

rough, with lumps of paint called impasto. Although wet oil paint initially dries by evaporation of a solvent like turpentine, chemical changes are responsible for long-term changes in its behavior. Oil paint dries by cross-linking which builds chemical bonds between long-chain molecules. The more cross-linking, the less flexible the layer. Drying of the paint also entails some shrinkage. In very thick films, like those of many Abstract Expressionists, internal stresses from the drying of uneven thicknesses of paint pull the paint layer, and the whole canvas, out of plane.

A relatively flexible new oil paint film expands and contracts with the expansion and contraction of the canvas in changing relative humidities. As the paint layer ages and becomes more brittle, its elasticity can no longer keep up with dimensional changes of the canvas and cracks form to accommodate the stresses. With extreme shrinkage of the canvas, particularly at RH levels above about 80%, the edges of the cracks are pushed together, often resulting in the creation of "tenting", little pup-tents of paint coming loose from the support. In normal cracking, the little islands of paint between the cracks tend to cup; that is, the edges of the cracks lift up from the support. As cycling of relative humidity continues, the cupping grows worse, and cleavage, that is, physical separation between layers, often occurs at the edges or intersections of the cracks.

---

[18] Hackney, Stephen, and Hedley, Gerry. "Measurements of the Aging of Linen Canvas." *Studies in Conservation* Vol. 26, p.1-14 (1987)

Eventually the cupping and cleavage lead to flaking of the paint. Here, as with many other kinds of objects, the aging of the structure is a direct result of harmful environmental change.

The last layer of a painting is the varnish. Traditionally, painters have waited a year before varnishing their paintings to give them time to dry. Some paintings have never been varnished; others have been varnished repeatedly through the years. The varnish layer performs several useful functions. It enhances the colors of a painting. As paint layers age, they tend to become more matte, and require varnishing to bring out the original colors. Varnish can also give the painting surface gloss. This is often confused with the phenomenon of the saturation of colors, but is not the same. Using a sprayed rather than brushed varnish, a skillful conservator can varnish a painting without leaving a shine. The degree of gloss of a painting surface can be controlled to whatever level is felt to be most appropriate for the style and condition of the painting. The third purpose of a varnish layer is to protect the painting. Varnishes protect the paint from air pollutants and allow safe cleaning of dirt from the surface.

Traditional varnishes, natural resins like dammar and mastic, discolor with time and become less soluble. The process is inevitable, but is speeded by light, particularly ultraviolet. The aging process also makes the layers somewhat cloudy; this loss of transparency has often led people to revarnish over the existing discolored layer and its accompanying dirt as an easy method of improving the appearance of a painting. The changes in color of varnish layers, particularly in the case of multiple layers, cause extraordinary changes in the color of paintings, changing sunny-day seascapes into storms at sea, and changing blue-eyed people into brown-eyed ones. Even slight discoloration diminishes the contrast between colors in a painting and reduces greatly the sense of depth, particularly in a landscape.

There is a small number of synthetic materials used by conservators as varnishes that are extremely light resistant and do not change color with time. These synthetic varnishes have a tendency to take on a static charge which causes dust to stick to them. Although some viewers say that synthetic varnishes look "plastic", the appearance of a varnish layer depends more on its thickness and the skill with which it was applied than on its chemical composition.

The aging of paintings is therefore a complex sequence of events, depending on the relative responses of each of the layers. If the RH of the environment of a painting cannot be controlled properly, the painting should be protected in other ways, chiefly by containerization, to buffer RH changes. Attaching a backing to the reverse of the stretcher of a painting is a non-controversial procedure that has been estimated to slow the aging of a painting by five to eight times, based on its capacity to slow down RH changes and to reduce pollutant levels. Paintings that have been framed under glass for long periods show an even further reduction in the rate of cracking and weakening of the canvas. Certainly few conservators would recommend this for paintings on exhibition, but the issue underscores the importance of RH control in the preservation of paintings.

A common treatment for badly deteriorated paintings has for slightly over a century been lining with a wax-resin adhesive. Lining consists of adhering a new canvas to the reverse of the existing one. (This is not the same as a transfer, which involves removing the existing support before attaching a new one. Transfers are in recent times seldom done. "Relining" properly refers to the removal of an existing lining and the addition of a new one.) Because wax is a good moisture barrier, wax-lined paintings are very stable in changing relative humidities. Their rate of deterioration as indicated by the formation of cracks slows almost to a halt. In the above-quoted tests, exposed wax-resin impregnated canvas behaved very similarly to enclosed samples.

Contemporary paintings with exposed raw canvas are unfortunately in for a hard time. Exposed canvas responds to changes in relative humidity even faster than painted canvas, and the large size of many of these paintings creates huge overall changes in dimension from even small RH changes. Exposure to light and air pollution causes darkening of the canvas which throws off the color values of the design. Weakening of the canvas from light exposure will eventually make proper tension impossible, and make major treatment of the painting necessary. Major treatment of such paintings is extremely difficult because the treatment materials that are used on traditional paintings will stain the raw canvas, and even surface cleaning can change the texture of the canvas. In short, a cavalier attitude in the care of these paintings will undoubtedly contribute to unrecoverable changes in their appearance, major treatment expense, and an almost inevitable loss of value. Few artists or dealers inform potential purchasers about conservation problems in these paintings, few collectors are aware of the precautions they should be taking to protect their investment, and the deterioration of contemporary works is often blamed solely on the experimental and irresponsible attitudes of the artists.

Acrylic paints were developed partially to provide a more permanent paint than traditional drying oils. Although acrylic paints retain their flexibility for long periods, they are not without problems. They remain very soft, and can be slightly sticky when warm. Dirt tends to stick to their surfaces. Because acrylic paint remains soluble in mild solvents, acrylic paintings are difficult to clean. Sudden environmental changes can cause cracking, as can exposure to freezing temperatures. Some styles of contemporary paintings, with large flat areas of color, are particularly difficult to treat because they show every defect. The smallest scratch, hole or crack is very evident, and toning the loss satisfactorily, almost impossible. Many contemporary paintings are routinely sent back to the artist for restoration, raising all kinds of dilemmas. If an artist in 1985 reworks a painting of 1950, is it the same painting or a later one? If original techniques are partially responsible for the problem that made the restoration necessary, how will the additional work affect the condition of the piece in the future? In the case of works by living artists, most conservators would rather do the work themselves in consultation with the artist, since conservators know more about the aging of materials and their interaction, and the artist knows more about the structure of the works.

Paintings on wood panels present some similar problems to those on canvas, since the wood also expands and contracts but in a different pattern. The crackle patterns of panel paintings are quite different from those of canvas paintings, but the process of cracking, cupping, cleavage, and paint loss is the same (See Fig. 24). Paintings on panel also suffer from warping of the panel, and from cracking of the panel due to misguided efforts to stop the warping (See Figs. 18, 19). RH control of galleries, or placement of panel paintings in controlled cases, is the best solution to these problems. Interestingly enough, the first major effort in museum climate control was in galleries of panel paintings in the National Gallery in London, where before World War II one technician worked almost year-round to treat flaking paint on panel paintings. When, during the war, the paintings were housed in a naturally stable environment, his work gradually decreased to nothing. This experience convinced the museum administration to install air conditioning.[19]

---

[19] Plenderleith, H. J., and Philippot, P. "Climatology and Conservation in Museums" *Museum* Vol.13, p. 255 (1960)

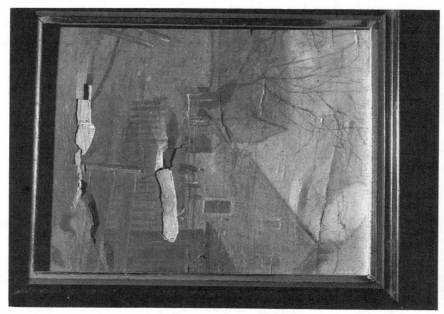

Fig. 24 William Sidney Mount, *Long Island Farmhouse* (shown sideways). This is a small (approx. 5 x 4 -inch) oil painting on wood with a bad case of tenting paint, due to the shrinkage of the panel. This problem is unusual for the artist; perhaps he considered this just a quick sketch and did not prepare the panel in his usual manner. The condition in general is not unusual. Courtesy an anonymous museum.

Picture Frames

Good quality picture frames are more and more being treated as fine arts objects by conservators and collectors. They have the classic problems of composite objects. Frames commonly consist of a wood base covered with gesso and gilded. As the wood expands and contracts, the gesso cracks and falls off. Three-dimensional ornamentation of frames is usually either carved from wood or molded from a material called "compo". This also becomes quite brittle with age. Frames perform an important service by protecting their contents from handling; in doing so they suffer, and in being repaired they often suffer again.

The gilding of frames is usually gold leaf; although some frames that appear gold-colored are silver-colored metal leaf toned yellow, only real gold retains its luster and color. Frames are often repaired with bronze powder paints that start out about the same color as the gold, but within a year can darken to a murky brown. Unfortunately many gilded frames with local damage from abrasion are painted all over with bronze paint. These kinds of repairs are a false investment. Good frames are valuable, both in purely monetary terms, and in terms of what they contribute to the appearance and physical security of a painting.

Frames should be cleaned only with a soft brush. Damp rags or furniture polish can easily wipe off the gold leaf. When a painting or print is off the wall, the frame should be examined to see if the corners are tight, if the rabbet is secure, and if the ornamentation is solidly attached. (The rabbet is the little ledge that holds the edge of the painting.) Any ornate frame needs padding if it to be laid face down on a table or leaned against a wall. Movers' blankets, pieces of carpeting, or any other kind of pads should be used to protect ornate frames. Proper care and treatment of frames is an important part of managing a paintings collection.

Furniture

The preservation of furniture has several pitfalls, only one of which is the warping and cracking of the wood. Much historic furniture has been used throughout its history, only retiring when it enters a museum (although even in museums, historic furniture often holds vases of flowers and other decorations), and therefore is marked by long years of wear, damage, and alteration. In the past, most furniture was joined with glue rather than with hardware; the failure of glue joins from RH fluctuations has necessitated repeated repair, and repairs were commonly done with nails or screws in the mistaken notion that they were stronger than glue joins.

Many conservators are therefore faced with furniture with loose joins weakened even more by splintering of the wood from nails and screws that have worked loose.

Furniture is usually built on a wooden structure but almost always includes more than one material. The presence of veneer, gilding, inlay of various materials, metal hardware, paint, upholstery, and other materials like leather or marble used as desk- or tabletops contributes complications to the preservation of furniture. Historic furniture also has problems derived from aging of the finishes, since traditional wood coatings, like traditional varnishes for paintings, become brittle, cloudy, and discolored with time. Complications due to a mixture of materials carry over from treatment to the long-term care of furniture.

No treatment can protect furniture from deterioration from the same sources that caused previous problems. RH fluctuations or RH levels other than those the piece is acclimated to will cause further loosening of joins, warping, and cracking. New French polish (the traditional shellac-based furniture finish) will darken and become cloudy and brittle just as the old finishes did if exposed to high light levels, particularly ultraviolet. Because of the impracticality of containerizing furniture to reduce climatic fluctuations, there is little other than environmental control that can be done to prevent continuing problems in the preservation of wood furniture. At the very least, good furniture should be moved away from direct sunlight and radiators.

Sparing application of a hard paste wax to furniture is permissible, and will protect the surfaces when pieces are in use, but will not protect against changes in relative humidity.

Fine old furniture in a private setting cannot usually be kept out of use. This creates difficulties for its maintenance. The traditional training of conservators generally does not accommodate the idea of making an object strong enough for use; craftsmen who repair furniture, on the other hand, may not be aware of the long-term consequences of some of their repair techniques, the importance of preserving the history of the piece, or the need to document their work. In the last ten years or so, furniture conservators have become much more sophisticated in combining the best of both worlds, and there are now some conservators who are interested in treating fine furniture that remains in use without compromising its historic and documentary value.

Contemporary Works

Collectors of contemporary art, whether of paintings, sculpture, crafts, costumes, or photography, may have difficult problems including plastics made for short-term use, unknown fabric finishes, quirky materials in sculpture, and extremes of size. The identity of many materials that turn up in contemporary art is unknown, and

very little is known about the aging characteristics of even the materials that can be identified. Much has been made in the popular press about the casual attitudes of some contemporary artists toward the survival of their art, and much in these articles is undoubtedly true. However, even the most conscientious artist finds little help in art school in learning to use traditional materials properly, and artists who wish to use materials of their own time would find little guidance anywhere. In short, museums, private collectors and conservators face difficult and unprecedented technical problems with many contemporary works. Examination of these pieces by a conservator before acquisition is crucial in avoiding pieces with inherent vice and in providing proper care for others.

Ethnographic Objects

Ethnography is a term that tends to be used as a substitute for the now mostly unacceptable term "Primitive Art". Ethnographic conservators are therefore those who treat African, Oceanic, and Native American collections, as well as Pre-Columbian objects. To confuse matters, the term ethnography in other parts of the world refers to what Americans would call folk art. In either case, the practice of ethnographic conservation includes the idea of preserving objects in their "as-used" rather than "as-created" state. This means that remains of foodstuffs in a basket, for example, should be preserved rather than cleaned off, and that ceremonial additions to objects should be left in place. The concerns of ethnographic conservators in preserving signs of use even when they might be considered as somewhat disfiguring have become more widespread in the field of conservation. Anyone involved in the care of collections that are not traditional fine arts should be aware of the debate on this subject, as conservation decisions are clarified by curatorial input. Many treatments turn out to be compromises between the two points of view of ethnography and fine arts, attempting to preserve historic evidence while maximizing the aesthetic impact and physical stability of the piece.

Functional Objects

The concerns of art conservation are being applied more and more to fields like musical instruments where previously restoration had been carried out with traditional crafts methods and approaches. The modern field of conservation is clearly based on the needs of the fine arts, yet conservators are attempting to adapt their methods, materials, and strategies as well as ethical constraints to objects as disparate as locomotives, space capsules, historic gardens, and historic canned foods. These efforts require cooperation among many different parties in an atmosphere of mutual respect; they are frustrating as well as challenging. Conservators have to learn to be flexible and innovative without giving up their principles.

Books

The care of books has complications of all kinds. Books are objects of mixed materials - paper and ink, cardboard, leather, textiles, glue and other adhesives, gilding and sometimes other metals. This means that the different parts react differently to RH changes and, although it may take a long time for moisture to permeate the structure of a tightly-closed book, the rippling of pages that accompanies drastic changes can cause destructive stresses on the whole structure of the book. Poor quality paper and acidic leather bindings contain the seeds of their own destruction. Books are often the victim of pests, and their lack of visibility even in home bookcases makes this particularly damaging.

The traditional life of a book involves periodic rebinding that includes replacement of most of the functional parts. This general approach contradicts modern conservation practice that emphasizes the retention of everything old, yet books are functional objects which may have no value if they cannot be opened and read. These contradictory requirements make the proper care

of valuable books a complex matter.

The care of books that are primarily of informational rather than historic value is not as theoretically complex a task, but the numbers of books extant and their poor lasting qualities make the job a monumental one. Librarians, archivists, and conservators who work with them have become extremely sophisticated in the management of varied library collections, often proposing a wide range of strategies from microfilming and customized book boxes to labor-intensive hand rebindings and custom-designed support stands for books on exhibition.

For people with their own book collections, environmental control to eliminate the most extreme RH levels combined with the use of book boxes for fragile books will offer a great deal of protection. Proper physical handling is vital: because modern books are not often considered truly valuable items, few people have been taught the proper way to turn the pages of a book so as to avoid creasing or soiling the pages. Even the acid-related deterioration of paper and leather proceeds much slower if the materials are not flexed.

Musical Instruments

Musical instruments are composed of the widest possible

variety of materials in alarmingly stressful configurations. Many like drums or banjos have skin materials tightly stretched; others have metal, gut or horsehair strings under tension. Stretched membranes and strings also put the bodies of the instruments under stress. Stretched skins often split from the shrinkage of the skins in low relative humidities. Such splits are very difficult to repair even when only appearance is a concern; when sound is at issue, only replacement can be satisfactory. Unfortunately, the replacement of the skins with new ones almost inevitably entails the destruction of physical evidence of the original materials and attachment methods. This is a classic example of the dilemma of dealing with musical instruments.

Wooden instruments are usually joined with animal glue, and the strength of the joins deteriorates rapidly in either very high or very low relative humidities; the weakening of glue joints is a common problem for string players, who get used to playing on instruments with gaps in seams. Unlike modern instruments, many historic wooden instruments are highly decorated. If paintings on panel are difficult to preserve without warping or cracking, painted harpsichord cases present even more difficulties. Treatments like the impregnation of paint layers with adhesives or repairs of splits may change the sound of the instruments.

Frequently played metal instruments are not susceptible to much tarnishing because they are frequently wiped with soft cloths, but, in collections, they suffer more. Instruments that stay unused tend to gather dust, and it may be difficult to remove dust:removal from such complex objects. Various moving and vibrating parts are made of fragile materials like plant reeds or animal quills. Felt pads in and under the keys of are susceptible to moth damage.

To avoid damage, strings should be loosened just to tautness for exhibition or storage. Dust covers are vital. PDB should be used inside pianos where necessary to avoid moth damage.

The many ills of musical instruments are familiar to musicians who have the freedom to replace strings, reeds, drumheads, and valves when necessary. The problems are compounded in collection instruments by a desire to preserve all original materials. The tuning and playing of a musical instrument puts various physical strains on the object, yet an instrument that cannot be played loses much of its historic value, not to mention its capacity for providing pleasure. Recent professional concerns in this area have resulted in recommendations that all possible physical evidence on original instruments be preserved to facilitate the production of replicas made with techniques identical to those of the original, but with new materials. This recommendation may be difficult to carry out in many settings. However, in dealing with musical instrument collections, it is important to understand the physical and ethical concerns inherent in treating functional objects, and to consult experts before any radical work is undertaken.

Scientific Instruments, Guns, etc.

Preservation of historic functional objects like microscopes, guns, and cars has often been carried out with the intent of putting all parts of the object in optimal working order as seen in their modern counterparts. This may mean replacing old handmade screws with uniform modern ones, repatinating , and in general removing all signs of wear. Conservators tend to reject these activities as destructive of historical evidence and as unwise in terms of the physical strain they place on already weakened materials. In highly specialized areas like these, standards in museums may be quite different from those among private collectors.

Chemically Incompatible Materials

Paintings are an extreme example of objects in precarious equilibrium because of differences in their physical response to moisture. There are other combinations of materials that are chemically incompatible. Metal and wood objects of various kinds are often difficult to preserve unchanged because the acids from the wood accelerate the corrosion of the metal. Lead is the most sensitive metal to acids and is thus most in danger here. Metal and wood pieces should probably be kept in an environment drier that what would ordinarily be recommended for the wood alone in order to slow the process of corrosion.

Leather and metal, particularly copper, is a bad combination because the fatty acids from tanning or from later treatment with oily dressings react to form a green waxy corrosion at points of contact. Iron will also react, but more slowly; the iron rust will in turn speed deterioration of the leather. Shells on leather often suffer efflorescence of salts from reaction with the same acids.

Textiles with metallic threads present a difficult problem. Although gold threads retain their luster over long periods, silver or copper threads corrode badly. Since the removal of corrosion inevitably entails either abrasion or treatment with corrosive chemicals, the treatment *in situ* of metallic

threads in textiles is generally
impossible. Many metallic threads
are complex structures of paper,
solid or plated metals, and/or silk,
making treatment additionally
difficult. For any textiles with
silver or copper threads still
untarnished, protection from air
pollution is vital.

Assessing a Specific Collection

Assessing the needs of specific collections entails more than a consideration of the materials that make up the objects. Other considerations like the construction and condition of the objects, their history, size, previous treatments, and even subject matter, should be taken into account.

Some pieces, for reasons that no one can predict, behave in a way atypical of their type. Every conservator has seen examples of one painting that has problems shared by no other painting by the same artist, or objects that behave differently from dozens of virtually identical ones. Although it may or may not be possible to treat the cause of the problem, a completely stable environment can be expected to help slow down the course of almost any kind of deterioration; objects like these should probably be maintained in special climate-controlled cases, no matter what the state of climate control for the rest of the collection. A conservator with long experience in a collection may be the only one who can identify pieces like this.

Some artists, for example, Reginald Marsh and Andrew Wyeth, used painting techniques that make many of their paintings subject to a kind of deterioration exemplified by the eruption of pinpoint dots of paint. Thomas Hart Benton was another artist whose paintings have peculiar structural problems because of the artist's technique. The conservators involved with these pieces treat them repeatedly, but cannot "cure" the problem at its source. In this situation, strict control of temperature and relative humidity may be the best treatment, and a specially designed case is the likely choice. A conservator experienced in examination of the kinds of objects in a collection should be able to identify these pieces after surveying a collection carefully and reading existing treatment and condition records.

The condition of a collection may change the requirements for environmental control and other measures of collections care. Textiles are perhaps the most obvious example. A machine-made coverlet of the late nineteenth century may be as strong as a modern one, capable of being rolled for storage, handled, and hung freely for exhibition. A silk embroidered picture from the same period may be so fragile, with rips and loose fragments, that it cannot be handled at all, and the slightest breeze (or sneeze) would produce disaster.

Differences in condition may justify completely different conditions of exhibition, storage, and handling. Some pieces are strong enough for a travelling exhibition; others may be strong enough for exhibition but not for travel. A third group may be in such poor condition that the pieces must be laid on shelves without being moved until they can undergo major treatment. A painting with flaking paint can be laid flat on a shelf; loose flakes on a sculpture will not be aided by gravity in the same way. Anything with flaking paint will be safer with the most stable environment possible.

Few objects will continue to deteriorate actively in an optimal environment. Bronzes with active bronze disease need a lower relative humidity to halt the progress of crystal growth than bronzes with no bronze disease need to stay disease-free. Likewise, mold-infested paper needs a lower RH to stop the mold growth than would be needed to prevent mold growth on a mold-free piece.

Many collections have a kind of clinic set up in a safe undisturbed place with containers capable of the best possible RH control where pieces with obvious condition problems await the visit of a conservator. With this capability, a vast majority of collection material may be considered safe with a much less rigorously controlled environment than would be required for the most fragile and sensitive pieces.

Previous treatments have a major effect on the response of pieces to their environment. The inability of materials added during treatment to respond in the same way as the object during shifts in relative humidity is often the reason why certain treatment materials are considered inappropriate. Inflexible fillings on wood that do not allow for opening and closing of cracks can cause additional cracking. Plaster fillings on bronzes hold moisture next to the surface of the metal and enhance corrosion. Some leather dressings can promote mold growth. Iron repair rods in stone or plaster pieces can cause major damage when high relative humidities cause corrosion and consequent swelling of the metal. The "cradling" of paintings can cause widespread cracking of a wooden panel in fluctuating relative humidities. In an ideal environment, none of these treatments would be harmful. It is a measure of how little conservators expect of current standards in climate control that all these treatments (except perhaps leather dressings in a small number of cases) are considered totally unacceptable in modern practice.

The lining adhesive of a painting has a major effect on its behavior. A painting lined with a wax-resin adhesive or with wax alone is much less responsive than an unlined painting to changes in relative humidity. The behavior of the wax as a barrier against moisture exchange with the air slows down the cracking of paint to a small percentage of its usual rate. On the other hand, paintings lined with animal glue respond even more radically to RH changes than unlined paintings. Judgments on the advisability of climate control for paintings should rely strongly on occurrence levels of the two types of linings.

Ripped paintings that have been repaired with a patch on the reverse instead of a full lining will distort much more quickly in shifting RH levels than in steady ones. Stretched paper and textiles are at extreme risk from fluctuations in RH. Hygroscopic materials like paper or textiles containerized with insufficient hygroscopic buffers can undergo mold growth from condensation with shifts in temperature and relative humidity. Textiles sandwiched between glass or Plexiglas® and paper that is framed touching glass are both common examples of this.

The history of an object is another factor in determining the optimum RH and temperature levels for it. Anything taken directly from a dry environment, like polychromed wood Kachina dolls, should have a very different RH from a polychromed wooden statue taken from an unheated European church. Objects from the deserts of Peru or Egypt would likewise be better preserved in an environment similar to the one that has preserved them for up to several thousands of years. Particularly in the case of mummies, in which biological deterioration is always a possibility, low RH levels are recommended.

On the other hand, objects which have become acclimated to an environment different from their native one may respond badly to the changes when put into their "proper" environment. Lacquer objects, for which a quite high RH is customarily recommended, may crack when put into this environment if they have become acclimated to a low RH.

A large portion of ethnographic collections consists of pieces that originated in hot and humid climates. A very gradual initial change to a more easily maintained level is required, both for practical purposes (no museum can maintain a rain forest atmosphere) and because high levels of temperature and relative humidity cause high rates of deterioration. A prudent strategy for bringing these objects into a temperate climate would be to import them in the summer, containerize them and allow for a gradual lowering of RH in the fall, while inspecting them periodically for problems. For objects being brought from dry countries, import in the winter would be prudent.

A museum in the New York area with a well-known collection of carriages had stored it for many years in unheated barns. Expensive environmental controls were prepared for the move of the collection inside. Unfortunately, well-intentioned staff and consultants had decided, based on reading the literature, that 50% would be the ideal RH level. When the carriages were brought into their new space, the wood started to crack and the paint to flake off almost immediately. The fact was that outdoors near the ocean, the average RH year-round was around 70%, and the pieces suffered in a sudden shift to a lower level.

The size of pieces may be an important factor in standards for care. Moving large sculpture and large paintings is quite a different activity from moving smaller ones. Heavy sculptures in particular should be moved only by people who specialize in this in order to avoid damage to the object and its surroundings as well as to avoid injury to personnel. RH changes that make a 25 x 30-inch painting slightly slack on its stretcher will produce much larger ripples if the painting is 8 x 10 feet. Paintings that hang close to the floor are much more susceptible to staining from being splashed with floor-cleaning solutions or dented by the edge of a vacuum cleaner. Lighting large pieces evenly may also be a major problem. Framing and mounting pieces larger than the standard four-by-eight-foot size of many manufactured sheet materials may entail considerable additional expense.

Very small objects need special handling as well. The temptation to carry these things around in a pocket or brown bag must be resisted. Mounting or

containerization of very tiny objects will prevent loss or damage. Any object made of many small parts, like micromosaics or beaded costume accessories should be containerized in some way, even if just in a flat tray or box, in order to prevent loss of any small parts that may come loose.

Subject matter of objects or paintings may be an important reason for changing customary display methods in a museum. Paintings or sculptures of nudes are common targets of vandals, and should be protected either behind Plexiglas® or glass or displayed well out of reach. Pieces with controversial subject matter should receive similar protection.

Collections of pieces with little monetary value may be particularly difficult to care for because of a lack of interest in them and the general unavailability of money for their care. In the case of a series of portraits of college presidents or elected officials, there may be an overriding obligation to preserve them in good condition without a corresponding high monetary or even sentimental value. Just because expensive treatments or environmental controls are out of the question, these thing should be protected as well as possible from physical damage. Ripped paintings can be very expensive to repair. A less than professional treatment which may be tempting under the circumstances may be followed by a far more costly treatment to undo the poor one whenever the next treatment becomes necessary. It may be worth attempting to enlist the aid of family members of the subjects of the portraits or other interested parties in order to provide a minimal level of care that will prevent the need for greater expenditure in the future.

One other type of inexpensive object which may require a treatment that costs more than the object is one in which poor condition, evident or not, is the reason for the low purchase price. These pieces are a primary reason why many conservators recommend that purchasers ask for expert advice before buying something rather than waiting for later.

Collections of travel souvenirs have unique problems that are complicated by the fact that even a minor treatment will probably cost more than the purchase price of the object (although not if the cost of the trip is factored in!). Such souvenirs may or may not be of the same techniques or materials as the originals. Leather or wood may not have been tanned or seasoned with traditional methods and may therefore be even more sensitive to changes in relative humidity than one would expect. An object sold as a copy of a ceramic may have been made of plaster molded and painted with acrylic paint; water in such a piece would seep through the plaster and cause the paint to peel off in sheets. Metals may have been painted in imitation of natural patinas; such paint may be dissolved by common adhesives or cleaners.

Polychromed wooden sculptures from Indonesia, the Caribbean, and other hot and humid parts of the world may exhibit immediate and disastrous flaking of paint during the first few weeks of cold weather in the fall. Frequent calls to conservators at this time of year complain of the flaking and ask for an inexpensive way to stop it. The answer is not encouraging. The treatment of an inexpensive item is no less time-consuming or expensive than that of a precious object; it may be more difficult.

The subject of environmental control has received a great deal of attention in museums in the last ten or twenty years. The emphasis has more recently started to spread to historic houses and to private collections. While curators, collectors, and administrators are trying to learn as much as they can about ultraviolet filters and air conditioning, it is important that they not lose sight of the unique needs of their collections. Optimal conditions depend on the specifics of the objects, their histories and their current conditions, not on the recommendations in a book. Knowledgeable examination of a collection is an important part of implementing a program of environmental improvement.

Postscript: If You Want to Do More

Non-conservators who have done all they can for their collections may still want to do some hands-on treatment of objects in their care. Within some rather strict limits, there are jobs that are safe for non-conservators. Aside from some informal training and someone to call on when something unexpected happens, these projects require a clean space where objects can be left undisturbed, unbumped, un-dripped-on, unsplattered, and, preferably, locked in. Cleanliness of both hands and surroundings is particularly important for paper and textiles, marble, and plaster, light-colored porous objects that are difficult to clean.

You will need space that has good ventilation because fumes from even relatively safe solvents should not be allowed to build up. (For more toxic solvents, an open window does not provide enough ventilation.) You will require a variety of tools and supplies, some of which must be reserved for conservation work. Stocking the right materials may take a lot of trouble and expense, as some conservation materials are difficult to buy in small quantities.

You will need undisturbed spans of time when you can concentrate without running for the telephone, and you will need the temperament for it. This is difficult to describe, but doing even minor treatment takes a certain compulsive, attentive manner of operation that some people simply cannot muster.

If you think you can cope with all this, try to get a conservator who will be willing to help you. Offer them their usual *per diem* rate for consultation time and assure them, if you can, that pieces that need their expertise will be sent to them for treatment. Demonstrate as well as you can a deep and abiding respect for the objects in your care. In case you haven't guessed, conservators do not have much sympathy with the idea that if you own something you have the right to destroy it, so do not express this notion if you wish to get a conservator to help you.

This is quite a touchy matter. Imagine, if you can, asking your doctor for advice on how to perform a minor surgical procedure on yourself or a member of your family. You may have to prove your patience or your persistence before a conservator will agree to help you. If conservators tell you a certain process is risky, believe them. If what they assign to you as a possibility seems too tedious, take my word for it: conservation work *is* tedious. You may like the idea of cleaning dirt off the surface of a painting, but doing it the way a conservator would, with a barely damp cotton swab one tiny area at a time, is not necessarily fun. For every moment of excitement in conservation there are hundreds of repetitious, frustrating and unrewarding ones. If this does not seem appetizing to you, stay away from the whole business and pay someone else to do whatever needs doing.

For framed textiles or paper, unframing, examination, and rematting and framing are important activities that can often be done by careful amateurs with supervision. There are books and articles that will help get you started, although even in this area, it would be better to do the reading first, then get a conservator to look over your collection *before* you begin. Backing and securing paintings in their frames properly may be another activity that dedicated amateurs can do, although there is little written material to help you, because every painting and frame will differ so much from the next.

There are plenty of books and articles that explain how to do somewhat more complex procedures like cleaning or repairing ripped paintings or repairing broken ceramics. It is undoubtedly true that a careful person good with their hands can do some of these procedures on some objects without inflicting any damage. But without a skilled examination, it may be impossible for an amateur to judge exactly which pieces these are. Many of these books recommend that at a certain point, pieces be set aside for a conservator to look at. I think it is more helpful if a conservator looks at the pieces first and perhaps does some tests *before*, rather than after, you tackle the work. Promising to be careful does not help when you do not know what to be careful of, or what to do if something unexpected happens.

Out of all the things you should keep in mind to get a conservator on your side and to protect your collection, one of the most important ones is not to apply furniture polishes, oils, waxes, fixatives, insect repellents, cleaning solutions, varnishes, or any other substance. Some of these things are appropriate; others can be damaging, particularly over a long period of time. Some furniture waxes like Renaissance wax are formulated for long-term use. Many others contain materials like silicones that are virtually impossible to remove in the future and can make other treatments impossible. Over-application of waxes, very common for zealous housekeepers, results in a thick sticky layer that traps dirt and gradually masks the original appearance of the surface. Polishes containing linseed oil stay sticky for long periods while they harden chemically (like the paint films of oil paintings), incorporating dirt in the layer and becoming gradually harder and harder to remove. Materials similar to original furniture finishes may confuse later attempts to determine the original appearance of a piece, to clean down to the original surface, or to duplicate the appearance of it.

Oily or waxy materials applied to the surface of paintings can have even more deleterious effects. If they are applied to paintings on paper or cardboard, they can be ruinous. There are a small number of commercially available varnishes that are appropriate materials for long-term use, but if they are applied to the wrong paintings, they can permanently alter the appearance of the piece. Manufacturers of commercial products can also change their formulations without notice, so any use of a commercial product should be checked with a conservator first.

Materials designed for the care of household items like furniture or silver are often excellent for the purposes for which they were made, that is, for maintenance of household items which are in use; they are seldom designed for use on any pieces that are meant to be preserved permanently. Many can interfere with future conservation treatments, and some can accelerate damage after the period of time for which they were designed is past. If you are committed to putting something on something you want to keep, call a conservator before you do it, and give them a chance to convince you not to.

I know that polishing or waxing or putting leather dressing on something can make you feel good for providing some needed loving care. There should be plenty of other things in this book that will keep you busy. Perhaps the most important is still the first: look at your collection and enjoy it. These things you have, whatever they are, that you have chosen to preserve, have something of their own to offer. Once you learn to see signs of deterioration and instability and learn what to do to minimize damage, it is important to relearn how to look at the whole object without seeing the dust and the fading, to participate in the life of the object and appreciate its beauty, its history, and the other people whose lives have touched it.

Further Reading

The following are a small number of relatively non-technical and easily obtainable books on conservation topics. Most conservators can furnish more detailed bibliographies on a particular subject; many of these books have their own bibliographies.

Clapp, Anne F. *Curatorial Care of Works of Art on Paper, Third Revised Edition.* New York: Lyons and Burford,1987.

Dolloff, Francis W. and Perkinson, Roy L. *How to Care for Works of Art on Paper.* Boston: Museum of Fine Arts, 1971.

Ellis, Margaret Holben. *The Care of Prints and Drawings.* Nashville: American Association for State and Local History, 1987.

Keck, Caroline K. *A Handbook on the Care of Paintings.* New York: Watson-Guptill Publications, 1965.

Mailand, Harold F. *Considerations for the Care of Textiles and Costumes.* Indianapolis: Indianapolis Museum of Art, 1980.

McGiffin, Robert F., Jr. *Furniture Care and Conservation.* Nashville: American Association for State and Local History, 1983.

Reilly, James M. *Care and Identification of 19th-Century Photographic Prints.* Rochester: Eastman Kodak Co., 1986.

Smith, Merrily A. *Matting and Hinging of Works of Art on Paper.* Washington, DC: Library of Congress, 1981.

Stolow, Nathan. *Conservation Standards for Works of Art in Transit and on Exhibition.* Paris: Unesco, 1979.

Thompson, Garry. *The Museum Environment, Second Edition.* London: Butterworths, 1986.

Weinstein, Robert A. and Booth, Larry. *Collection, Use and Care of Historical Photographs.* Nashville: American Association for State and Local History, 1977.

Zycherman, Lynda A., and Schrock, J. Richard. *A Guide to Museum Pest Control.* Washington, DC: Foundation of the American Institute for Conservation of Historic and Artistic Works and the Association of Systematics Collections, 1988.

Sources of Supply

The following list includes both manufacturers and retailers. Some firms are both; others sell their own products only in large quantities.

Archivart (Formerly Process Materials Corp.), 301 Veterans Blvd., Rutherford, NJ 07070 (800) 631-0193, NJ (201) 935-2900.

Manufacturer of Archivart® archival products for preservation and restoration.

Art Preservation Services, 253 East 78th Street, New York, NY 10021 (212) 794-9234.

Supplier of instruments to monitor and control environment, consultation on environmental control.

Belfort Instrument Co., 727 S. Wolfe Street, Baltimore, MD 21231 (301) 342-2626. Manufacturer of meteorological equipment including RH monitors and data loggers.

Carus Chemical Co., 1001 Boyce Memorial Drive, Ottawa, IL 61350 (800) 435-6856. Manufacturer of Carusorb® filtration medium.

Conservation Materials Ltd., 1165 Marietta Way, P. O. Box 2884, Sparks, NV 89431 (702) 331-0582.

Supplier of conservation tools and materials.

Conservation Resources International, Inc., 8000 H Forbes Place, Springfield, VA 22151 (800) 634-6932.

Manufacturer of archival storage products.

Delta Designs Ltd., P. O. Box 1733, Topeka, KS 66601 (913) 234-2244.

Designer and manufacturer of museum storage equipment.

Garrison/Lull, Box 337, Princeton Junction, NJ 08550 (609) 259-8050.

Consultation on the museum environment.

General Eastern Instruments Corp., 50 Hunt St., Watertown, MA 02172 (617) 923-2386.

Supplier of sophisticated humidity measurement equipment.

W. L. Gore & Associates, Museum Products, P. O. Box 1550, Elkton, MD 21921 (301) 392-4440.

Manufacturer of silica gel tiles.

W. R. Grace & Co., Davison Chemical Division, P. O. Box 2117, Baltimore, MD 21203 (301) 659-9010/9242.

Manufacturer of silica gel.

Hollinger Corporation, P. O. Box 8360, Fredericksburg, VA 22401 (800) 634-0491.

Manufacturer of archival storage products.

Humidial Corp., 465 North Mt. Vernon Avenue, P. O. Box 610, Colton, CA 92324-1111 (714) 825-1793.

Manufacturer of color change humidity indicators.

Kennedy-Trimnell Co., Inc., 109 North Kenilworth, Oak Park, IL 60301 (312) 386-6476.

Manufacturer of humidity control modules.

Lab Safety Supply Co., P. O. Box 1368, Janesville, WI 53547-1368 (800) 356-0783.

Supplier of safety equipment.

Light Impressions Corp., 493 Monroe Avenue, Rochester, NY 14607-3717 (800) 828-6216; New York State (800) 828-9629.

Manufacturer and supplier of archival supplies.

Lighting Services Inc, 150 East 58th Street, New York, NY 10155 (212) 838-8633.

Manufacturer of lighting track and regular and low-voltage fixtures.

Lightolier, 100 Lighting Way, Secaucus, NJ 07094 (201) 864-3000.

Manufacturer of lighting track and regular and low-voltage fixtures.

Littlemore Scientific Engineering Co., Railway Lane, Littlemore, Oxford OX4 4PZ, ENGLAND.

Manufacturer of ultraviolet meters.

Madico, Inc., P. O. Box 4023, 64 Industrial Parkway, Woburn, MA 01888 (617) 935-7850.

Manufacturer of filtering window films and material for shades.

Micro Climate Technology Inc., 4180 Morris Drive Unit 11, Burlington, Ontario L7L 5L6 (416) 637-7888

Manufacturer of relative humidity control modules.

Mogul Corp., P. O. Box 200, Chagrin Falls, OH 44022 (216) 247-5000.

Mogul's "Steam SAFE" program provides analytical services and advice on managing safe steam humidification.

National Fire Protection Association, Batterymarch Park, Quincy, MA 02269 (800) 344-3555.

NFPA is a source for information on all facets of fire protection.

Paper Technologies, Inc, 25801 Obrero, Mission Viejo, CA 92691 (714) 768-7497.

Manufacturer of archival papers and other supplies for conservators.

Photo Plastic Products, Inc., P. O. Box 607638, Orlando, FL 32860-7638 (407) 886-3100.

Manufacturer of archival photograph storage enclosures.

Printfile, Inc., Box 100, Schenectady, NY 12304, Distributor of photographic storage supplies. (518) 374-2334

Distributor of archival photograph storage enclosures.

Purafil, Inc., 2654 Weaver Way, Doraville, GA 30340 (800) 222-6367.

Manufacturer of Purafil® filtration medium and equipment, analysis and consultation on air cleaning and monitoring.

Qualimetrics, Inc. (Formerly Science Associates, Inc.), P. O. Box 230, Princeton, NJ 08542 (800) 247-7234, NJ (609) 924-4470.

Manufacturer and distributor of instruments for measurement of light and RH.

Rohm and Haas, Independence Mall West, Philadelphia, PA 19105 (215) 592-3000.

Manufacturer of Plexiglas® products.

Silver Care Products, 3535 Hoffman Road East, St. Paul, MN 55110 (800) 328-1449.

Supplier of 3M Silver Protector Strips.

Solar Screen, 53-11 105th Street, Corona, NY 11368 (212) 592-8223.

Manufacturer of roller shades, fluorescent tube jackets, E-Z bond® window film.

Talas, 213 W. 35th Street, New York, NY 10001-1996 (212) 736-7744.

Supplier for general conservation and archival supplies. Carries Archivist pens, British standard blue cloths.

Taylor Made Co., P. O. Box 406, Lima, PA 19037 (215) 566-7067.

Manufacturer of protective pouches for archival and photographic collections.

3M Energy Control Products, 3M Center, St. Paul, MN 55144-1000 (800) 328-1449.

Manufacturer of Scotchtint sun control window film and optical lighting film.

University Products, Inc., P. O. Box 101, 517 Main Street, Holyoke, MA 01041 (800) 628-1912, in Mass. (413) 532-9431

Manufacturer and supplier of general archival and conservation supplies.

Venture Lighting International, 32000 Aurora Road, Solon, OH 44139. Tech. info.: (800) 338-6161. Ordering: (800) 437-0111.

Manufacturer of specialty light bulbs, specializing in tungsten-halogen bulbs.

Verilux, Inc., 12 Laurel Lane, P. O. Box 1512, Greenwich, CT 06830 (203) 869-3750.

Manufacturer of full-spectrum fluorescent tubes.

Sources of Information

The American Association of Museums (AAM)

1225 Eye Street, NW

Washington, DC 20005

(202) 289-1818

AAM is the membership organization for museums and museum personnel. AAM publishes *Museum News* and some books on museum topics and sells books from other publishers. AAM also accredits museums.

The American Association for State and Local History (AASLH) 172 Second Avenue North, #102 Nashville, TN 37201 (615) 255-2971

AASLH is a membership organization for historical agencies, historical societies, history museums and their staffs. It publishes a series of Technical Reports as part of its journal *History News*. AASLH also publishes a variety of books, some of them on conservation-related topics.

The American Institute for Conservation of Historic and Artistic Works (AIC)
1400 16th Street, NW
Washington, DC 20036
(202) 232-6636

AIC is the membership organization for American conservators. It publishes a technical journal and a newsletter for members, as well as brochures entitled *Guidelines for Selecting a Conservator, Conservation Training in the United States* and the *Code of Ethics and Standards of Practice* (available free of charge). AIC is in the process of instituting a referral service.

The American Society for Heating, Ventilation, and Air Conditioning Engineers (ASHRAE)
1791 Tullie Circle
Atlanta, GA 30329
(404) 636-8400

ASHRAE is the membership organization for HVAC engineers. They have a publication program and regional groups that hold periodic meetings.

Center for Safety in the Arts (CSA)
5 Beekman Street, Suite 1030
New York, NY 10038
(212) 227-6220

CSA is a clearinghouse for research and education on hazards in the arts. Its services include the Art Hazards Information Center that answers telephone and mail inquiries, a newsletter, *Art Hazards News*, consultation, lecture programs, etc. CSA also publishes and sells books, data sheets, and pamphlets on relevant issues.

Canadian Conservation Institute (CCI)
1030 Innes Road
Ottawa, Ontario, CAN K1A 0C8

CCI publishes an extremely useful series of *Technical Bulletins* (available free of charge) on topics related to collections care including relative humidity, lighting, and environmental monitoring.

Cornell Cooperative Extension
Insect and Plant Disease Diagnostic Office, Department of Entomology
5140 Comstock Hall
Cornell University
Ithaca, NY 14853-0999
(607) 255-3144

Cornell Cooperative Extension is an excellent source for information on insect damage and for insect identification. The usual fee is $5.00 per sample.

New York State Conservation Consultancy (NYSCC)
2199 Saw Mill River Road
Elmsford, NY 10523
(914) 592-6726

Funded by a grant from the New York State Council on the Arts, NYSCC publishes a series of Conservation Bulletins on subjects like the care and storage of metals, textiles, and paintings, when to call a conservator, etc.

Northeast Document Conservation Center (NEDCC)
Brickstone Square, Building 100
Andover, MA 01810-4099
(508) 470-1010

NEDCC publishes a series of hand-outs on topics related to the care of paper-based materials icluding photographs and archival materials.

The Society for the Preservation of Natural History Collections (SPNHC)
5800 Baum Blvd.
Pittsburgh, PA 15206

SPNHC is an organization for those interested in the development and preservation of natural history collections. SPNHC publishes a journal, *Collection Forum*, and the *SPNHC Newsletter*.

Sample Record for Paintings

courtesy The Brooklyn Museum

THE BROOKLYN MUSEUM
188 Eastern Parkway
Brooklyn, New York 11238

Painting Record . . . .
Department of Paintings
and Sculpture

Artist:

Title of work: Place executed:

Medium (please list types of paint, manufacturers, and number of paint layers if structure is complex; be as fully descriptive as possible):

Support:
canvas......................; cotton duck......................; other..
preprimed.................; unprimed.................; primed by artist (please list materials used,
manufacturer, and number of layers)...

Please indicate if this painting is varnished (partially? entirely?):

Name of varnish used:

If any special techniques were employed in the making of this work, please describe the materials and methods used:

Are there any special instructions for the installation or maintenance of this work?

If appropriate, please discuss title:

Sample Record for Paintings, courtesy The Brooklyn Museum

Is there any documentation you care to provide on the personal, social, or symbolic reference in this work?

Are there any exceptional circumstances or incidents that relate to the making of this work or its subsequent history?

If there are studies or preliminary drawings for this work, or if this is a study for another work, please indicate titles of these related works and collections:

Place and date this work first publicly shown:

Places and subsequent exhibitions:

Through whom was it first sold?

Previous collections (also include private individuals to whom the work has been lent, eg. another artist):

Where has this work been published, reproduced, discussed, or mentioned?

Have you written about the work (include published and unpublished material)?

....
Date

....
Signature

INDEX

abrasives 168
absolute humidity 25, 26, 27
abstract paintings 93
acid
    acetic 98, 99, 100
    formic 98, 100, 105, 110, 167
    hydrochloric 98
    nitric 98, 200
    sulfuric 98
acid rain 111, 115
acid-free cardboard 106, 206
Acid-free folders 193
acid-free glassine 192
acid-free materials 102, 103, 106, 194
acid-free tissue 207
acidic backings 194
acidic cardboard 198, 209
acidic materials 189, 194, 204, 206
    durability of 103, 104
acidic paper 106, 191, 192, 194, 220
    aging 190
acidity 103, 106, 222
    and light 68
    and pollution 68
    and RH 39, 68
    effects on books 220
    effects on canvas 212
    effects on collections 39, 98, 107, 111, 147, 148
    effects on copper 222
    effects on corrosion 222
    effects on DEAE 60
    effects on lead 222
    effects on leather 39
    effects on metals 222
    effects on paper 39, 68, 189, 190, 192, 194
    effects on photographic materials 198
    effects on shells 208
    effects on stone 172
    effects on textiles 204
    of barkcloth 180
    of baskets 179
    of cardboard 103
    of leather 185, 187, 188
    of paper 102, 111, 133, 189, 191
    testing for 103

acids 44, 98, 107, 160, 161
    from construction materials 160
    from fly specks 137, 140
    from perspiration 148, 160
    from pollution 98
    from PVC 168
    from wood 56, 107
    in cleaning solutions 162
    in dust 112
    in oils 164
    neutralizing 108
    organic 98, 159, 163, 167, 208
    sources of 98, 189, 191
acrylic (sheet) 75, 80, 81, 168
acrylic paint 214, 229
Activated charcoal 113
adhesive residue 194
Adhesive tape 148, 154, 192, 194, 199
adhesives 33, 192, 220, 229
    aging 147, 170
    animal glue 34, 217, 220, 221, 227
    effects of pesticides on 134
    effects on paper 194
    for barrier films 108
    for ceramics 170
    for lining paintings 226
    of collages 195
    on stamps 197
    pesticides in 117
    pollution from 97, 99, 100, 105
    staining from 192, 195
    wax 226
    wax-resin 214, 226
administrators 229
African art 219
African sculpture 85, 162
    oily residues on 138, 142
African "bronzes" 164
aging 33, 71, 82, 121
    from light 67, 97
    from pollution 97
    from RH 97
    of adhesives 147, 170
    of books 220
    of canvas 211, 212
    of cellulose nitrate 200
    of coatings 69, 217, 218

NOTICE

To the best of the Publisher's knowledge the information contained in this book is accurate; however, the Publisher assumes no responsibility nor liability for errors or any consequences arising from the use of the information contained herein. Final determination of the suitability of any information, procedure, or product for use contemplated by any user, and the manner of that use, is the sole responsibility of the user.

This book is intended for informational purposes only. The reader is warned that caution must always be exercised when dealing with chemicals, products, or procedures which might be considered hazardous. Expert advice should be obtained at all times when implementation is being considered.

Mention of trade names or commercial products does not constitute endorsement or recommendation for use by the publisher.

About the Author

Barbara Appelbaum is a partner in Appelbaum and Himmelstein, a New York conservation firm which she co-founded in 1972. The firm provides a wide range of conservation services including the treatment of individual paintings, objects, and textiles. Consultation is also provided for institutions and private collectors on various aspects of collections care.

The firm has developed a reputation for treating objects of odd composite materials, such as gilded and painted leather screens, reverse paintings on glass, and hair embroideries, as well as more conventional paintings and objects. In addition, they have developed, using techniques and materials previously used for twentieth century paintings, a method for treating severely deteriorated silk textiles, including flags and banners and embroidered pictures on silk and velvet.

The partners have performed conservation assessments and collection surveys for a large number of institutions and private collections around the country, and consult on environmental control and museum design for conservation. Ms. Appelbaum and Mr. Himmelstein have published and lectured widely on their textile conservation methods, on conservation surveys, on various aspects of environmental control, and on other technical subjects.

Ms. Appelbaum received an undergraduate degree in Japanese Art History at Barnard College, and a Certificate in Conservation from the Conservation Center of the Institute of Fine Arts at New York University. She was an Assistant Conservator at the Brooklyn Museum for a number of years, primarily working on painted wooden objects and other materials such as leather, ivory, basketry, textiles, and ceramics.

Ms. Appelbaum also taught a course on collections Management in the Museum Studies Program of New York University for fourteen years. She was on the Board of the American Institute for Conservation (A.I.C.), the American professional organization for conservators, for five years, and served as chair of the A.I.C. committee on Accreditation and Certification. She is also a member of the Editorial Board of *Art and Archaeology Technical Abstracts*.